WORD AND SPIRIT

The Indiana Series in the Philosophy of Religion
Merold Westphal, general editor

WORD AND SPIRIT

A Kierkegaardian Critique of the Modern Age

RONALD L. HALL

The King's Library

INDIANA UNIVERSITY PRESS
Bloomington and Indianapolis

The paper used in this publication meets the minimum requirements of American
National Standard for Information Sciences—Permanence of Paper for Printed
Library Materials, ANSI Z39.48-1984. ∞™

Manufactured in the United States of America

Library of Congress Cataloging-in-Publication Data

Hall, Ronald L., date
    Word and spirit : a Kierkegaardian critique of the modern age /
Ronald L. Hall.
    p.   cm.—(The Indiana series in the philosophy of religion)
    Includes bibliographical references and index.
    ISBN 0-253-32752-0 (alk. paper)
    1. Kierkegaard, Søren, 1813–1855—Contributions in philosophy of
the self.   2. Kierkegaard, Søren, 1813–1855—Influence.
3. Philosophers, Modern.   4. Self (Philosophy)   5. Postmodernism—
Religious aspects—Christianity.   I. Title.   II. Series.
B4378.S4H35   1993
198'.9—dc20   92-14596

1 2 3 4 5   97 96 95 94 93

For Maggi, Amy, and Erin

Irony as a [mastered moment] manifests
itself in its truth precisely by teaching us
how to actualize actuality, by placing the
appropriate emphasis on actuality. In no
way can this be interpreted as wanting to
deify actuality in good St. Simon style or
as denying that there is, or at least that
there ought to be, a longing in every
human being for something higher and
more perfect. But this longing must not
hollow out actuality; on the contrary, life's
content must become a genuine and
meaningful element in the higher
actuality whose fullness the soul craves.
Actuality hereby acquires its validity, not
as a purgatory—for the soul is not to be
purified in such a way that stark naked,
so to speak, it runs blank and bare out of
life—but as history in which consciousness
successively matures, yet in such a way
that salvation consists not in forgetting all
this but in becoming present in it.
Actuality, therefore, will not be rejected,
and longing will be a sound and healthy
love, not a weak and sentimental sneaking
out of the world. The romantic longing
for something higher may well be
genuine, but just as man must not
separate what god has joined together, so
man also must not join what God has
separated, but a sickly longing such as this
is simply a way of wanting to have the
perfect prematurely. Therefore actuality
acquires its validity through action. But
action must not degenerate into a kind of
fatuous indefatigableness; it ought to have
an apriority in itself so as not to lose itself
in a vapid infinity.

Søren Kierkegaard

CONTENTS

ACKNOWLEDGMENTS

This book focuses on the bearing of a single, small, dense, and exasperating text on a (the) single but comprehensive philosophical (existential) question: what it means to be a human being, or more exactly, what it means to be (fully) human. That text is Kierkegaard's (Author A's) "The Immediate Erotic Stages" found in Volume I of *Either/Or*. I have reflected on and wrestled with this issue for more than twenty years.

I did not become obsessed with this text on my own. As a graduate student, I was afflicted with it by William H. Poteat, an extraordinary teacher to whom I owe a profound if equivocal thanks. Not only did Professor Poteat introduce me to Kierkegaard via this enigmatic text in *Either/Or I*, he provided me with an indispensable framework for reading Kierkegaard, derived in part from Kierkegaard but mostly from his own genius. In so doing, Professor Poteat helped set the course of my intellectual life. Although I have, in moments of frustration, cursed him for this affliction, my gratitude to him is profound and in the final analysis goes much deeper than I can say. I wish to thank Professor Poteat for making very helpful suggestions on an earlier draft of this book but at the same time to exculpate him of any responsibility for its mistakes, blunders, excesses, and shortcomings.

Even though I acknowledge these meditations as my own, I did not work them out alone. Accordingly, I have two more acknowledgments to make.

First, to my friend and colleague, R. Taylor Scott, I owe a profound debt for providing the personal and intellectual companionship without which I would not have been able to complete this book. Because of Taylor's unwavering support over the years, the academy has not been for me as lonely a place as it has been for many academics I know.

Nor have I been alone in my life away from the office and the classroom. My wife, Maggi, and my two daughters, Amy and Erin, have provided a fabric of moral support that has been indispensable not only for my academic life but for my life. Over the past few years, the question "How's your book coming?" has become as routine a greeting from my family as "How was your day?" Well, I am happy to say, it is finished. In gratitude for their encouragement, for their belief in me as a philosopher as well as a husband and father, I dedicate this book to them with my deepest thanks.

Portions of these meditations have been previously published as follows: A section of chapter 3 appeared in slightly different form as "Language and Freedom: An Analysis of the Demonic in Kierkegaard's *Concept of*

Anxiety," *International Kierkegaard Commentary*, vol. 2, edited by Robert L. Perkins (Macon, Ga.: Mercer University Press, 1985), pp. 153–66. A section of the Introduction to chapter 4 and a section of the Epilogue appeared in slightly different form as "The Irony of Modern Thought: An Analysis via Kierkegaard's *Concept of Irony*," *Soundings* 71, no. 4 (Winter 1988), pp. 601–18. A section of chapter 5 appeared in slightly different form as "Michael Polanyi on Art and Religion: Some Critical Reflections on *Meaning*," *Zygon: Journal of Religion and Culture*, 17, no. 1 (March 1982), pp. 9–18.

I am grateful to Francis Marion University for providing financial assistance for this project.

ABBREVIATIONS

The following abbreviations have been used in the text for works cited more than once.

AA   Crites, Stephen. "Pseudonymous Authorship as Art and as Act." *Kierkegaard: A Collection of Critical Essays.* Edited by Josiah Thompson. Garden City, N.Y.: Anchor Books, 1972.

BD   Redner, Harry. *In the Beginning Was the Deed: Reflections on the Passage of Faust.* Berkeley: University of California Press, 1982.

BI   Maston, Floyd. *The Broken Image: Man, Science and Society.* Garden City, N.Y.: Anchor Books, 1966.

BN   Sartre, Jean-Paul. *Being and Nothingness: A Phenomenological Essay on Ontology.* Translated by Hazel E. Barnes. New York: Washington Square Press, 1966.

CA   Kierkegaard, Søren. *The Concept of Anxiety.* Translated by Reidar Thomte and Albert B. Anderson. Princeton, N.J.: Princeton University Press, 1980).

CH   Eliade, Mircea. *Cosmos and History: The Myth of the Eternal Return.* New York: Harper Torchbooks, 1959.

CI   Kierkegaard, Søren. *The Concept of Irony: With Continual Reference to Socrates.* Edited and translated with introduction and notes by Howard V. Hong and Edna H. Hong. Princeton, N.J.: Princeton University Press, 1989.

CR   Cavell, Stanley. *The Claim of Reason: Wittgenstein, Skepticism, Morality, and Tragedy.* New York: Oxford University Press, 1979.

DUW   Auden, W. H. "Dichtung und Wahrheit." *Homage to Clio.* New York: Random House, 1955.

DW   Spengler, Oswald. *The Decline of the West.* Abridged edition by Helmut Werner; English abridged edition by Arthur Helps; translated by Charles Francis Atkinson. New York: Modern Library, 1932.

E/O I, II Kierkegaard, Søren. *Either/Or,* volumes I & II. Edited and translated by Howard V. Hong and Edna H. Hong, with introduction and notes. Princeton, N.J.: Princeton University Press, 1987.

HC   Arendt, Hannah. *The Human Condition.* Chicago: University of Chicago Press, 1958.

HG	Boman, Thorlief. *Hebrew Thought Compared to Greek*. London: SCM Press, 1960.
JLA	Austin, J. L. *How to Do Things with Words*. Edited by J. O. Urmson. New York: Oxford University Press, 1965.
JRS	Searle, John R. "The Word Turned Upside Down." *New York Review of Books*. October 27, 1983.
JS	Taylor, Mark C. *Journeys to Selfhood: Hegel and Kierkegaard*. Berkeley: University of California Press, 1980.
KB	Grene, Marjorie, editor. *Knowing and Being: Essays by Michael Polanyi*. Chicago: University of Chicago Press, 1969.
KK	Grene, Marjorie. *The Knower and the Known*. London: Faber & Faber, 1966.
KP	Mackey, Louis. *Kierkegaard: A Kind of Poet*. Philadelphia: University of Pennsylvania Press, 1971.
KPA	Taylor, Mark C. *Kierkegaard's Pseudonymous Authorship: A Study of Time and the Self*. Princeton, N.J.: Princeton University Press, 1975.
LI	Derrida, Jacques. *Limited Inc*. Evanston, Ill.: Northwestern University Press, 1988.
LS	Steiner, George. *Language and Silence: Essays on Language, Literature and the Inhuman*. New York: Atheneum Press, 1958.
LV	Ihde, Don. *Listening and Voice: A Phenomenology of Sound*. Athens: Ohio University Press, 1976.
MB	Berman, Marshall. *All That Is Solid Melts into Air: The Experience of Modernity*. New York: Penguin Books, 1988.
MED	Descartes, René. "Meditations." *The Philosophical Works of Descartes*. Translated by Elizabeth S. Haldane and G. R. T. Ross. Vol. I. London: Cambridge University Press, 1968.
MP	Polanyi, Michael and Prosch, Harry. *Meaning*. Chicago: University of Chicago Press, 1975.
OC	Wittgenstein, Ludwig. *On Certainty*. Edited by G. E. M. Anscombe and G. H. Von Wright and translated by Denis Paul and G. E. M. Anscombe. Oxford: Basil Blackwell, 1969.
OG	Derrida, Jacques. *Of Grammatology*. Translated by Gayatri Chakravorty Spivak. Baltimore, Md.: Johns Hopkins University Press, 1976.
PA	Grene, Marjorie. *A Portrait of Aristotle*. Chicago: University of Chicago Press, Phoenix Books, 1963.
PF	Kierkegaard, Søren. *Philosophical Fragments*. Originally translated and introduced by David F. Swenson; new introduction and commentary by Niels Thulstrup; translation revised and commentary translated by Howard V. Hong. Princeton, N.J.: Princeton University Press, 1962.
PI	Wittgenstein, Ludwig. *Philosophical Investigations*. Translated by G. E. M. Anscombe. New York: Macmillan, 1968.

PK   Polanyi, Michael. *Personal Knowledge: Towards a Post-Critical Philosophy*. New York: Harper Torchbooks, 1964.

PM   Poteat, William H. *Polanyian Meditations: In Search of a Post-Critical Logic*. Durham, N. C.: Duke University Press, 1985.

PP   Pascal, Blaise. *Pensées*. Introduction by T. S. Eliot. New York: E. P. Dutton, 1958.

PW   Ong, Walter. *The Presence of the Word: Some Prolegomena for Cultural and Religious History*. New York: Simon & Schuster, Clarion Books, 1970.

RH   Caputo, John D. *Radical Hermeneutics: Repetition, Deconstruction, and the Hermeneutic Project*. Bloomington: Indiana University Press, 1987.

SUD   Kierkegaard, Søren. *The Sickness Unto Death: A Christian Psychological Exposition for Upbuilding and Awakening*. Edited and translated by Howard V. and Edna H. Hong, with introduction and notes. Princeton, N.J.: Princeton University Press, 1983.

TD   Polanyi, Michael. *The Tacit Dimension*. Garden City, N.Y.: Anchor Books, 1966.

WJ   Pitkin, Hannah. *Wittgenstein and Justice: On the Significance of Ludwig Wittgenstein for Social and Political Thought*. Berkeley: University of California Press, 1972.

WORD AND SPIRIT

PROLOGUE

KIERKEGAARD'S CRITIQUE OF THE MODERN AGE

> A human being is spirit. But what is
> spirit? Spirit is the self. But what is the
> self? The self is a relation that relates
> itself to itself or is the relation's relating
> itself to itself in the relation; the self is
> not the relation but is the relation's
> relating itself to itself.
>
> (S. K.)

Søren Kierkegaard is our modern prophet: with ruthless literary cunning, he rails and rages against us, exposing our deep-seated despair and our incessant flights from reality; and with love and concern he calls us to faith and to ourselves.

His prophetic critique of the modern age[1] focuses on *spirit*. Operating from behind the mask of his pseudonymous authorship, he says in one place, "The basic concept of man is spirit,"[2] and in another, simply that spirit is identical to self.[3] But even though spirit is self, and spirit is the basic concept of man, Kierkegaard also thinks that it is possible for us to be spirit-*less*, to lack a self, or more precisely to fail to be the self each of us already essentially is. This means that the self each of us already essentially is can fail, in varying degrees, to be existentially actualized, or what is the same thing, can fail, in varying degrees, to be historically thematized and freely appropriated as our own. To express this hermeneutical circle[4] in a slightly different way, Kierkegaard's claim is that we human beings can fail to be fully human, or that we, as persons, can fall short of a fully personal existence.

What we can fail to do, however, we can also succeed in varying degrees at doing, provided that we have the resources and most importantly the *will* to do so. For Kierkegaard, *choice* is an indispensable element in the existential actualization of the given actuality of our existence. When choice is allowed the transcendence it requires, when it is vested with its rights, we are enabled to actualize reflectively and reflexively the prethematic given actuality of our pre-reflective being-in-the-world. Although the full existential actualization of the actuality of ourselves is rare, it is not an impossible possibility. By virtue of the power of choice, each of us, on occasion, and to some degree, can come to ourselves, can become the self that each of us already essentially is. In this choice we remain the same self and yet, paradoxically, we are radically transformed. In the choice of ourselves, what each of us already essentially is gets taken up and appropriated as our own. As Kierkegaard puts it: "He remains himself, exactly the same as he was before, down to the most insignificant feature, and yet he becomes another, for the choice penetrates everything and changes it" (E/O II,223).

Insofar as Kierkegaard places *freedom* at the very center of spirit and self, his view is consistent with the biblical narratives.[5] The Bible depicts our human fallen state, our alienation from God, the world, and ourselves as a function of our (negatively free) refusal positively to appropriate freedom. According to the biblical myth, freedom is not the enemy of human being; quite the contrary. Our original sin is not our presumption positively to exercise freedom, rather, it is the opposite: our sin is not our *use* of freedom, it is our *misuse* of it. This misuse of freedom, however, dialectically testifies to what it excludes: sin is a sign of our capacity for positive freedom. From the biblical perspective then, freedom is fundamental to human being, so fundamental that even its denial testifies to its positive reality.

Yet the Bible also tells us that our misuse of freedom, our disobedience and rebelliousness, our refusal to be transparently grounded in the power that constituted us, leads inevitably to despair.[6] Only the positive appropriation of freedom can save us from this fate; only in such an appropriation can we existentially actualize the self that each of us already is, the self as the spirit we both are and are called to be.

Such a positive appropriation of freedom, and the actualization of the self as spirit that such an appropriation entails, is possible, on Kierkegaard's analysis, only from within *faith*.[7] For Kierkegaard, faith is fundamentally a *relation*. It is just this relation that spirit requires for its full existential actualization. Recognizing this helps us to grasp Kierkegaard's point in having Anti-Climacus say both that "the self is a relation" and in the same breath that it is not the relation (SUD,13). What I shall take him to mean here is that spirit does not constitute a relation but is constituted *in a relation*, namely, the relation of *faith*.

For Kierkegaard, faith is not only a relation, it is a double relation, and involves a double movement. Faith, first and foremost, is a self/God relation. This relation is radical and absolute. As Kierkegaard puts it, to live in faith is to exist before God; to exist before God, moreover, is to be related to God as the absolute center of one's life. Such an absolute relation to the Absolute is established when, in faith, we choose to respond positively to God's call and enter into a binding *covenant* with him. Second, faith is a self/world relation. In order for us to be absolutely related to the Absolute (God) in faith, we must be torn *asunder* from all of our absolute relations to the relative (the world); we must root out from ourselves every trace of idolatry. Spirit drives us toward transcendence and sunders us from the world. This sundering of ourselves from the world is not an end in itself; rather, it is but a temporary and teleological suspension of the immanent for the sake of the transcendent. This uprooting suspension allows spirit the transcendence it needs for us to take our place, as spirit, *before God*. Being radically displaced from the world in order to be radically placed before God in faith opens new possibilities for self-understanding. In this new understanding, a radically new self/world relation is thematized. The New Testament characterizes this new relation as one in which the self is *in, but not of*, the world.

Because faith establishes simultaneously two relations, the self/God relation and the self/world relation, it requires a *double movement*. The first movement of faith *sunders* us from our absolute relation to the world in order to place us before God. In the second movement of faith, a positive self/world relation is established, a transformed *bonding* of ourselves to the world. The world is given back to us from the hands of God and we receive it back in faith by taking it up as the palpable context of freedom that our existence as spirit requires. In faith, then, we are not called to leave the world for God, but to take up a dialectical *sundered/bonded* relation to it. In summary, to exist in faith is to exist within a radical covenantal bonding to God *and* to exist within a dialectical sundered/bonded relation to the world. In such a relation of faith, we come to ourselves as spirit and root out of our existence every trace of despair (SUD,14).

In addition to the claim that each of us is constituted as self and as spirit within a relation, or better, within the double relation and within the double movement of faith, Kierkegaard also asserts that "the self is a relation that *relates itself to itself*" (SUD,13, italics added). As I read this, it means that each of us can exist in any fully actualized sense as spirit and as self only to the extent that we are self-conscious and have some degree of reflection and self-understanding. That is, each of us can exist as spirit only if we have consciously thematized, to some extent, our historical, concrete givenness in terms of the categories and requirements of the double movement of faith. To be a self we must choose ourselves; but to be enabled to do this, we must understand ourselves as having that capacity. To understand this more fully, we must understand ourselves in terms of the double movement of faith and its double relation to God and to the world. In order for us to come to ourselves in faith, we must consciously choose not only to be absolutely related to God, we must also choose our place in the world, that place that we have already been given prior to our thematized self-understanding. To receive the world back in faith, we must take up that place in the world as our own. As Kierkegaard puts it, when the individual chooses himself, he "becomes conscious as this specific individual with these capacities, these inclinations, these drives, these passions, influenced by this specific social milieu, as this specific product of a specific environment. But as he becomes aware of all this, he takes upon himself responsibility for it all" (E/O II,251). I will return presently to this claim that the self can relate itself to itself only through conscious, reflective self-understanding and choice.

Kierkegaard's critique of the modern age centers on his charge that modernity is essentially faithless, selfless, and spiritless. His judgment echoes his modern prophetic predecessor, Pascal, who so incisively recognized that we moderns are a restless, rootless, and placeless people. Indeed, Kierkegaard could not agree more with what Pascal said of our modern predicament: "Man does not know in what rank to place himself. He has plainly gone astray, and fallen from his true place without being able to find it again. He seeks it anxiously and unsuccessfully everywhere in impenetrable darkness."[8]

I will take it for granted that Kierkegaard and Pascal are correct that the modern age is profoundly spiritless, that we moderns are deeply alienated from ourselves, and that we live in a kind of atmosphere of cultural and personal despair. What I want to explore, with Kierkegaard's help, is the particular character of this modern spiritlessness, the peculiar twists of the modern resistance to, and ultimate denial of, spirit. I will make the case that Kierkegaard also wants to make, namely, that the denial of spirit in the modern age is ironically dependent on the impact of Christianity. If this is true, then this dependence will enable us to mark a major difference between modern and pre-Christian forms of spiritlessness.

What Christianity managed to do was to take the idea of spirit from its Hebrew antecedents and radicalize it in such a way that for the first time it was irreversibly posited as a world-historical force. It might seem that this radical and irreversible positing of spirit would have produced a situation in which spiritlessness would be impossible. For Kierkegaard, however, this is not so. Indeed, the positing of spirit brought with it an ironic possibility of spiritlessness that had not existed in pre-Christian paganism, a possibility that we in the modern age move ever closer to realizing. This ironic possibility that Christianity indirectly introduced to the world was the possibility of a spiritually qualified spiritlessness. For Kierkegaard, a denial of spirit—for example, in paganism—is one thing, but the spiritual denial of spirit is quite another. This latter kind of spiritlessness that has invaded the modern age Kierkegaard characterizes as *the demonic*. In what follows, I will take Kierkegaard's lead and explore and investigate the idea that the spirit of the modern age is essentially demonic and that our modern and post-modern predicament is an ironic consequence of Christianity.

In saying that I am following Kierkegaard's lead in this critique, I am obliged to say something about the relation between Kierkegaard himself

and the pseudonyms through whom he speaks. While I agree that we
must always be careful not to identify Kierkegaard with his pseudonyms,
it is just as much of a mistake to think that Kierkegaard himself is completely absent from his pseudonymous works. Kierkegaard speaks *indirectly*
though his pseudonyms in such a way that what is said by them is often
what Kierkegaard is asserting himself. Most often the difference between
Kierkegaard and the pseudonyms is in what each does with these assertions. For example, Kierkegaard clearly does not share Author A's celebration of the musical/demonic in *Either/Or I*; quite the contrary: A is an
aesthete; Kierkegaard, through A, is attempting to wound aestheticism
from behind. Yet A also asserts that the advent of Christianity radically
changed human consciousness; surely Kierkegaard agrees with this, although the changes that are the most important, for Kierkegaard, are
inserted subtly and in an offhand way through A's voice, while A himself
concentrates on an aesthetic interpretation of these changes. The upshot
here is that we must be careful not to think that Kierkegaard has no voice
in and behind his pseudonyms. In fact, one of the central claims of this
book is that Kierkegaard is trying to get his readers to grasp the importance of speaking in their own voices; he does this ironically by not speaking *directly* in his own; it does not follow, however, that he does not speak
at all. My task is to ferret out Kierkegaard's own voice and to show its
critical bearing on modernity and the post-modern reaction to modernity.

To prepare you for what is to follow, allow me to introduce, in a highly
programmatic outline, some of the central concepts and distinctions that
have guided my reflections. Of necessity, these preliminary remarks will
be convoluted and dense. I will spend the chapters that follow elucidating
them.

A Kierkegaardian distinction that figures centrally in this book is one
that is not usually given a lot of attention in commentaries on Kierkegaard's thought. This distinction, most clearly made by Kierkegaard in
Either/Or I, is between the *psychical and the pneumatic* (or spiritual) qualification of spirit. Kierkegaard makes this distinction in order to point out
the differences between the pagan understanding of spirit—especially as
that is found in the most perfect expression of paganism, namely Greek
consciousness—and the Christian understanding of spirit. For Kierkegaard, the key differences are as follows: in pagan (Greek) consciousness,
spirit is psychically qualified, that is, qualified as soul; in Christianity spirit
is pneumatically qualified, that is, properly qualified as spirit. What this
means is that in paganism spirit, as "psyche" (soul), as psychically qualified, is understood as resting in a *static* harmony and accord with the sensuous world. In Christianity, by contrast, spirit is understood as existing
in a *dynamic* opposition, strife, and discord with the sensuous.

As I might just as well have put this, the contrast that Kierkegaard
draws between the psychical and the pneumatic qualification of spirit is

ultimately a contrast between two radically different sets of assumptions about the nature of the spirit/sensuous relation. I will call these differing sets of assumptions *world-pictures.*

I am using the term 'world-picture' here in a way that is similar to the way that Wittgenstein uses it. He says of a world-picture [*Weltbild*], "it is the substratum of all my enquiring and asserting."[9] As I will interpret them, world-pictures are frameworks that we both use and inhabit, that we both have and live in and from. World-pictures operate at both the tacit and the explicit levels of our awareness. At the tacit level, they thematize our historically given, concrete, embodied existence for us; and at the explicit level, they provide the resources necessary for us to appropriate as our own a coherent and meaningful account of our existence, an intelligible self-understanding. In such an appropriation, we come to relate ourselves to ourselves. We might call a world-picture a kind of world-story that we find ourselves in when we come to self-consciousness, and that we are also called on either to appropriate as our own or to reject for some other picture. A world-picture is a fabric of concepts, analogies, metaphors, and models, the interweaving of which defines for us not only our sense of the world, but our sense of our place in that world. Such world-pictures make themselves manifest in a culture in different forms. These forms range all the way from the myths and legends of a people to highly reflective philosophical theories.

I will take Kierkegaard's contrast between the psychical and the pneumatic qualification of spirit to be a contrast between two radically different world-pictures, two deeply held sets of assumptions about the nature of the relation of the self and the world. Given Kierkegaard's identification of spirit and self, I will take the self/world relation to be synonymous with the spirit/sensuous relation. Moreover, I will take both of these ways of expressing the same relationship to parallel another relation that figures prominently in *Either/Or I*, namely, the relation between idea and medium.

The fundamental difference, for Kierkegaard, between the psychical world-picture and the pneumatic world-picture is that the former figures the self/world relation in terms of *visual* analogies, models, and metaphors, and the latter figures the self/world relation in terms of *auditory* analogies, models, and metaphors. Insofar as the psychical world-picture is dominated by the visual and the pneumatic world-picture is dominated by the auditory, the former thematizes the self/world relation as *static* and the latter thematizes the self/world relation as *dynamic*.

This contrast between the psychical and the pneumatic will enable us to sort out the various senses of *immediacy* that are at play in Kierkegaard's thought. In preliminary outline, let me say that immediacy is an idea of presence, and that there are a variety of such ideas, and a variety of ways immediacy can be mediated or expressed. (This way of speaking no doubt causes some consternation, but I am convinced that no sense can be made of an unmediated immediacy.) I will focus on three senses of immediacy—sensuous, reflective, and existential. What is immediately present to the senses is sensuous immediacy; what is immediately present to thought is reflective immediacy; what is immediately present within reflection and within the historical continuity of past and future, actuality and possibility, is existential immediacy. To complicate matters, there are two senses of sensuous and reflective immediacy, but only one sense of existential immediacy. Sensuous and reflective immediacy can be either psychical or pneumatic; existential immediacy can only be pneumatic. All forms of sensuous and reflective immediacy, both psychical and pneumatic, are *aesthetic*; only the immediacy of the historical present is *existential*. Psychical/aesthetic sensuous and reflective immediacy find their perfect expression in the static, visual, medium of the plastic arts. Pneumatic/aesthetic sensuous and reflective immediacy find their perfect expression in the dynamic, auditory medium: either music per se, or some other medium that has become musicalized; pneumatic/existential immediacy finds its perfect medium of expression in felicitous speech.

Kierkegaard provides us with some heuristically powerful suggestions to help us understand. In *Either/Or I*, in his (A's) discussion of the relation between idea and its medium of expression, he contrasts three media: the plastic arts (architecture, painting, and sculpture), speech, and music. His argument is that in each of these media a different relation exists between idea and its sensuous expression. I will say that the three relations between sensuous medium and idea exemplified in these three media embody three different ways that the self/world, spirit/sensuous relation can be thematized, namely, as psychical/aesthetic; as pneumatic/aesthetic; and as pneumatic/existential.

A common feature of all aesthetic media is that they are limited to a "present tense." That is, aesthetic media cannot express the historical process in time. By contrast, speech has the resources for expressing three tenses, past, present, and future. This capacity for expressing the historical process in time is what makes speech a concrete medium; it is what makes it existential as opposed to aesthetic. Even though music takes place in time, it cannot express historical continuity; it is over as soon as it sounds. In the plastic arts, the present does not unfold in any sense; it is simply before us all at once, as spatially determined. Both music and the plastic arts are thus limited to only a present tense, even though the "present" expressed in the former medium is dynamic and the "present" expressed by the latter is static. Because of its structure of tenses, the medium of speech is the only medium that can express historical continuity.

In focusing on the contrast between the aesthetic and the existential[10]— a contrast I take to be at the heart of Kierkegaard's thought—I must forego a detailed discussion of Kierkegaard's analysis of the differences within the existential mode. These are differences between the ethical and the religious and, within the religious, differences between religiousness A and B. Although these differences will be taken into account, I will be primarily concerned to contrast an existential self-understanding (or, more specifically, the Christian self-understanding, religiousness B, which I take to be paradigmatically defined as existence before God and synonymous with personal existence) to the modern aesthetic musical/demonic self-understanding which suppresses, inhibits, and ultimately destroys the existential presence of spirit in the world.

On Kierkegaard's reckoning, the plastic arts of classical sculpture and architecture perfectly embody a *psychical/aesthetic* model for thematizing the self/world, spirit/sensuous, relation. The plastic arts are, of course, *visual and spatial* phenomena. When these arts serve as the models of the spirit/sensuous relation, self and world are depicted as existing in an essentially *static* relation of harmony and accord. In contrast to the plastic arts, speech and music provide us with *pneumatic* models for thematizing the self/world relation. Music and speech are not visual but *auditory*. When these phenomena serve as the models of the spirit/sensuous relation, the self and world are depicted as existing in an essentially *dynamic* relation of opposition and exclusion. As Kierkegaard has Author A remark: "In antiquity, the sensuous found its expression in the mute stillness of sculpture; in the Christian world, the sensuous had to burst out in all its impatient passion" (E/O I,98).

Both speech and music are dynamic and auditory and, as such, fall within the sphere of the pneumatic world-picture: music is a pneumatic/aesthetic medium and speech is a pneumatic/existential medium. The radical difference between the two lies in their formal properties as media; this difference in turn issues in two radically different but equally pneumatic models for thematizing the self/world relation. I will argue that, because of its special resources—resources conspicuously absent from music—speech provides a perfect model for thematizing a dialectical, sundered/bonded, self/world relation. As such, speech is the perfect medium for expressing the Christian spirit. By the same token, music, lacking these resources, provides a model for thematizing a very different self/world relation—a relation that, from the Christian point of view, is a *mis-relation*. Even though this mis-relation is pneumatically determined, that is, even though it is a relation that presupposes a pneumatic world-picture as its necessary context, I will say that it—as a *mis*-relation—is a perversion of spirit in its positive (Christian) sense. Following Kierkegaard, I will call this spiritually determined perversion of spirit *the demonic*. Music is as perfectly suited to expressing the demonic perversion of spirit as speech is perfect for expressing spirit in its positive (Christian) sense.

In saying that music is the perfect medium for expressing the demonic, I hope I will not be understood to be saying that all music is demonic. Neither I, nor A, nor Kierkegaard would argue that all music is demonic.

Rather, the claim that we would all agree on is simply that music has the demonic as its absolute subject. This does not, of course, mean that all music expresses the demonic. Clearly, spirit, in its positive Christian sense, *can be,* and often is, expressed in music, but not absolutely. For its absolute expression, spirit requires speech. Just as clearly, speech can express the demonic—as we will see, it does in Faust; but it is not in speech that the demonic finds its absolute medium. If the demonic is to be expressed in its absolute sense, it must be in music; just as spirit can be expressed in its absolute sense only in speech. Neither Kierkegaard nor I would be forced to banish music from the religious; we would only point out that it cannot be at the center of the religious. Or, to put this liturgically, music has a proper function in worship as a prelude, a sermon hymn, an anthem, a postlude, etc., that is, music must be subordinated to the service of the word—the scripture readings and the sermon; and to the service of the table—where the word is made flesh.

There is an inescapable irony implied in the claims I have been making. The irony is that Christianity not only brought forth a world-picture in which spirit was able to burst forth in all of its positive existential reality and power, it also, and in the same stroke, made a demonic perversion of spirit possible. This dialectical consequence was unavoidable: when Christianity introduced spirit into the world it also introduced the potential for the demonic. Modernity, as we might put it, is the illegitimate child of Christianity. Brought forth as a possibility by the advent of spirit, the modern age has turned spirit against itself; it has become demonic through and through.

I must now turn from the contrast between psychical and pneumatic world-pictures, aesthetic and existential ideas and media, to consider another vital assumption at work in Kierkegaard's thought. Kierkegaard assumes that there is a given actuality prior to thematic reflection. This is the assumption behind the claim that our task as persons is to actualize actuality. This actuality that we are called on to actualize is our concrete, embodied existence in the world.

I will take the bedrock actuality of human existence to consist of a plexus of activities to which we as human beings are uniquely given prior to reflection and thematization. The sense in which this plexus of activities is prior to reflection is logical not existential; that is, our concrete human existence is never world-picture-neutral; it never stands outside of some, however primitive, thematization of it. Yet the very idea of thematization makes no sense unless there are certain bedrock elements of our existence that are *given* to be taken up and appropriated. These bedrock elements of human existence can be abstracted and phenomenologically described.

If we were phenomenologically to describe what we uniquely do and are given to doing as human beings, as persons, we might include the following activities: human beings and only human beings engage in telling stories, praying, asking questions, answering them, promising, describing something, commanding, getting married, having a conversation, and so on. What is striking in any such list is the centrality of speech. As a matter of phenomenological description, then, bedrock to our concrete human existence is the fact *that we speak*. Following J. L. Austin's terminology, I will say that the most fundamental human activity is the *speech-act*.[11]

Like Austin, I will also take the paradigmatic speech-act to be enacted in the first person singular active voice, indicative mood. That is, I will take the paradigmatic speech-act to be something like "I promise," since every speech-act is a form of giving one's word to some other. We as human beings are not only able to speak, we are able to speak in our own voice; we are able to say with felicity, "I promise," to confess, "I did it," to voice our regret, our delight, our despair, and our hope. At the heart of what we do uniquely as persons is our capacity to speak in the first person, to speak in our own voice.

Our first person speech-acts *intend* a dialectical self/world relation. Or to put this differently, the self that we are called to be, the self as spirit, the self that is constituted in a relation, is *given* within the first person speech-act. (I am only following Kierkegaard's lead here: through Author A, Kierkegaard has suggested the startling claims that man's most basic concept is spirit, and that *language is absolutely qualified by spirit and is therefore the authentic medium for expressing the idea, namely, man's essential idea, spirit* [E/O I,65,67].) Even though the self that we are called to be, the self as spirit, the self as concrete 'I,' is present in our felicitous speech-acts, prior to its being thematized, it is only incipiently present. Our task as persons is to thematize this incipiently present self into a self-understanding that will enable us to actualize its incipient actuality. Apart from being thematized and appropriated, spirit remains a merely human *possibility*, an unactualized actuality.

Although the self that is present in its concrete existence is *related* to the world, it is still only an incipient self, and its world only an incipient world, until it becomes a self that *relates itself to itself*. That is, a self comes to itself only if it has a degree of self-consciousness.[12] Only on this condition is the self able to take up, make explicit and appropriate, the self/world relation that it is already in, both precritically and ultimately acritically. For Kierkegaard, without such self-consciousness, it is impossible for a self to actualize its incipient actuality.

My claim is that my incipient actuality as a speaker can be vested with its full existential actuality, that is, appropriated as my own, only within a world-picture that provides the conceptual traction required for this existential appropriation. As Kierkegaard remarks: "Not until spirit is posited is language installed in its rights" (E/O I,66). Such a world-picture must be one in which self and world are depicted as fundamentally and essentially *historical*. This is precisely the way that self and world are depicted within the pneumatic world-picture.

Insofar as I live pre-reflectively as a speaker, I also live pre-reflectively within temporality and contingency. These elements, however, do not add up to the full actuality of *historical* existence any more than my words alone add up to a full-blown speech-act. Something more is required if the self is to be a self that relates itself to itself. These given elements must be taken up as my own. This requires reflection, self-consciousness, and choice: it requires that my existence be thematized into a world-story that becomes my own story. World-pictures provide the conceptual resources for such thematizations.

Allow me to give an example. In order for me successfully to engage in the ordinary practice of making a promise to someone, in order for the telos of that act to be fully realized, I must not only enter the relation established by my act, but also relate that relation back to myself; I must make the relation my own. In order to do this, I must have a thematic conception of myself, others, and the world, that will allow my act its full reality. I must have a world-picture in which promising has a place, that is, I must have a historical world-picture. If I do not have a conception of the world as historical, of myself as free and responsible, I cannot, in any full-blown sense, promise something to someone. Promising, that is, requires some measure of self-knowledge and self-possession. In a promise I am required to know what it is to promise something, to know what I am doing, and most importantly, I am required to take myself and the other to be vested with the necessary powers and capacities to engage in that act. While I cannot know all of the consequences my promise may entail for it to succeed and for it to be *my* promise, I must not only know that I am responsible in relation to those consequences, I must actually accept them as my own. If my world-picture provides no conceptual room for me to make sense of this appropriation of responsibility, if it allows no conceptual room for making sense of the contingencies in the world that give rise to both the possibility and the necessity of promising, if it allows no room for freedom, and so forth, then the practice of promising is called into question.

As well as being indispensable for the actualization of our given actuality, our thematizations of our existence may preclude this actualization. As Kierkegaard has it, this was exactly the case in the Greek consciousness. The Greek world-picture was psychical, preventing spirit from becoming fully actualized and speech from being vested with its rights. For example, when a Greek audience watched a performance of Sophocles' tragedy *Oedipus Rex*, they no doubt appreciated and admired the efforts of Oedipus to determine his own destiny, to exercise freedom, to act. That is, they appreciated in him precisely what they knew existentially to be a given, namely, that human beings routinely and quite unselfconsciously and unproblematically engage in the practice of declaring themselves in their choices, decisions, and actions, and conduct their lives as if they had at least some measure of influence over their destiny. Yet their world-picture precluded them from thematizing what they concretely knew in their lives. Even though these practices of making and declaring decisions concerning the future, of making promises, resolves, commitments, and so forth, were at least incipiently present in ordinary Greek life, we can say that the Greek imagination had no resources in its world-picture wherein these practices could be given traction. In fact the resources of the Greek psychical world-picture only allowed a thematization of the course of the world and of human affairs in terms of fate. In the psychical world-picture there is no place for *contingency*, and hence no resources for understanding and appropriating the freedom and self-determination that seem to be implied in the activities of our ordinary life. The fact, however, that Oedipus is a hero shows the ambivalence that the Greeks surely felt toward the world-picture in and from which they lived: on the one hand, this pre-modern picture provided order and stability for them; on the other, it meant that there was no place for freedom and no place for any measure of self-determination. According to the Greek world-picture, freedom spelled chaos, impiety, and disorder, so every hint of it had to be banished, even if this required a radical reinterpretation of our ordinary life.[13]

The Greeks experienced the agony and tragedy of being caught in an ironic conceptual-existential contradiction. Spirit was present in Greek life, but because Greek consciousness was psychically qualified, this could not be acknowledged without contradiction. The Greek psychical world-picture could accommodate the given actuality of spirit only by thematizing it as soul. As soul, spirit remained repressed and submerged in the harmony and accord of the Greek cosmos; it was in this sense that Greek culture was essentially spiritless. Apart from being set within a different, a pneumatically qualified, world-picture, spirit could not come forth in its full existential actuality and dynamic power. The pneumatic world-picture that would have provided the resources for thematizing a positive place for spirit was simply *unavailable* to the Greeks. At this point in history, the pneumatic world-picture had not been introduced into the human imagination; this had to wait for Christianity.

Unlike the Greeks, the dominant world-picture that we in the modern age have and live in and from is pneumatic. Modern culture is, in this respect, qualified by Christianity. It was Christianity that introduced spirit into the world and thereby introduced the pneumatic world-picture. The fact that the modern age is essentially pneumatically qualified does not entail, however, that it accords spirit its rightful place. Indeed, it is Kierkegaard's contention that the modern age is spiritless. However, the spiritlessness of modernity is essentially different from that in Greek and pagan cultures. In the psychical denial of spirit there is a certain innocence; the modern denial of spirit is a willful rejection of spirit that ironically gets its energy, power, and rationale from spirit. Because of this ironic twist in the modern denial of spirit, because it is, as it were, a spiritual denial of spirit, Kierkegaard identifies modern spiritlessness with the *demonic*.

Kierkegaard's *Either/Or I* provides us, I think, with two very helpful interpretive models for understanding our distinctively modern form of spiritlessness. These models are represented by two legendary figures: Don Giovanni and Faust. What makes these two figures paradigmatic of the demonic is that they both express in their own distinctive ways a spiritually qualified spiritlessness: Don Giovanni is demonic sensuality and Faust is demonic reflection or demonic intellectuality. Don Giovanni and Faust are different, but only superficially. As Kierkegaard puts it: Faust "reproduces" Don Giovanni (E/O I,99). This reproduction is a function of the fact that Don Giovanni and Faust are simply mirror images of one another; both feed off of the same spirit/sensuous (mis)relation.

Even though Don Giovanni and Faust are spiritually qualified figures, and therefore exist dynamically, neither of them exists within the dynamics of speech. This is so despite the fact that Kierkegaard says that: "Faust, as a reproduction [of Don Giovanni] has an intellectual-spiritual quality. The power of a seducer like this is speech: that is, the lie" (E/O I,99). The idea of Faust falls outside of speech in a much more subtle way than does the idea of Don Giovanni.

Clearly, the idea of Don Giovanni—that is, the idea of a completely de-spirited, dynamic, sensuality, the sensuous perpetually emptying itself of idea—falls outside of speech and squarely within music. Indeed, such a sensuous immediacy is the absolute subject of music, and classically expressed in Mozart's *Don Giovanni*. Faust, on the other hand, is idea without sensuous immediacy, a kind of sensuous-less spiritual immediacy, a discarnate intellectual immediacy. As such, Faust, as the idea of pure idea, requires for its expression a reflective medium, a medium like the medium of speech.

I will argue, however, that the idea of Faust, as much so as the idea of Don Giovanni, falls inside of aesthetic immediacy and hence, in a subtle but essential sense, outside of speech. The aesthetic immediacy of Faust and that of Don Giovanni are different to be sure: one is sensuous, one is intellectual. Yet, in another, more important, sense, they both fall within the same immediacy, namely, the aesthetic immediacy of the fleeting moment. That is, both Faust and Don Giovanni are pneumatic/aesthetic figures. As pneumatically qualified, the aesthetic moment they express is not the aesthetic moment of psychical stasis and repose; rather, it is the fleeting moment of restlessness and tumult.

Even though pneumatically qualified, both Faust and Don Giovanni fall outside of spirit in its positive, existential sense. Spirit in this latter sense exists within a *historical present*. A historical present is marked as much by its *continuity and reflection* as it is by its *immediacy*. The historical present is immediacy *within* continuity and *within* reflection. The historical present

is that dynamic moment that is stretched between, and essentially connected to, actuality and possibility; that dynamic moment that is anchored
within the actuality of the past and oriented within the horizon of possibilities that constitutes the future. Spirit requires a setting of historical
time and a medium that can express the historical process in time; a medium that has the resources to express *existential immediacy/continuity*. That
medium is speech.

As I will show, even though Faust appears to find his medium in speech,
in the final analysis this, like Faust's life itself, is a deception, a *mere* appearance: Faust, as much as Don Giovanni, is an *aesthete*. I will argue that
Faust is as much qualified by the dynamics of the musical as is Don
Giovanni: Don Giovanni does not speak, he sings; Faust does not speak
either, he poetizes; his existence is lyrical, and in the end a "reproduction"
of the musical; in Faust "everything ends in music"; his words, his life, are
"full of sound and fury" but signify nothing. The perfect medium for this
demonic expression of spirit is not felicitous speech; rather, it is speech as
"the lie," speech as a vehicle of concealment and destruction, speech as
lyrical deception, and ultimately *speech as music*. In their common rejection
of speech in favor of the musical, both Don Giovanni and Faust negatively
witness to the essential connection that Kierkegaard draws between word
and spirit: to deny spirit is to deny speech—or better, one way to deny
spirit is to deny to speech its authority, legitimacy, and efficacy and to seek
to escape its world-establishing implications.

The malaise of the modern age, as I shall argue, is rooted in the fact
that it does not find its center of gravity in the dynamics of the speech-act
but in the dynamics of *music*. Music provides no resources within itself for
establishing the dialectical self/world relation that spirit, as spirit, demands. In a musical culture, speech withers, but along with it, spirit. Even
though we may continue to *exist* as incipient spirits, that is, to engage routinely in this or that speech-act before some other, when our dominant
self-understandings go against the grain of this practice, eventually spirit
itself will be called into question and we will begin to disappear as persons.

But enough of preliminaries and promises. Let us begin.

I

SENSUALITY AND SPIRIT

> The basic concept of man is spirit, and
> one should not be confused by the fact
> that he is also able to walk on two feet.
>
> (S. K.)

'Pneuma' is the Greek word that is most properly translated as 'spirit,' while 'psyche' is the Greek word for 'soul.' Both of these words are etymologically connected to breath, or, more specifically, to the breath of life. As the *Oxford English Dictionary* has it, 'psyche' means, in its primary sense, breath; it is derived from the infinitives 'to breathe,' 'to blow' (later), 'to cool'; hence life (identified with or indicated by the breath); further, the *OED* says of 'psyche' that it is "the animating principle in man and other living beings, the source of all vital activities, rational or irrational, the soul or spirit, in distinction from its material vehicle, the soma or body." The *OED* defines 'pneumatic' along similar lines as belonging to air or wind, breath or spirit.

Although both 'psyche' and 'pneuma' mean in their root senses 'breath' they are by no means synonymous. As with any term, the sense and meaning of 'psyche' and 'pneuma' are context dependent; they arise within, and are at home in, a particular form of life. The form of life in which 'psyche' seems to have its home is what we might call the *natural world*, just as 'pneuma' seems to have its home in what we might call a *historical world*. Accordingly 'breath' has a different sense and meaning in a natural conceptual neighborhood than it does in a historical one. One difference between the two senses of 'breath' that Kierkegaard implicitly trades on in *Either/Or I* may be expressed as follows: (1) breath, as psyche, is rooted in the rhythmic, life-sustaining, natural phenomenon of breathing in and breathing out, of inhaling and exhaling, and so is thought to be the very sine qua non for biological life; (2) breath, as pneuma, is the vehicle that carries and conveys our words, the breath of speech as it were. Of these two meanings of breath, the one that comes to have primacy in the world-picture that rules a cultural life determines that picture or that culture as being, in Kierkegaard's words, either *psychically qualified* or *pneumatically qualified*.

A major aim of "The Immediate Erotic Stages" is the exploration and elaboration of this distinction between a psychically and a pneumatically qualified world-picture. My aim is to elaborate and interpret this distinction even further. I will show that Kierkegaard's suggested contrast between psychical and pneumatic world-pictures is critical for making sense of the contrast he also wants to explore between pagan and Christian understandings of the spirit/sensuous, self/world relation. Moreover I will point out that this contrast can be fruitfully interpreted as paralleling the distinction that we make in the human sensorium between *visual* and *auditory* phenomena. That is, I will show that the psychical picture of the self/world relation is derived from a set of interwoven models, analogies, and metaphors abstracted from the phenomenon of seeing, just as the corresponding pneumatic picture is formed by abstracting from the phenomenon of hearing. As it turns out, the psychical and the pneumatic pictures of the self/world relation find their historical embodiment in Classical Greek and Judaeo-Christian cultures respectively.

In the enigmatic text of *Either/Or I*, under the literary disguise of Author A, and in his characteristic maieutic style, Kierkegaard boldly asserts the startling and seemingly outrageous thesis that the Christian picture of the self/world relation—a picture that was concretely introduced into the human imagination in the event of the Incarnation—marked the first time that sensuality, in its full existential power, became fully imaginable and fully realizable. In a key passage from this section of *Either/Or I*, A says:

> Sensuality is posited as a principle, as a power, as an independent system first by Christianity, and to that extent Christianity brought sensuality into the world. But if the thesis that Christianity brought sensuality into the world is to be understood properly, it must be comprehended as identical to its opposite, that it is Christianity that has driven sensuality out of the world, has excluded sensuality from the world. . . . I could add one more qualification that perhaps emphatically shows what I mean: sensuality was placed under the qualification of spirit first by Christianity. This is quite natural, for Christianity is spirit, and spirit is the positive principle it has brought into the world. (E/O I,61)

I will take A's claim that Christianity was the first to introduce into consciousness a world-picture in terms of which sensuality was fully imaginable and fully realizable, indirectly to communicate Kierkegaard's own understanding of the unique impact of Christianity on the human imagination. The positing of sensuality was an indirect consequence made possible by this impact. What Christianity posited directly was spirit; but this Christian spirit was posited in dialectical opposition to the sensuous; and, as contrary to the sensuous, this spirit was imagined to be in fundamental strife and conflict with it. In order for Christianity to posit spirit in this tension with the sensuous, it had to *sunder* it from its pre-Christian, pagan admixture within the sensuous. But Christianity posited spirit as such in order to establish a new *relation* between spirit and the sensuous, a new self/world relation, a relation that *bonds* the two in such a way as to allow spirit its full reign, its freedom, its transcendence, as well as its place, its context, its world. This relation that Christianity posited in the event of the Incarnation we may call a *dynamic synthesis* of spirit and the sensuous, a *dialectical* self/world relation.

According to Kierkegaard, the elements of this dynamic synthesis, namely, spirit and the sensuous, or self and world, were already present in the world before the advent of Christianity, but they existed in what may be called a *static synthesis*. As Kierkegaard puts it, the relation between spirit and the sensuous here "is not contrast or exclusion"; rather, in their static synthesis, spirit and the sensuous exist in "harmony and consonance" (E/O I,62). And he goes on to say that it was in this latter manner that spirit and the sensuous were related in paganism, and particularly so in paganism's most perfect expression, namely, in Greek culture (E/O I,62).

When Christianity broke the pagan static synthesis of spirit and the sensuous completely apart by introducing a picture of that relation in which the spirit and the sensuous were at once radically *sundered* and radically *bonded* in a dynamic synthesis, certain indirect consequences followed. The most important such consequence is that the event of the Incarnation brought possibilities that did not exist, and were not even conceivable within, paganism. One such possibility that we in modernity know only too well is that Christianity made it possible to picture spirit as absolutely sundered from, with no bonding within, the sensuous; and the sensuous as absolutely sundered from, with no bonding to, spirit. Christianity introduced, then, the possibility that both spirit and the sensuous could exist not only as principles and powers but as *separate, independent, and self-contained systems*. Christianity introduced, in other words, the possibility of *a demonic self/world relation*.

In the demonic world-picture, the sensuous is depicted as excluding all traces of spirit and yet as dialectically informed by the very same rebellious and disobedient spirit that is perpetually disengaging itself from it. This is the idea of demonic sensuality, the idea of a spiritless world perpetually slipping away into the temporal flux of the immediate moment of sensuous perception. The other side of this demonic self/world alienation is the idea of spirit in and of itself, spirit as completely disengaged from the sensuous, spirit as pure idea, pure reflection. In this demonic depiction, spirit is pictured as completely turning away from the sensuous world and into itself, into the dynamic immediacy of its ever changing stream of consciousness. For Kierkegaard, demonic spirit, no less than the demonic sensuality that is its counterpart, is opposed to and lies outside of spirit in its positive (Christian) sense. From the point of view of Christianity, then, demonic reflection is, like demonic sensuality, a spiritually qualified spiritlessness.

We must remember in all of this that, for Kierkegaard, spirit is self. For him, to exist as spirit, as self, is to reach the telos of human being, to realize a fully personal existence. This means that if Christianity was the first to posit a radical sundered/bonded relation between the sensuous and spirit and that if only in such a dialectical relation of exclusion and appropriation spirit can come forth in its full existential power and reality, then it follows that Christianity also was the first to posit self in its full existential reality and power, the first to posit personal existence in its fullest sense. This is exactly what Kierkegaard is suggesting. In concert with this, my assertion is that Christianity accomplished this innovation by being the first to introduce into the human imagination a world-picture which provided the conceptual and metaphorical resources necessary for spirit (self) to gain the traction necessary for its full constitution and concrete expression in the world.

The historical context of the Christian innovation is well known. The early Christians came to believe that Jesus of Nazareth revealed and embodied in his life and teachings the decisive expression of spirit in its most radical and concrete reality and power. In him, it was thought, the radical dialectical synthesis of spirit and the sensuous was normatively achieved and revealed once and for all. What I am taking this to mean is that the early Christians became convinced that the sundered/bonded self/world relation that spirit requires for its full expression found its unsurpassable model in Jesus.

I realize that this makes the Christian movement sound a bit pretentious. Can we really believe that it was not until Christ arrived that spirit (self, personal existence) came into the world? On the face of it, this bold claim seems not only false, but outrageously so. Surely we would want to say that spirit (persons, selves) was in the world before Christianity! Yet Kierkegaard's claim is that Christianity was the first to introduce spirit into the world. The arrogance and audacity of such a claim tempts us to dismiss it out of hand.

To mitigate these reservations to some extent I must reemphasize an important point. When Kierkegaard says that Christianity was the first to posit spirit in the world I take him to mean only that Christianity· was the first to bring spirit (self, personal existence) into its full existential actuality. That is, I do not think that Kierkegaard is saying that Christianity created spirit ex nihilo. Rather, for Kierkegaard, Christianity first posited the world-picture which provided the conceptual and metaphorical space necessary for the expression of spirit in its full existential reality and power. I say this because it is Kierkegaard's argument that the possibility of spirit (self and personal existence) was already incipiently present in the world *before* the advent of Christianity, indeed before the advent of the

Hebraic antecedents to Christianity. The incipient reality of spirit was, however, unable to come forth into its full existential actuality and power without a world-picture that would authorize and ratify it.

Spirit was, and has always been, incipiently present in the human per se; it is ineluctably manifest, I want to claim, in the existential speech-acts to which we as humans are given: the acts of naming, calling, answering, and so forth. Therefore when I say, with Kierkegaard, that Christianity brought spirit into the world for the first time, I mean only that Christianity brought into the world for the first time a world-picture that was able to awaken spirit from its dreaming slumber; that was able to provide a framework in which we could ratify and authorize its already present presence within our lives; a framework in which we could actualize the actuality of spirit. Again, the incipient reality of spirit is inexpungibly present in the dynamic web of relations established in the practice of speaking, hearing, and responding to one another. In providing a world-picture in which this presence could be ratified and authorized, Christianity brought spirit into its own; gave it, as it were, the conceptual and metaphorical traction it needed to allow it to come forth in its full existential actuality and power.

I cannot deny that, even with these qualifications, the claim that Christianity brought spirit into the world for the first time still seems audacious. My only response is: "So be it!" After all, as Kierkegaard remarks, "Boldly ventured is half won." Let us then venture forth.

Spirit as Psyche

A psychically qualified world-picture situates spirit within a *cosmos*. As cosmos, the world is pictured as a closed, fixed, static, and finite structure of order. In this picture, an eternal and an impersonal principle of being, a *logos*, is imagined to be the timeless source of the cosmic order. As such, the cosmos is pictured as having no beginning and no end; in it there is no essential place for novelty and no essential place for contingency. The metaphors and models that represent a cosmos are essentially visual and spatial. The preeminent such metaphor is the circle, which by its very nature is without beginning or ending and is closed, finite, self-contained, and static.

In a cosmos, even the paradigms of temporal succession are cyclical and thus closed, finite, self-contained, and essentially timeless. It was this picture of temporal succession that Plato was relying on when he said of time that it is "the moving image of eternity." In such a cosmic picture of time, novelty and contingency are denied their ontological rights. This denial is the consequence of picturing time as an eternally repeating cycle of nature; that is, as a result of picturing time as exemplifying the rhythms of breathing in and breathing out, growth and decay, birth and death; of picturing the movements of time as embodying the rhythmic cosmological cycles of the seasons, the eternally repeating orbits of the sun, the moon, and the stars. Within such a picture of time, as a pattern of eternal repetition, novelty and contingency have no place.

When "time" is pictured as moving in a circle, then it follows that what has been (the past) will be again, and that what will be (the future) already has been. Here the categories that are definitive of historical time, namely, the past and future, are rendered problematic. What do the concepts 'past' and 'future' mean in an ontological picture wherein it is assumed that what has been will be again, that is, that the past is the future? And what of the future, since what will be has already been? Here the future is also the past and the past the future and so time becomes not only unreal but our everyday existential experiences of the passing of time, of novelty and contingency, become illusions. As Mircea Eliade has put it, the assumptions of a cosmic picture of the world lead finally to the abolition of historical time: "insofar as an act (or an object) acquires a certain reality through the repetition of certain paradigmatic gestures, and acquires it through that alone, there is an implicit abolition of profane time, of duration, of 'history.' "[1]

If we can forgive Eliade's identification of history with "profane" time, a questionable identification from the biblical perspective, his work can be very helpful in providing us with a phenomenological description of the cosmological world-picture. As he describes it, this picture of the world as a cosmos is a picture which prizes archetypes, repetition, and participation. He finds this picture dominant in what he calls "primitive" or "traditional" cultures. These terms, however, are not meant in any pejorative sense, nor do they reflect the depth or sophistication of such "primitive" or "traditional" cultures. Indeed he finds this picture of reality as cosmos to be operative in one of the most advanced and civilized cultures that we have ever known, namely, that of the golden age of ancient Greece, the age of Greek philosophy. But not only does he think that this picture of the real was operative on a more or less tacit level, as most pictures of the real operate, he thinks that in Greek culture it was given its most sophisticated expression wherein its premises and their implications were formulated and made explicit in an unprecedented way. This formulation is nowhere more eloquently expressed than in Plato's theory of forms (CH,34).

What Eliade means by saying that the implicit ontology of primitive and traditional cultures has a Platonic structure is just that the real in these cultures, as for Plato, is paradigmatically represented in terms of archetypes, that is, in Plato's language, *eternal forms*. As he puts it, according to the ruling assumptions of this picture of the real "an object or act becomes real only insofar as it imitates or repeats an archetype. Thus, reality is acquired solely through repetition or participation; everything which lacks an exemplary model is 'meaningless,' i.e., it lacks reality" (CH,34).

In this Greek picture, reality is eternal and the eternal is *immutable*. As immutable, the eternal cannot be created or destroyed; the eternal does not come into or go out of existence. Or what is the same thing, the eternal is ahistorical. As such, the realm of concrete individuals and particulars, both of which come into and go out of existence in the temporal order of history, are relegated to a status of less than ultimately real. We have here the expected corollary to an ontology of the eternal. Temporal individuals and particular objects and acts come into and go out of existence and so, by definition, are not eternal, not immutable, that is, not real. That individuals and particular objects and acts exist at all is due only to their participation in the eternal.

Paradoxically what is true of individual things in this ontology of the eternal is true also for human, temporally embodied, individuals. As Eliade has pointed out, this ontology implies that individual human beings have a tendency to become archetypal and paradigmatic. "This tendency," he says, "may well appear paradoxical, in the sense that the man of a traditional culture sees himself as real only to the extent that he ceases to be himself (for a modern observer) and is satisfied with imitating and repeating the gestures of another. In other words, he sees himself, i.e., as 'truly himself,' only, and precisely, insofar as he ceases to be so" (CH,34).

In this picture of the real, the primary archetype of the eternal is *logos*. As Thorlief Boman has noted, "It is a self-evident presupposition to the Greek that in the things in the world and primarily in its very progression a *logos*, a perceptible, knowable law, governs, which first makes possible knowing and understanding in the human *logos*."[2] Indeed, we might say that because *logos* represents the very heart of the real, namely, eternal form and order, that it comes to stand, for the Greeks, as the very essence of the cosmos. Perhaps then we need to say something more about this Greek word for 'word.'

The Greek word 'logos' derives from the verb 'lege' meaning to say, or to speak. Boman's work is again helpful here. He claims that another root came to govern the final determination of the meaning of 'logos' for the Greeks. That other root is 'leg,' which means "to gather," or "to put together in *order*," or "to *arrange*" (HG,67). This other meaning, rather than the association with speaking, gradually became the dominant meaning of 'logos.' More and more logos was uprooted from the lively dynamic act of speaking—and hence from the embodied speaker—and came to stand for the eternal and fixed order of the cosmos.

In the Greek imagination, it was thought that logos tells us, in the words of Plato, "how a being is."[3] Logos then becomes the very key to Greek thought, at least insofar as it follows the Platonic tradition. In this Platonic tradition, the object and lure of thought is *being*, what truly *is*. What truly *is* is eternal, immutable, indestructible, static, at rest, harmonic, and peaceful; it is apprehendable only through a passive theoretical intuition of the mind's eye. Although, in the Platonic scheme, reality can be apprehended by human knowers through philosophical reflection, it is in no way dependent on any *personal ground* for its establishment. For Plato, reality is wholly objective. As the eternal, immutable, and objective arrangement and order of the cosmos, *logos* simply names an *impersonal ontological principle*.

While it is certainly beyond my competence to say why the Greeks pictured the world and the self in this way, I can certainly note that the picture that they had and lived within is connected to the place that *vision* had in their imaginations as a metaphor and model of the real. In his marvelous book *Listening and Voice*, Don Ihde has remarked:

> The Greek thinking was conceived in the world of light, in the Apollonian visual world. . . . The Greek language expresses this identification of 'seeing' and 'knowing' by a verb which means in the present *eidomai*, 'appear,' 'shine,' and in the past *oida*, 'I know,' properly, 'I saw.' Thus the Greek 'knows' what he has 'seen.' Even the Greek verb meaning "to live" is synonymous with "to behold light." Before philosophy and deep in the past of Greek experience the world is one of vision. In this sense, visualism is as old as our own cultural heritage.[4]

It is no wonder that an imagination of such an orientation finds its perfect companion in visual models and motifs. The basic phenomenological characteristics of sight indicate this compatibility quite clearly. Ordinary seeing, although it takes place in time and is dynamic in that sense, is essentially, that is, in its abstract structure, *atemporal*. If we abstract from the concrete temporal and embodied phenomenon of seeing to examine the structure of sight and the structure of what is seen, we notice something very important: what is seen is *spatial* and therefore has in the structural relation among its parts no intrinsic temporal successiveness; the spatial *gestalt* is before the passive eyes of the beholder as a complex integration of parts all of which are determinately there all-at-once, every part simultaneously co-present and hence, in a certain sense, *eternal*. Don Ihde's remarks on the static character of vision are helpful: "If I look at a calendar on the wall, it stands out as motionless and mute, and in relation to it I detect only a massive nowness. Its appearance neither dramatically *comes into presence* nor *passes from it* in its motionless state" (LV,94).

Let me emphasize again that I am talking about an abstracted structure of vision and not the concrete activity of seeing something. The latter is hardly static; rather, because it is an essentially embodied activity, it pulsates with a dynamic orienting motility, with the dynamic kinesthetic intentionalities of my posture, focus, attention, and so forth. William H. Poteat in his work *Polanyian Meditations*—a work that I judge to be definitive on this issue—remarks on this aspect of the dynamic activity of seeing. One of the examples he uses in his phenomenology of the visual is

his experience of sitting in his study and looking at an expressionist canvas
that is hanging on the wall. He says:

> What do I see? Even though I maintain the stasis of my posture in relation
> to what is before me, I am aware that the field of what I see is anything
> but static. There *is* a center to my vision. But there are lines of intention-
> ality that run away from it in all directions. I feel, even though in fact
> unmoving, profoundly drawn to, 'moved' toward, but also, insofar as I wish
> to see the *canvas*, 'repelled' by the margins of my visual field that them-
> selves lie on all four sides beyond the limits of the painting. What I see
> here is surfaces pervaded with dynamism. (PM,57)

Yet having said this Poteat goes on to give an account of what is seen
that is similar to and advances Ihde's account. He says that "the 'time'
during which my unmoving gaze is fixed upon what is before it and the
'time' through which the visible scene 'unchangingly' *endures* is indistinguishable from eternity" (PM,57). Elaborating the implication of this
claim, Poteat says: "The propriety of making this claim is further en-
dorsed when I remark another, perhaps the unique, feature of the visual
field before my fixed gaze: its dynamism notwithstanding, every 'part' of
that determinate surface, bounded by the frame of my open eyelids, is at
once sensuously and simultaneously co-present with every other 'part'"
(PM,57).

We may be inclined to agree with Ihde and Poteat that what is seen, in
the examples of the calendar and the canvas, has a kind of static endurance through time in that it does not temporally unfold before us in any
essential sense. The question may arise, however, as to whether the case
in favor of the interpretation of visual phenomena as essentially static and
eternal has been unduly prejudiced by the examples of the calendar and
the canvas both of which are admittedly static spatial phenomena without
any internal dynamism. Are there not other examples of visual/spatial
phenomena where something is seen as "going on" before our eyes? For
instance what about the phenomenon of watching a house burn?[5] Certainly it appears that we have here a visual dynamism that is not simply
the dynamism of the activity of embodied seeing, but a dynamism that is
in the spatial object itself. What is seen seems to unfold before us; the
house that is burning is literally passing away right before our eyes.

In order to make the case for the claim that the abstracted structure of
vision and the essentially spatial structure of what is seen therein are atemporal, I must contrast the visual with the auditory.[6] This anticipates a
more elaborated discussion of the auditory that will follow when the focus
is on speech and music. For now I will concentrate on the differences
between two dynamic phenomena, one visual, one auditory: watching a
house burn and listening to a piece of music.

Music is ordered, motival, sound; as such the sounds of a musical per-

formance form a dynamic pattern. This dynamic pattern is formed as
sounds unfold within a temporal motif. This unfolding is internal to the
musical performance itself and not some secondary quality imposed by the
listener. As Ihde puts it, "there is no way in which I can escape the sense
of a 'coming into being' and a 'passing from being' in the modulated motions of sound. Here temporality is not a matter of 'subjectivity' but a
matter of the way the phenomenon presents itself" (LV,94). Just as the
essential and defining element in vision is space, so the essential and defining element of sound is temporality: the elements of an auditory phenomenon, like a musical performance and unlike the elements of a visual
phenomenon, do not present themselves all at once, simultaneously, in a
fixed, static, and eternal pattern; rather the elements of an auditory phenomenon are given as essentially temporally successive, as unfolding, as
sequential.[7]

How then is the visual phenomenon of watching a house burn, a phenomenon that takes time and in which things pass away in space/time,
essentially different from the auditory phenomenon of listening to a musical performance? The difference is really rather obvious and has to do
with the difference between two different ways that the parts of the phenomenon are given, namely, on the one hand, as spatially given, all at
once, and on the other, as temporally given, successive and sequential. If
we freeze one frame in the phenomenon of watching a house burn, take
a picture of it, as it were, what the phenomenon *is* is clear: we have before
us a house burning or someone watching a house burning. At any given
moment a self-contained totality is *present*; each spatial frame is self-contained and complete; or at least the phenomenon could (without violating
the appearance as a whole) be imagined as composed of such shots seen
successively. So the apparent dynamic movement is really a succession of
self-contained wholes each complete in itself.

This is very different in the case of listening to a musical performance.
If we freeze one "frame" in this phenomenon, i.e., one note in the melody
line of a score, we do not have before us music, much less a complete
piece of music, or a musical performance; we have an isolated sound. Because this freeze frame would be an instant, to make it analogous to the
visual phenomenon, the single note would have no endurance as in a single note held by a performer over several moments. This isolated sound
would not be recognizable as music precisely for the reason that Kierkegaard cites, namely, that music has within itself time as its essential element. If all of the parts of a piece of music were sounded all at once, we
would not have music but noise. What makes music music is just the temporal and motival succession of its sounds.

With these qualifications, it seems reasonable to maintain that the abstract objects that we passively behold before our eyes in a visual/spatial
perception are self-contained and essentially atemporal. If this is true,
then visual/spatial models and metaphors derived from this abstracted

sense of vision have exactly the characteristics that define the real in Plato's metaphysics. The real, for Plato, is fixed, static, self-contained, complete, and eternal. I do not mean to suggest simply that Plato's ontology finds visual metaphors congenial, but that Plato's ontology took the turns it took owing to the preeminence of the visual in his imagination. Vision, I want to claim, was for Plato and for Greek culture generally the dominant sense, and therefore the meaning of 'sensuous,' that is, what is given to the senses, was defined for them by their hypertrophication of vision as the primary metaphor for the real. This is so even though, for Plato, what is "seen" in the truest sense is not what is seen with embodied eyes but with the introspective "eyes of the mind."

Let us return now to our discussion of Kierkegaard's attempt to characterize the sensuous/spirit relation in the ancient Greek, psychically qualified, picture of the real. We can now say that for the Greeks the primary metaphors and models for making sense of that relation were essentially visual and spatial.

When the sensuous is understood primarily as a visual/spatial phenomenon, as the Greeks understood it, and when it serves as the medium in which spirit is expressed, a certain spirit/sensuous relation is presupposed. Moreover spirit and the sensuous themselves are both qualified in this relation. The visual/spatial qualification of spirit and the sensuous turns spirit into psyche or soul, the sensuous into static space, and qualifies the relation between the two as one of harmony and accord.

I am using 'sensuous' and 'spirit' here as Kierkegaard does, as exactly analogous to 'medium' and 'idea.' Remember that for Kierkegaard "man's most basic concept is spirit" (E/O I,65). Therefore, in a psychically qualified picture of spirit and the sensuous, that is, where the real is modeled as a visual/spatial phenomenon, both idea (soul) *and* medium (the sensuous) get visually/spatially qualified. This means that idea gets transformed into a visual, spatial *surface* that endures through time in a static eternity. This visual/spatial qualification of the idea is reflected in our ordinary ways of speaking. When we say of a painting or of a piece of sculpture or architecture that it has beautiful lines, shapes, contours, colors, and the like, we imply that its ideas of order, form, beauty, etc., are expressed *in*, or perhaps better, *on*, the surfaces of the medium. This is idea and medium as psychically qualified, that is, this is idea as inconceivable outside of its immediate and immanent synthesis with its visual, spatial, sensuous medium. The souls of things and human beings then are so *integral* to their sensuous expressions in the psychical/aesthetic relation that they form with their visual, sensuous embodiments what can best be characterized as a relation of harmony and accord.

The psychical/aesthetic relation between idea and medium in which idea and medium exist in an immediate and static synthesis can be contrasted with a relation between idea and medium, spirit and the sensuous, in which the idea dynamically transcends its medium. In this latter relation, the medium is constantly being negated, constantly overturning itself, constantly appearing and disappearing, constantly *pointing beyond itself*, to the idea, and the idea is constantly outrunning its medium of expression.

Kierkegaard finds the paradigms of the psychical/aesthetic relation of idea to medium in the visually and spatially determined media of classical painting, sculpture, and architecture. A more extended discussion of these latter two paradigms is to follow; for now we can introduce the following remark by Kierkegaard:

> Neither in sculpture nor in painting is the sensuous a mere instrument; it is rather a component. It is not to be negated continually, either, for it is continually to be seen conjointly. It would be a strangely backward consideration of a piece of sculpture or of a painting if I were to behold it in such a way that I took pains to see it independently of the sensuous, whereby I would completely cancel its beauty. In sculpture, architecture, and painting, the idea is integral to the medium, but the fact that the idea does not reduce the medium to a mere instrument, does not continually negate it, expresses, as it were, that this medium cannot speak. It is the same with nature. Therefore, it is properly said that nature is dumb, and architecture and sculpture and painting; it is properly said despite all the fine, sensitive ears that can hear them speak. (E/O I,67)

In contrast to these paradigms, Kierkegaard finds the paradigms of the dialectical relation of idea to medium in music and in speech. He says that in language,

> the sensuous is reduced to a mere instrument and is thus annulled. If a person spoke in such a way that we heard the flapping of his tongue etc., he would be speaking poorly; if he heard in such a way that he heard the vibrations of the air instead of words, he would be hearing poorly; if he read a book in such a way that he continually saw each individual letter, he would be reading poorly. Language is the perfect medium precisely when everything sensuous in it is negated. That is also the case with music; that which is really supposed to be heard is continually disengaging itself from the sensuous. (E/O I,67–68)

I will have more to say about the dialectic of the auditory, that is, the dialectic of music and speech, when we turn the discussion to the pneumatic world-picture.

I noted above that Kierkegaard asserted that painting, sculpture, and architecture were like *nature* in being dumb, in being unable to speak, or as I can now put it, in being unable to point beyond themselves and reduce themselves to mere instrumentalities. The order in nature then, as Kierkegaard understands it, is itself a paradigm of the psychical/aesthetic relation of idea and medium. To put this differently it would be fair to say that the psychical/aesthetic relation between idea and medium is essentially *organic*.

When we consider organic systems we are immediately aware of the ordered integration of the elements within those systems. We are also aware that each system can become an integral part of a larger system and that nature itself integrates every subsystem into a cosmos of harmony and accord. Here cosmos is pictured as an ecological system, each part delicately balanced with every other; to upset one part is to upset the whole. It is not surprising that modern day ecologists find their heroes in premodern, that is, psychically qualified, civilizations which were, as they say, "more in tune with nature than we are."

The psychical/aesthetic picture of the organic relation of spirit to the sensuous substantially buries spirit in the sensuous, transforming it into a substantial life-principle or psyche. This psyche is seamlessly bonded to its sensuous embodiment as wetness is to water, as heat is to fire, as lightness is to air, and as solidness is to the earth. Indeed, so thoroughly immanent is the soul in its sensuous embodiment that its sundering from that substantial embodiment is literally inconceivable. Such a sundering would be as inconceivable as abstracting the spatial component from a visual phenomenon, as inconceivable as abstracting roundness from the spatial configuration of a circle, real or imagined. Here idea (eidos) is the intrinsic form of the sensuous object by virtue of which that object is what it is.

I must warn, however, that it is a mistake to claim that in the psychically qualified picture of the real the sensuous and spirit are organically or naturally *bonded* if this is taken to imply that spirit and the sensuous are already two ontologically distinct elements present in the world and already sorted out from each other. This is precisely what is not the case. In the psychical world-picture spirit and the sensuous are as yet not two fully formed distinct elements that are in need of being bonded. Although the psychically qualified, visualist world-picture does not allow a place for spirit and the sensuous to exist as *two* categorically distinct elements, there is an implicitly recognized place within that picture for what we might call an incipient, pre-sundered distinction between these "two" elements. In their psychical relation, however, these incipiently distinct, pre-sundered elements are imagined to be perfectly matched, belonging and fitting together as a fetus "fits" into and is at home in its womb, as a vein "fits" into the leaf it feeds.

In the psychically qualified picture then it is not only unthinkable to sort out spirit (soul/psyche) from its sensuous embodiment, it would be a violation of the cosmos to seek to do so. Indeed it would be correct to say that the psychical picture not only does not provide room for the positing of spirit and the sensuous as sundered (and bonded), the picture itself is a concerted effort to block that sundering and to establish a vision of the real in which idea and medium exist in perfect harmony and accord. In a cosmos, spirit is pictured as perfectly *at home* in its sensuous embodiment (E/O I,47).

This psychical "bonding" of form to matter is so complete because so completely informed by visualist metaphors and models. This psychical bonding of spirit and the sensuous shows itself in even the most concerted attempts at abstraction within the psychical world-picture. It is even present, as Spengler has noted, in Greek mathematics. Spengler says: "The Classical mathematician knows only what he sees and grasps. Where definite and defining visibility—the domain of his thought—ceases, his science comes to an end. . . . The alpha and omega of the Classical mathematic is construction . . . that is, the production of a single visually present figure." In a similar vein Spengler remarks how Pythagorean numbers are bonded to the finite world: "The number 1 . . . was also the symbol of the mother-womb. The digit 2, the first true number, which doubles 1, was therefore correlated with the male principle. Finally, the holy 3, the combination of the first two numbers, represented the act of procreation. . . ."[8] The classical Greek mind then was simply unable to avoid picturing numbers as representing finite magnitudes and visible figures. For the Greeks therefore, and for any psychically qualified picture of reality, idea or intelligible form, even if abstractly represented in mathematics, retains its "bonding" to the visual, and hence immanently and spatially conceived, sensuous world.

This perhaps sounds a little more like Aristotelian metaphysics than it does Platonic. After all, so the standard textbook interpretation goes, it was Plato who held that intelligible forms are separable from sensuous particular things and Aristotle who claimed that forms have no separate or separable existence.[9] Of course Aristotle did not for one minute think that there were no ideas, no universals, no souls, no intelligible forms. Rather he insisted, with Plato, that knowledge would be impossible if there were no ontological categories or intelligible forms into which reality is organized and systematized and in terms of which it is eternally grounded.[10] These forms, however, are not, for Aristotle, separable from their sensuous embodiments, the matter these forms order. According to Aristotle the sensuous embodiments of intelligible forms are necessary for human knowledge of the eternal. As Kierkegaard might put it, the Greek psychically qualified picture of the relation between spirit and the sensuous is no better represented than in the Aristotelian metaphysics of the ordered harmony and accord of form and matter.

This difference between Aristotle and Plato is, however, only apparent. Though Plato claims that forms are separable and essentially separated from the visible world of sensuous particulars that participate in them, he does not manage to divest himself of visualist assumptions, assumptions that lead him finally to fail to make his claim good. I say this because, for Plato, the apprehension of the forms is an essentially visual performance,

even though the organ of this "vision" is the mind's eye. Vision by its very
nature, even an abstracted vision of the soul, requires spatial (however
abstracted) objects that are statically and eternally present before the
"eyes." Plato cannot get away from at least an analogy between the sensible and the intelligible. In a telling case in point Plato compares the intelligible form of the Good to the sun in the visible world. He remarks in
the *Republic* as follows: "It was the Sun, then, that I meant when I spoke
of that offspring which the Good has created in the visible world, to stand
there in the same relation to vision and visible things as that which the
Good itself bears in the intelligible world to intelligence and intelligible
objects."[11]

We may conclude that even Plato's ardent attempt to separate the forms
from the sensibles falls victim to his tacit reliance on visual metaphors and
models. His reduction of thought to introspection, to a theoretical vision
of the mind's eye, shows this decisively. For Plato, thought, in its highest
form, is contemplation; and contemplation is a kind of spectation, a kind
of mental seeing of mental objects in a mental space. Plato's theory of
forms then retains its Greek visualist starting point. As such, the ideas or
forms retain an inexpungible, if only an analogical, relation to the spatial
and visible sensuous world. Even for Plato, forms and sensibles exist in an
essentially psychical/aesthetic relation of static immediacy. Indeed, this was
necessary for Plato's theory of forms to make sense, for otherwise it would
not have been possible for him to speak coherently of "beholding" the
forms, in the original tactile and thus spatially sensuous sense of that term,
or even for that matter, for him to develop and hold a "theory" of the
forms at all, in the original visual and hence spatially sensuous sense of
that term.[12]

Spirit as Pneuma

The psychical world-picture dominated the ancient imagination until
the advent of Christianity. What Christianity effected was a shift in world-
pictures, a shift from the psychical picture in which the relation between
spirit and the sensuous was depicted as visual/spatial/static, to a pneumatic
world-picture in which the spirit/sensuous relation was depicted as audi-
tory/temporal/dynamic.

Christianity, however, did not posit the pneumatic world-picture ex
nihilo. Rather, what Christianity did was radicalize the faith it inherited
from its Hebraic ancestry. As the Christian movement understood itself,
the faith of Abraham, Isaac, and Jacob received its decisive and radical
expression in Jesus of Nazareth.

From the Christian point of view the Hebrews were the forebears of the
pneumatic world-picture insofar as they placed the *spoken word* (*dabhar*) of
Yahweh at the very center of reality. For the Hebrew the very name of

God is a speech-act: "I am." And yet owing to its preoccupation with itself as *a people* before God, the Hebrews did not develop fully a corresponding human "I am." That is, the Hebraic focus on the "we are" caused them not to attend fully to the development of a human "I-consciousness," a consciousness of themselves as individuals who speak before God as God himself speaks, that is, in the first person.

My argument is that only in a first person speech-act does spirit come forth in its essential sundered/bonded relation to the world. And from the Kierkegaardian perspective that I am taking, it was Christ who revealed this to the world for the first time. Indeed as the Christian reckons, it was in Christ that spirit received its most powerful and most decisive human expression for it was in Christ that the "I am" of Yahweh was made flesh and walked among us. And following Kierkegaard's suggestions, we can say that it was not until Christ—who spoke with authority—that the spoken word was fully vested with its rights, not until Christ that spirit found the medium it needed for its full existential expression.

Even so the Christian innovation would have been impossible apart from its Hebraic antecedents. Among the most significant contributions that the Hebrews bequeathed to Christianity were its picture of creation and its correlative picture of man as created imago dei. In the Hebraic imagination God is pictured as speaking the world into existence. In this picture God not only creates the world with his word but also sustains its continuity with it. Here everything that exists, including the self, is pictured as owing its existence to, and hence absolutely dependent on, the creative and providential *dabhar* of God. Here the paradigm of human action is established: to act is to speak as God speaks; in the act of speaking (*dabhar*) spirit finds its decisive expression in man. This spirit is *pneuma*, spirit as "the breath of speech." Spirit as pneuma, as Kierkegaard instructs us, must be sharply distinguished from spirit as *psyche*, spirit as the natural order of the cosmos. It is precisely spirit as pneuma that Christianity first posited. In the Christian world-picture a radically transcendent spirit becomes radically immanent in the world: the *dabhar*—and not the *logos*—becomes flesh.

The key difference between spirit as psychically qualified and spirit as pneumatically qualified lies in the ontological place that is accorded in each qualification to temporality. As we have said, in a psychically qualified picture of the world there is not only no essential place for the reality of time, there is a concerted effort to deny reality to anything temporal. In this picture, time is at best the moving image of a timeless eternity. In the pneumatic picture, time is no illusion; but not only is time itself real in the pneumatic picture, it is the necessary context for the appearance of the real. The positing of the pneumatic world-picture then provided the necessary conceptual context for spirit, in its dynamic and temporal transcendence, to appear in the world in its full existential actuality and power.

When I say that the pneumatic world-picture provides a context for the appearance of spirit in its full *temporal transcendence*, I am using 'temporal' in what I take to be its most coherent meaning, namely, as *historical*. In historical time, that is, in one way linear time, the temporal distinctions of past, present, and future find their most coherent expression as distinct realities. This is so since, as historically conceived, each moment of a temporal succession is unique, irreversible, and unrepeatable. This historical conception of temporal sequence allows the concept of past its full existential reality, for in historical consciousness, what is past, in both its positive and negative senses, in its pathos and relief, is present as really past, as really over and done. Also in historical consciousness, the future becomes present as that which has really not yet happened, as an awesome realm of possibility and contingency. The historical sense of future brings with it a sense of reality to novelty and contingency. In this consciousness, reality is no longer imagined to be complete and self-contained, closed and fixed, static and eternal. Now the world is pictured as essentially open, developing, unfolding, from its original creation to ever new creative possibilities. Here the future has come into its full reality as the double edged realm of *hope* and *dread*. Moreover, as the future opens us to possibilities it also presents these possibilities as in need of being actualized. Just at this point, the place of the individual as a free and responsible agent emerges at the very center of the real. In the dynamic movements of historical time, the agent's task is to transpose—in his choices—possibilities into actualities. Or in cryptic summary of all of this: historical consciousness is inescapably *anthropocentric*.

When time is real, or better, when reality is conceived as historical, reality itself appears as radically contingent. Here reality consists of both (future) possibilities and (past) actualities. What has become actual "came into existence" from real possibilities—possibilities that would have remained as such had it not been for the intervention of an agent whose act in the moment of the present brought that actuality into its full historical determination. In the historical picture of reality then, what is and what will be are determined by and are contingent upon what is said and done. Another way to put this is to say that in the historical picture every reality is *subjectively grounded* in the irreversible and unrepeatable acts of either God or of God's human counterpart, imago dei man. The introduction of this picture of reality as historically and subjectively grounded was clearly an ontological innovation of enormous import.

In the psychically qualified picture of reality as cosmos and in the pneumatically qualified picture of reality as history, the key metaphor is *the word*. In the pneumatic picture, however, 'word' means something decisively different than it meant in its psychical rendering. In the Hebrew language the word for 'word,' that is, *dabhar*, was essentially connected to the dynamic *act* of saying and speaking. This is unlike the case with the Greeks whose word for 'word,' *logos*, strayed from its root connection to the dynamic act of speaking finally to mean the impersonal, rational, and static principle of cosmic order. The root connection of the Hebrew word for 'word' to the dynamic act of speaking, however, remained firm. We can begin to see this when we note that the meaning of *dabhar* is not only 'word' but also 'deed.' As Boman has pointed out, " 'Word' and 'deed' are . . . not two different meanings of *dabhar*, but 'deed' is the consequence of the basic meaning inhering in *dabhar*" (HG,65).

For the Hebrew, the paradigmatic act of speaking is the *dabhar* of Yahweh. Yahweh's word brings the world into existence and his fidelity to his word sustains it. As such, the word of Yahweh becomes for the Hebrews the metaphor and the measure of the real. W. H. Poteat goes to the heart of the matter when he says:

> What we *can* say is that for the Hebrew *dabhar* was always the spoken—more exactly the *speaking*—word; and the speaker of the (just now) speaking word was paradigmatically Yahweh. And it was the *authenticity* and *fidelity* of this speaking word of Yahweh, who calls everything into existence when he speaks, and was the touchstone and the test of *every* word—whether it be authentic, real, and meaningful, or on the contrary empty . . . And this speaking word is not only the *measure* of reality; it is in its very utterance that reality takes up its abode between men and God and among men—literally hanging upon the "breath of God." W. H. Auden has said: "A sentence uttered makes a world appear." (PM,116)

Poteat goes on to draw perhaps the most fundamental differences between the Greek *logos* and the Hebraic *dabhar*. This difference is that *logos* stands for an order that is eternally and *impersonally* established, while *dabhar* stands for an order that came into existence and remains so only in relation to the spoken word of Yahweh, and so is historically and *personally* established. He says of *dabhar* that it does not, as *logos* is thought to do, "replicate the particular *logoi* of an eternal and finite text, and by so doing, conform to *what is the case*, that is, to what is by virtue of this, eternally true" (PM,119). "For the Greeks," he goes on to say, "words get their meaning in being parts of 'an immutable and impersonal mode of discourse' related to some ultimate principle of impersonal rational order; for the Hebrews words get their meaning in being expressions of the personal" (PM,116).

For the Hebrews, Yahweh speaks and the world appears. As the Psalmist has put it: "By the word of the Lord were the heavens made, and all their host by the breath of his mouth" (Psalms 33:6); and in another verse: "For he spoke, and it came to be; he commanded and it stood forth" (v.9). As the paradigmatic speaker, God's *dabhar* stands as the model of human being. For the Hebrews, then, it was not only God who makes the world appear; it is anyone who speaks with the aim of approximating the felicity of God's *dabhar*. In this sense, the spoken word is at once enormously powerful and at the same time, at least in the mouths of human beings, extremely dangerous. Yahweh is faithful to his words but the Israelites knew all too well that humans, who imitate his speech, often are not. As Poteat has put it, the Israelites "knew full well the difference between, on the one hand, words that were real doings and makings and, and, and on the other, *mere* words, feckless and inefficacious words not attended by the "felicities" (PM,119). And, quoting Boman, he goes on to remark that the Israelites know

> "of very promising words which did not become deeds; the failure in such instances lies not in the fact that the man produced only words and no deeds, but in the fact that he brought forth a counterfeit word, an empty word or a lying word which did not possess the inner strength and truth for accomplishment or accomplished something evil." A counterfeit, empty, or lying word is a disowned or unowned word, hence a *mere* word—that is, speaking quite directly, "sound and fury signifying nothing." (PM,120)

As its creator, as the one who speaks the world into existence from nothing, Yahweh radically transcends the world. When the Torah says, "Hear, O Israel: The Lord our God is *one* Lord," it does not mean that Yahweh is the most important being among many beings. Rather what this means is that Yahweh is not *a* being at all; in some important sense we might say he is ultimately no-thing. This way of speaking is meant to point out the fact that Yahweh is pictured as radically transcending every being as its ultimate source and ground. As such God is not *of* the world; instead the world exists by his word, by his command, and is as such *in his faithful keeping*; the very existence of the world depends on him absolutely. Perhaps what is meant by claiming that God created the world out of nothing is just this: that without God there would be nothing.

In the Bible, Yahweh is pictured as radically transcendent and absolutely other than the world. As such this biblical picture strictly prohibits the idolatry of identifying Yahweh with any particular place, person, or thing *in* the world. In this picture, God is the absolute and the world is the relative. Faith in God is just an absolute relation of commitment to the absolute and a relative commitment to the relative. This latter relativizing of the world is the very heart of the spirit's transcendence of the world, of its qualification as spirit.

In the Christian picture, according to which the self and the world are essentially relative and essentially and transparently grounded in the radically transcendent power which constituted them, spirit receives its proper telos. Here spirit is called to *sunder* its absolute relation to the relative and to take up an absolute relation to the Absolute. The paradox in this is that the individual, historical self is relative and hence this call is a call for an absolute *bonding* of the relative to the Absolute. The paradox of joining the temporal and the eternal is deepened in that the telos of the spirit also demands an essential but relativized *bonding* of the relative to the relative, an appropriation by the self of the world, an appropriation by spirit of the sensuous. More exactly, because the self's relation to the world is relative and not absolute, we can say the the telos of spirit is realized only insofar as spirit takes up a dialectical *sundered/bonded* relation to the world.

In this dialectical picture, not only does spirit come into its own as sundered from its sensuous worldly embodiment, the sensuous gets posited as the necessary ground of the positive appearance of spirit in the world. Even though spirit, as temporally transcendent, is sundered from the sensuous, it also appropriates, of necessity, the sensuous world it excludes. In this appropriation, the temporal world is received from the hands of the Eternal. For the first time the self/world relation becomes personal. In this dialectic the self comes to relate itself to itself and to its place in the world.

In the pneumatic world-picture, God is pictured as the radically transcendent ground of all that is, including the self and as radically immanent within the world. Just because God is the ground and source of everything that is, he is able freely to *present* himself in any place, at any time, and through any person or act, thing or event. And so he does. He is pictured as present in the most unlikely of places and times and in and through the most unlikely of peoples and events. He chooses an unlikely people to be "his people" and "tents among them"; he travels with them in their exodus to their unlikely "promised land"; he chooses an unlikely person in whom to make the radically transcendent nature of spirit decisively incarnate.

In each of these choices there is a manifestation of the transcendent within the immanent that does not allow an idolatrous identification of the two. This refusal of spirit to be identified with the world or with anything immanent forms the context of the struggle of the early Hebrew people with the nature religion of Baal and Baaleth, a religion that threatened to replace the Hebraic picture of God as transcendent with a picture of him as immanent within the natural order, the cycles of fertility and season. It is this transcendence of spirit that is embodied in the New Testament's report of Jesus' apocalyptic remark about his own radical spiritual *displacement*: "The foxes have holes and the birds have nests, but the son of man has no *place* to lay his head." The faithful life that Jesus embodied was certainly a life lived *in and for the world*, but it was just as surely not a life *of the world*.

Because of the radical temporal transcendence and dynamic nature of spirit as pneuma, it cannot appear fully within the static, visual, and spatial media of expression. A new medium is required. Spirit as both radically transcendent of the world and essentially incarnate in it requires for its full appearance a medium that has within itself the resources for expressing a dialectical sundered/bonded relation of self to the world. Spirit requires a medium that is able to express transcendence and immanence simultaneously. That medium, Kierkegaard suggests, is the auditory medium of speech.

The pneumatically qualified picture of spirit as radically transcendent and dynamic imagines spirit as perpetually disengaging itself from the sensuous. This disengagement of spirit from the sensuous is analogous to the relation of the content (what is to be heard) and the medium of expression of that content in a motival auditory phenomenon. Consider again the elusive moment of an *immediately present* sound in such a phenomenon: in the temporal succession of sounds in an ordered auditory medium each sound comes into existence in the moment and, just as quickly, goes out of existence. These momentary sounds are constantly passing away but always in the service of expressing some idea. The ideas that are expressed *through* the pneumatic media of motival sound are, like spirit, never statically before us in the way that the ideas expressed in a visual phenomenon are; pneumatically expressed ideas never rest *in* the sensuous as they do in a psychically qualified medium. Yet the ideas expressed through the pneumatic media are nevertheless present; the difference here is between a temporal and a spatial presence. This difference does not imply, however, that the pneumatic temporal presence, because it is forever passing away, is not real; indeed the presence of sound is as palpably real as anything can be: sounds resonate within the world, within our bodies, within our very bones.

As vision and space are the dominant metaphors for the psychically qualified picture of the self and world, so hearing and time dominate in a pneumatically qualified picture. This contrast parallels, I have already claimed, the contrast between the Greek *logos* and the Hebrew *dabhar*. Recall that for the Hebrew the word (*dabhar*) is also *deed*; it is something happening, something going on, dynamic, temporally thick. *Dabhar* bespeaks *movement* for the Hebrew, no less than *logos* bespeaks rest and repose for the Greek. As Walter Ong has put it, for the Hebrew, "word [*dabhar*] is not an inert record but a living something, like sound, something going on" (PW,12).

Hearing is to vision as *dabhar* is to *logos*. The heart of this distinction is in the fact that temporality is as essential to the structure of hearing as timelessness is essential to the structure of vision. Sounds come into being and pass away; they are related in a temporally unfolding span. Sounds arise from a field of contingent possibilities and come into an *immediate presence* and pass away from that presence. Again, this sharply contrasts with a visual pattern that is fixed, static, and timelessly eternal. In an auditory pattern, the sonic elements are given as essentially temporally successive, as unfolding, as sequential. This distinction between the essential structures of vision and hearing holds, I have argued, despite the contingent fact that the actual phenomenon of seeing something endures through time and hence takes time. As Don Ihde has remarked, "*Sound reveals time*" (LV,103).

The key difference that relying on the auditory makes here is that it provides a new way of figuring the relation of idea to medium. Here spirit (idea) is pictured as constantly breaking out of its sensuous expression, or, as Kierkegaard puts it, what is to be heard is "continually disengaging itself from the sensuous" (E/O I,68). Only an auditory medium can properly express the sensuous/spirit relation as one of contrast, exclusion, and strife. Yet this is just the nature of spirit as it was posited by Christianity: in Christ spirit was manifest in its radical *transcendence*. (And we must not let ourselves be confused by the fact that he also walked on two legs.) Only an auditory medium can express this temporal transcendence. As radically transcendent, spirit cannot be captured *in* its sensuous expression—this would be idolatry. Here spirit is as radically transcendent of the sensuous as soul is radically immanent in it in its pre-sundered mode of existence within the psychically qualified, visualist picture of the real.

Sonic media are perfect for expressing transcendence because they have within themselves time as an essential element. Sounds unfold within a temporal horizon of protension and retention.[13] In a dynamic succession of sounds, the idea is constantly breaking out of its sensuous medium and the medium constantly annulling itself. The *present moment* in such a temporal span comes into being by annulling the immediately preceding present moment that protended it, only to give way itself to the next present it protends, and then to fade into a past that is retrotended in every new present. And so it is with the temporally unfolding sounds in an auditory phenomenon; and so it is with the spirit and the sensuous in a pneumatically qualified world-picture.

Although music and speech are both auditory and have the resources for expressing transcendence, for "negating" the sensuous, they are at the same time fundamentally different. This difference is crucial for Kierkegaard and for his critique of modernity. I will turn to this difference in the last section of this chapter. To anticipate, I will argue that even though both music and speech are sonic media and thus have the resources for expressing a *sundered* self/world relation, they differ as to their resources for expressing a dialectical *bonding* of the spirit/self within the world. I will argue that speech has in its formal structure bonding resources that are absent in music. These resources, in combination with its resources for expressing transcendence, make it the perfect medium for expressing transcendence in its radical and paradoxical incarnation.

Failing to notice the presence of these bonding resources in speech and their absence in music is as great an oversight as failing to see the similarities between them. It is the former mistake that led Walter Ong to say indiscriminately of both music and speech that they are, as sound, equally "evanescent" (PW,111). This characterization makes no adequate distinction between word and tone and we are left to think that each, like every sound, *merely* "perishes each instant that it lives" (PW,111).[14] While this characterization may be adequate for music, I will argue that it misses the essential dialectic of the speech-act.

One way to express the difference between what music is perfectly suited to expressing and what speech is perfectly suited to expressing is found in the distinction that Kierkegaard draws between two senses of the *immediate*, both of which are pneumatically qualified: "The immediate, qualified by spirit, can be qualified in such a way that it either comes within the realm of spirit, or is outside the realm of spirit" (E/O I,70). And he goes on to say that the immediate that falls within the realm of spirit can be expressed in music, but that it is not the absolute subject of music. Rather, the immediate that falls within the realm of spirit is the absolute subject of language (speech), and can only be expressed in its fullest reality by means of the medium of speech. He says:

> But if the immediate, qualified by spirit, is qualified in such a way that it is outside the realm of spirit, then music has in this its absolute theme. For the former immediacy, it is unessential for it to be expressed in music, whereas it is essential for it to become spirit and consequently be expressed in language. For the latter, however, it is essential that it be expressed in language, since it is qualified by spirit in such a way that it does not come within the realm of spirit and thus is outside the realm of language. But the immediacy that is thus excluded by spirit is sensuous immediacy. (E/O I,70–71)

The two spiritually qualified senses of the immediate are two senses of spirit, namely, spirit as spirit, the spirit that Christ incarnated, and spirit as the demonic spirit of worldlessness, that is, the demonic spirit that is "incarnated" in Don Giovanni and in Faust.

And to anticipate a bit further the argument of the last section, I will say that the immediacy of spirit is the dynamic moment that is incarnate within *historical continuity*, while sensuous immediacy is expressed in the disconnected *flux* of the moment, the essentially discarnate moment of perpetual vanishing. Because demonic, sensuous immediacy eclipses both past and future, it finds its perfect expression in the *aesthetic medium of music*; and because the immediacy of spirit is the historical, it finds its perfect expression in the essentially tensed *existential medium of speech*.

Before I explore these matters more fully, however, I want to turn to Kierkegaard's discussion of classical sculpture and architecture, which are, like music, aesthetic media, but; unlike music, are psychically qualified.

Architecture and Sculpture: Psychical Paradigms of Aesthetic Immediacy

It is in the service of making the distinction between the sensuous/spirit relation within a psychically qualified world-picture and that relationship within a pneumatically qualified picture that Kierkegaard devotes a good portion of the discussion in the "Immediate Erotic Stages" to the issue of the nature of the *classical* as that is defined in the worlds of painting, music, sculpture, poetry, and architecture. The ostensive focus of the exploration here is the relation between form and content in an aesthetic work, or as he also puts it, the relation between the idea and its medium of expression. This "aesthetic" discussion of aesthetics yields important interpretive dividends for understanding classical Greek culture as psychical/aesthetic and opens us to understanding what Kierkegaard means by saying that, in a psychically qualified picture of the world, the sensuous and spirit exist in an relation of *harmony and consonance*.

One way to classify an aesthetic work is in terms of its form—its medium—and in terms of its content—the idea it expresses. Sometimes works of art manage to match form and content, idea and medium, in a perfect harmony. For example, what makes Homer's *Iliad* a classical epic poem is that the content of the poem was the perfect epic subject, the Trojan War. There is here a "thoroughgoing mutual permeation" (E/O I,52) of form and content, idea and medium, the mutual intensity of both creating a happy, harmonious, and immortal unity.

In elaborating this notion of the absolute reciprocal interpenetration of form and content, idea and medium, Kierkegaard introduces a distinction between the *abstract* and the *concrete*, a distinction that is vital to the subsequent discussion. It is this contrast that figures more prominently in the discussion than the pretended focus on the issue of how to rank the classics. According to Kierkegaard, a medium can be either abstract or concrete, and the same obtains for the idea that it expresses. Sometimes works of art perfectly combine abstract medium and abstract idea; sometimes concrete medium and concrete idea are perfectly matched; nevertheless, abstract media can express concrete ideas and vice versa.

Catching us a bit off guard, given our modern tendency to associate the abstract with the intangible and the concrete with the tangible, Kierkegaard says of architecture that it is doubtless the most abstract medium. (As it turns out, architecture is the most abstract *psychical* medium but not the most abstract *pneumatic* medium; this is music.) Following this, he says that the ideas that receive expression in architecture are by no means the most abstract (E/O I,56). But how is this determination made?

The measure by which an idea and a medium are determined to be either abstract or concrete for Kierkegaard is the measure of the degree to which each is *permeated with the historical* (E/O I,55). The more concrete an idea or medium, then, the more it is related to our concrete historical existence and the more abstract the more removed from, or literally "taken out of," the historical. By definition here, the concrete is primary and the abstract is derivatively defined in terms of it, namely in terms of its relative distance from the concrete. The most abstract medium would be the one most removed from historical existence, and the same for the ideas it expresses.

The nature of historical consciousness has already been adumbrated in the preceding discussion in which the distinction between the Greek *logos* and the Hebrew *dabhar* was at issue. With this distinction in mind, perhaps we can understand why Kierkegaard says that architecture is the most abstract medium, though it expresses ideas that are more concrete because more related to history than, for example, sculpture.

Both architecture and sculpture, and for that matter, painting, are abstract media precisely because they, as *visual and spatial*, do not have time as an essential component. As I have already said, visual space is essentially atemporal; and this is so despite the fact that every visual/spatial object endures through time in a kind of eternity. All of the elements in a visual/spatial object are simultaneously and sensuously co-present and so can be "taken in" in a moment. Visual/spatial *Gestalten* are *statically present* to the eyes of the beholder. Since history is essentially temporal, we can readily understand that, as media, the spatially determined media are removed from the historical and hence are abstract despite their obvious tangibility.

Likewise we can just as easily grasp the analogies between sonic media and the historical. Like history, sonic media have time as an essential component. Neither the spoken word nor music stands before us in the same way that a cathedral or a sculpture does. In the latter two examples, all of the parts of the spatial objects are *statically present* out in front of us; whereas, in the former, as we listen to music or to someone speak we are in the midst of a different sort of immediacy: the sounds are *dynamically present* to us, but not as out in front of us; rather as all around us and indeed *in* us, and we in them; and more: what is present is present dynamically as fugitive to our grasp, forever outrunning itself in the moment of its performance.

This much should help us take a first step in understanding why Kierkegaard claims that architecture and sculpture (and painting) are abstract media. Each of these aesthetic forms is abstract because its medium is spatially static and hence removed from the historical which is by definition temporally dynamic. It would be a mistake to suppose, however, that both of the sonic media, music and speech, are equally close to the historical. Indeed, as I will explain in the next section, for Kierkegaard, speech, or as he puts it, language, is the most concrete medium, and music is the most abstract. This may sound strange since, as dynamic, one would think that music is close to the historical. As Kierkegaard says, however, music has "an element of time in itself but nevertheless does not take place in time except metaphorically. It cannot express the historical within time" (E/O I,57).

The distinctions that Kierkegaard is drawing here are distinctions of degree. His claim is that one medium or one idea can be more or less permeated with historical consciousness in relation to another. He says, for example, that the medium of architecture is more abstract than the medium of sculpture. Although not equally so, both of these media are abstract relative to speech; relative to each other, one is more abstract than the other. Again the paradigm of the concrete that Kierkegaard uses in making this determination is the historical.

For Kierkegaard, the center of concrete existence is within historical continuity—within its dynamically unfolding moments of past, present, and future. This historical continuity can find expression only in a medium that has the resources to express the past, the present, the future. This medium is speech. Hence, speech is the most concrete medium conceivable. And the most concrete idea is the idea most intimately connected to the historical—that idea, for Kierkegaard, is self. But what is self? When we remember that, for Kierkegaard, self is spirit—it is man's basic idea—we are again thrown off balance. It goes against the grain of our modern imaginations to think with Kierkegaard that *the most concrete idea conceivable is spirit*!

When we see that, for Kierkegaard, the concrete *is* the historical, we can understand why he has A claim that architecture is more abstract as a medium than sculpture even though it expresses more concrete ideas than sculpture. For the most part, sculpture—at least the sculpture that Kierkegaard is considering here, namely, classical (Greek) sculpture—is closer to the concrete than architecture because of its "human size." Sculptures stand before us, because their size is relative to our own, in a different way than does a building. Consider, for example, the sheer existential mass of a Greek temple, which looms over us and elicits in us the kind of awe that would be expected from an encounter with something that, in relation to our own concrete embodiment, overwhelms us. Sculptures, being closer to our human size, are more capable of being taken in by us, of being touched and handled. Venus de Milo stands before us in a less threatening, less alien way than the Parthenon. And yet, we must admit a relativity here: the Parthenon is relatively closer to the human than, e.g., Chartres or the World Trade Center Towers, precisely because it can be more readily taken in as it stands before our gaze; and certain sculptures are indeed more massive than others, but, however massive, every sculpture remains, by its very nature, readily available to the human embodied visual and tactile grasp.

Although more abstract as a medium than sculpture, the ideas architecture is able to express are more concrete than the ideas expressed in sculpture. Why is this? The reason is that sculpture, while it may begin within the historical world for its subject matter, ends by freezing or abstracting a moment from the temporally successive historical world in order finally to seek to capture its eternal essence. Consider the *Discabolis*: a moment in the discus throw—a temporal phenomenon—captured in its atemporal immediacy. The subject matter of sculpture thus is eternal form and not the historical; indeed the historical it cannot express. The historical thus can be no more than the occasion for *the presentation of the eternal*. Indeed only representative sculpture takes its point of departure from the historical. Abstract sculptures do not even attempt to freeze a moment in historical time; rather they begin by attempting to present immediately the abstract forms of line, mass, proportion, etc. For these reasons, the ideas that sculpture seeks to express are relatively abstract; that is, in relative degrees, removed from the historical.

This is not the case with architecture. Unlike sculpture, which is designed to be appreciated for its repose, beauty, and eternal form, architecture is more centrally a part of the historical world of action. The architect forms for us our worldly habitat, the place we live in; indeed, as we might say, the architect forms for us *the world*. The human world—as distinct from nature—is the public place for human action and for the conduct of human affairs; it is a polis, a city. If for no other reason than this, architecture bears a closer relation to the historical than sculpture. Great architectural works express the human love of the world; sculpture expresses a love of eternal, worldless, ideal forms.

Architecture, sculpture, and painting are all, as media, spatially static and therefore abstract in relation to the temporality of historical consciousness. In order to find a medium that is concrete and hence appropriate for expressing the human in all of its temporal, historical reality, we will have to seek it not in the (abstracted) world of visual and spatial form but in the auditory world that is constituted by temporal succession. The two suggestions for such auditory media that preoccupy Kierkegaard are music and speech. What he says in regard to these two media, perhaps surprisingly, is that music is the most abstract medium, and speech the most concrete.

Music and Speech: Pneumatic Paradigms of Aesthetic and Existential Immediacy

As I have said, both music and speech, as auditory phenomena, are intrinsically lively, dynamic, and timeful. They are in Kierkegaard's terminology *pneumatically qualified*. These two media are pneumatic ("spiritual") precisely because in both of them the sensuous is "negated." As Kierkegaard has Author A put the matter: "Language is the perfect medium precisely when everything sensuous in it is negated. That is also the case with music; that which is really supposed to be heard is continually disengaging itself from the sensuous" (E/O I,68).

I am interpreting this pneumatic "negation of the sensuous" to be a function of the fact that both music and speech are sonic media and hence temporally structured. As I have argued, time is an essential element in the structure of sound: the parts in a temporally unfolding pattern of sounds exist in a dynamic protensive/retensive succession. It is because of the temporal successiveness inherent in the sounds of music and speech that what is to be heard, namely, the idea, is constantly disengaging itself from the sounds that are its sensuous medium of expression. This is so because each sound in the dynamic succession of sounds in music and speech is constantly outrunning itself, constantly giving way to the next moment in the succession and to the next sound, and all of this in order to make way for the unfolding ideas that are constantly disengaging themselves from the succession of sounds/moments. This dynamic process, this movement of sounds, has the effect of *sundering* (in both music and speech, but in different ways in each) the idea (spirit) from the sounds; and this is so because the idea is expressed *through* the sounds, that is, through the notes and spoken words.

Because the sensuous medium of both music and speech is sound and as such has time as its qualifying element, these two pneumatically qualified media can be contrasted to the psychically qualified visual media of classical painting, sculpture, and architecture. Rather than enduring through time in a kind of static eternity, as in the case with these visual arts, the dynamic sonic/auditory medium in music and speech is constantly disappearing, constantly negating itself. Moreover, and unlike the case in the visual arts wherein the idea is seamlessly joined in harmony and accord with its sensuous medium, in music and speech idea and medium are in a relation of strife and exclusion. Kierkegaard's claim that both music and speech "negate" the sensuous is equivalent to the claim that music and speech express their ideas *through* a sensuous medium that passes away just at the moment that it comes into existence. The sounds that are *present* to the senses in music and speech are as elusive as time itself. When the sensuous is so qualified by temporality then it perpetually slips away, perpetually annuls itself for the sake of the idea. As Kierkegaard (Author A) puts it: "Language has its element in time; all other media have space as their element. Only music also occurs in time. But its occurrence in time is in turn a negation of the feelings dependent upon the senses" (E/O I,68).

In spite of these similarities, in spite of the fact that, as dynamic, sonic media, music and speech "negate the sensuous," they are, for Kierkegaard, fundamentally different. This difference is of as much ontological and axiological importance as are the similarities between the two. The heart of this difference is found in the two distinct senses in which music and speech "negate" or "annul" the sensuous. What seems implied by Kierkegaard's remarks, and my explicit claim, is that the formal properties of music and speech as media effect this difference. Because of this difference in formal structure, musical "negation" turns out to be an *aesthetic nullification* of the sensuous, while the "negation" involved in speech turns out to be an indirect *existential appropriation* of it.

Speech, according to Kierkegaard, is the perfect medium for expressing spirit as spirit, that is, spirit as it was first posited by Christianity. For Kierkegaard speech provides the necessary means for spirit to arrive at this telos, for spirit to arrive at its most positive, concrete actualization.

Music on the other hand is, for him, the quintessential medium for expressing the *demonic*. The demonic is a pneumatically qualified perversion of the positive sense of spirit. As I will interpret it, the positive sense of spirit, the sense of spirit that Christianity first introduced into the world, is spirit as essentially *incarnate* in the time and place of the sensuous historical world. This is the spirit that "negates the sensuous" and at the same time existentially appropriates it as the dynamic ground of its historical continuity. The demonic, by contrast, is the spirit that nullifies the sensuous world; the demonic is essentially *discarnate* spirit. Even though demonic spirit is discarnate and alienated from the sensuous, it nevertheless informs the sensuous world, but negatively. This produces what Kierkegaard calls *demonic sensuality*, that is, a dynamic but spiritless world. The medium of music is perfectly suited to expressing such a demonic sensuality, insofar as it, as medium, dynamically and perpetually empties itself of spirit, and insofar as it has no resources for providing spirit with a stabilizing ground within the world. The ideas that music is perfectly suited to expressing are, in Kierkegaard's (A's) words, "power, life, movement, continual unrest, continual succession" (E/O I,71). Kierkegaard calls the composite of these ideas "the sensuous in its elemental originality" (E/O I,56) and says that it finds its perfect expression in Mozart's *Don Giovanni*.

The key to what I mean by saying that music nullifies the sensuous world and speech existentially appropriates it, is found in the following cryptic remark that Kierkegaard has Author A make about the medium of music: "Music has an element of time in itself but nevertheless does not take place in time except metaphorically. It cannot express the historical within time" (E/O I,57). By contrast, Kierkegaard suggests that the wealth of speech is precisely its capacity for expressing the historical process in time. Because historical consciousness is essentially tensed, that is, stretched between its past, through its present, toward its future, it requires for its expression a medium that is itself essentially tensed. The medium perfectly suited to the expression of this historical situatedness is speech.

When we as persons—as concrete, particular, embodied individuals—say something *to* some other, at some time, *from* some particular concrete standpoint, we, of necessity, speak in a particular *tense*. The medium of speech, in other words, has a built-in formal structure of tenses and the act of speaking is always and inescapably connected to a singular historical context. As such, as both medium and as act, speech is inherently and of necessity tensed. This essentially tensed structure of the speech-act makes it the indispensable medium for the positing of, and for the expression of, the full reality of historical consciousness.

For us to exist within historical consciousness, we must be aware of and be situated within a concrete historical here and now. Because speaking is essentially tensed, it provides us with just what is required for this consciousness. When we speak in our own voice we not only acknowledge our embodiment in a particular time and place, we also insert ourselves into, and orient ourselves within, historical time. The acknowledgment of this given historical situatedness, and the historical orientation that speaking implies, provide to our words—to the otherwise merely vanishing and elusive moment of the here and now of our speech-acts—a stability and a continuity without which they would become completely disconnected from their concrete, temporal contexts of enactment. As essentially tensed, speech is equipped with the necessary resource for assuring that it will not collapse into a perpetual flux of immediate sounds disconnected from historical time and place. The tensed structure of the speech-act then makes it the perfect medium for expressing the dynamic but continuous flow of historical time. As such, the speech-act vests the historical with its ontological and axiological rights.

Although music has tempo within itself, and although it takes place within a perpetually disappearing "present," this is not the same thing as its having tenses. Again, it does not take place in time except in a metaphorical way. In music there is a "before," a "now," and an "after"—music is after all a dynamic and a pneumatically qualified medium. Yet these movements of tempo are not equivalent to the movements of history. What is yet to come in a musical performance is not the future, and what has just been played is not the past; music, lacking tenses, is unable to express historical succession and historical continuity. Rather, music, as sensuous sound, hurries along in perpetual vanishing, perpetually negating itself in absolute sensuous immediacy; and the musical idea, especially the musical idea par excellence, namely, Don Giovanni, hovers and dances in wild transcendent intoxication above the world, demonically animated, fueled, and informed by its perpetual negation of the sensuous—a negation that is taken as the ultimate liberation of spirit. Lacking a structure of tenses, or, as we might say, having only a "present" tense, and as such, not being anchored to any particular time and place, musical sounds, hurry along in a perpetual self-negation as the ideas expressed through them perpetually vanish into thin air.

One indication that music (lacking a past tense and a future tense) has no resources in its formal structure as a medium for expressing the historical process in time is the obvious fact that a musical performance is essentially repeatable; it is not tied to any concrete singular context of production. Again, a musical performance does not take place in time in any essential sense. Indeed, it is the wealth of music as an aesthetic medium that it can be, and is designed to be, repeated, to be performed over and over. This is of course distinctly different from the speech-act that has, as performed, a singular context of production.

Even though a musical performance is essentially repeatable, its mode of repetition is not psychical. In other words, even though the dynamic movements of before and after in a musical performance appear to be like the psychically qualified movements of the seasons and the planets, they are not. Musical repetition is not psychical, it is pneumatic. Unlike the psychically qualified eternal repetition of the cosmos, a repetition that is simply the moving image of a deeper eternal stasis, rest, and repose, musical repetition is the expression of radical flux, of constant movement, of movement through and through, of perpetual vanishing. This musical flux is absolutely deracinate, absolutely without connection to the stability of a continuous historical world.

Because of its character as repeatable, nothing can *happen*[15] in music—at least in the full historical sense of this term. Whatever happens in history is dated, unrepeatable, irreversible, and, as such, unique. A historical happening can take place only within a dynamic present that is *bonded* within a past actuality that has not "passed away" into nothing and oriented toward a future of radically open possibilities that are real and not merely apparent. Nothing can happen in music in this full historical sense precisely because it is unable to express either the actuality of the past or the radical openness of future possibility.

Music cannot express a historical sense of past since the historical past is not simply that which has completely passed away into nothingness. Rather, the historical past is the accumulation and sedimentation of what has gone before. Music leaves no trace behind once it is over. As Kierkegaard puts it, "[music] is over as soon as the sound has stopped and comes into existence again only when it sounds once again" (E/O I,102). By contrast, the speech-act establishes the past, the tradition in which we live and from which we orient ourselves toward the future. The historical past provides a context of continuity without which our identity is lost in the flux of the immediate moment. Indeed, without such an actuality of a historical givenness, we would not be able to act or to speak at all.

Although our words as dynamic, sonic phenomena "pass away," they pass into and become an inextricable part of *the (our) world*. The sounds of a speech-act may exist only as they are passing out of existence, as do the sounds of music, but the words of the speech-act have, as the notes of the music do not, the potential for being used to establish an actuality as intractable and as stable as we can imagine.

If music were able to express a sense of future that is historical and so radically open, then it would be true that it could express radical novelty, a quality implied by such an openness to possibility. As I will presently explain, novelty in its historical sense is the same as novelty in its most radical sense. It is because music lacks the resources for expressing the idea of novelty in its most radical form that it is impossible for anything really to happen in it. There is of course something "going on" in a musical performance—it takes place in time, but again in an unessential sense; that is, what is "happening" in a musical performance is not historical.

My claim is that because music lacks a formal structure of tenses, it is unable to express novelty in any radically historical sense. To be sure, every moment of the musical performance presents itself as having just come into existence, as being radically novel, as being present, and even as being unique; in music there is a sense of constant and perpetual renewal. On a deeper analysis, however, we find that this perpetual "novelty" is nothing like a historical (radical) novelty because, even though the sounds in a musical performance are perpetually coming into existence, the source from which these notes "come into existence" is not a radically open realm of possibility. The historical future is exactly such a realm of radical openness. In a musical performance what is to come next in the temporally unfolding performance is essentially fixed by the score before it is performed; what is to come is closed off from possibility.

While it may be true that each time we hear Beethoven's Fifth Symphony we are liable to pick up something "new," something we had not heard before, this reflects only our growing comprehension of the symphony's complexity and depth. Yet so long as it is the Fifth, it will not have a surprise ending, a different second movement, and so forth. We may await the conclusion of the symphony and be surprised by it only if we have never heard it before; but even then we do not await its ending anxiously sitting on the edge of our seats as though the ending is yet to be determined by the musicians or the conductor—as though it were being determined afresh just at the moment we are hearing it.

In this respect, listening to a musical performance is analogous to listening to a novel being read, or reading it. In both cases what will be in the novel (the future) and what is yet to be played in the music, what is yet to come, is essentially fixed. And even though what is yet to be in the case of the novel—where language is the medium—is more akin to the historical future than what is to be in the musical performance, neither expresses any radical sense of a historical future; neither expresses any sense of a radically open realm of historical possibility; hence neither expresses a radical sense of historical novelty. Ironically, then, novels cannot express historical novelty; and this is doubly so for music, for its medium is not a tensed language.

The impoverishment of music, when it comes to expressing the historical process in time, can be grasped when we recognize that music cannot tell a story. A story can be told thanks only to the resources available within the medium of language. Indeed, only to the extent that music has a verbal text (either in it or about it) can we think of the music as "telling a story." But even here it is the language that expresses the story, not the music. In an opera, for example, nothing really happens. When someone is killed on stage, we do not call the police because we know that this is not really an act that has transpired. We willingly suspend our disbelief in such cases. We know that what is going on is not real, not history, but play, or a play. Yet there would be no story, no simulation of action at all, if words were not present. Words are essential to the dramatic action. Yet even stories and plays, as narrative forms, only approximate the narrative form of history. As aesthetic, these narrative forms do not yet embody the *existential novelty* that history requires; for this the future must be radically open.

In respect to radical existential, historical novelty, the *composition* of a musical score, or the *writing* of a novel, as incomplete processes in time, embody an openness closer to history than the completed work of art. The composer in the process of composing has yet to determine how his score will end, and the same for the writer of the novel. This is also true in the case of a jazz session of improvisation wherein what is yet to be played awaits the determination of the musicians and is determined as they proceed. Such an openness is found in every temporally unfolding process, including painting, sculpting, or designing a building. As analogous as they are to historical novelty, however, these creative processes do not yet embody the radical openness to possibility that historical novelty requires.

One might say that historical novelty is existential and not aesthetic. The openness of a work of art to a new development is a function of how near it is to completion. In fact, the closer to completion the less possibility is at play. Once complete, a work of art is closed off from further possibility. At this point there is no longer any possibility for novelty within it. Because historical existence always moves toward a radically open future, possibility and novelty are permanent features of it; historical existence does not seek to close off possibilities and to come to rest; rather, historical existence is always opening itself to a horizon of new and expansive possibilities.

Where do we find radical historical novelty? The obvious answer is in *human action*. Human actions are novel, unique, irreversible, and unrepeatable. Every such action has a singular context of enactment; every action is dated, connected essentially to a particular time and place; every action is anchored in some individual with a proper name who chooses it, initiates it, who brings something new into existence through it, and who must bear its consequences. Or, to summarize, human actions are *radically free, and the human agent is radically responsible for what she has brought about.*

My claim is that the most distinctive embodiment of radical existential freedom is found in the human actions that are enacted by means of speech. That is, I want to contend that the paradigmatic expression of radical historical novelty and openness is found in the human speech-act. The model of the speech-act that I am using is *dabhar*. Speaking as *dabhar* is something dynamic, something happening in time. But *dabhar* does not only go on in historical time, it is the root and bark of historical time and without it the historical world of human action and the historical self as the free and responsible agent of actions could not come forth.

In adopting this model of speech as *dabhar* I am interpreting speech in a way similar to the interpretations of Arendt, Austin, and Wittgenstein, namely, as essentially connected to action. With Arendt, I am assuming that "speechless action would no longer be action."[16] With Austin, I am taking speaking to be the instrument indispensable for the performance of an array of actions that are distinctively human; with Wittgenstein, I am taking the meaning of speech to be essentially connected to its lively use. When we pay attention to our actual practices as speakers, the connections that Arendt, Wittgenstein, and Austin draw between speech and action strike us as obvious. This can only make us wonder why their observations to this effect have been received in the modern philosophic tradition as novel and innovative contributions to the philosophy of language.

As the formal structure of tenses in the speech-act situates a speaker within historical *time*, its distinctive *semantic and reflexive* resources situate a speaker within a fabric of relations that constitute his *place* in the historical world. The distinctive semantic and reflexive resources in the speech-act allow it to be used by a speaker to establish this historical sense of place by virtue of the fact that speaking not only *sunders* its ideas from its sensuous medium of expression—pointing to its ideas by transcending *to* them—but also by virtue of the fact that speaking establishes, at the same dialectical moment, a covenantal *bond* between the one who expresses those ideas and the one(s) to whom they are expressed; a bond that establishes the standpoint of the speaker concerning what the ideas are of, or about; a bond that ties the speaker to and within the world.

I must make it clear that I am using 'semantic' here in a very restricted sense. I will take a "semantic medium" to be one that expresses its ideas by "pointing beyond itself." In this respect, not all media are semantic. In some cases, the meaning or idea is expressed wholly *in* its medium. This is what I would call an organic or psychical medium of expression. Ideas are expressed not *in* a semantic medium but transparently *through* it. A semantic medium is, as Kierkegaard might put it, pneumatically qualified.

In the sonic media of both music and speech, the sounds direct our attention away from the sensuous *to* what is to be heard; both transcend *to* their ideas, both are semantic. And yet, the sense in which music and speech point beyond themselves as media, the sense in which both "negate" the sensuous, is radically different. This difference is all-important.

The heart of the difference between the semantic dimension of music and the semantic dimension of speech is that the latter points beyond itself by transcending *to* its idea, but always *from* its words, or more precisely *from* the sensuous particulars of the act of speaking, indeed, even more precisely, *from* the situated, embodied speaker. While it is true of music that it transcends *to* its idea, it does not do so by dialectically bonding the *to* within its *from*. Quite the contrary: a musical performance points *to* its idea precisely by *nullifying* its "from"—its connections to place and time, and to the musicians who perform it. Strangely enough, however, this nullification of the whence in musical transcendence is matched by a similar nullification of its "to" as well. Even though music "negates" the sensuous and transcends "to" its idea, the content of its essential idea is perpetual vanishing. As such, the "to" in musical transcendence, its essential idea, is a kind of dynamic and absolute "away from," a dynamic nothingness.

This difference between the transcendence of music and speech can bear repeating. Without a *reflexive grounding* in a concrete and situated "from," the "to" of musical transcendence is quite different from the "to" of the speech-act; the musical "to" perpetually nullifies the "from" and so cuts its idea off from the *whence* of its expression. In music the sensuous *whence* of the musical idea is perpetually slipping away into nothingness, perpetually vanishing; moreover, it is just this perpetual vanishing that is its idea. The speech-act, on the contrary, points beyond itself by reflexively *grounding* the "to" of its semantic transcendence solidly in the "from" of its historical context of enactment; such a grounding *bonds* the speech-act within a particular time and place and ultimately to some particular concrete, embodied speaker. This reflexive grounding of the speech-act vests the "to" of its from/to structure with its proper semantic rights, and the "from" with its proper reflexive rights. Words, in the felicitous speech-act, do not transcend to the nothingness of perpetual vanishing; rather they transcend *to* some external reality—to something, someone, to some historical possibility or actuality, and so forth; that is, the speech-act has the resources—as music does not—*to say something to some other about something*. As such, speaking, in its indicative, assertive mood, is not a perpetual nullification of the world; indeed, the very contrary. The "to" as well as the "from" in the from/to structure of the felicitous speech-act serve to establish bonds between the speaker and the world, as much so, in fact, as the very same structure serves to establish the speaker's transcendence.

Again the difference between the semantics of music, in which the sensuous particulars "point beyond themselves" *to* the ideas they express, and the semantics of the speech-act is that the "to" of the speech-act is inescapably *reflexive* while the "to" of musical transcendence is not. Because of its inherent reflexivity the speaker is an essential and pivotal element in the determination of meaning in the speech-act; the speech-act always, and of necessity, retrotends to the whence of its enactment—a whence that lies squarely in the situated embodied speaker herself. In music there is no such reflexive relation between the music and the musician. As we could also put this, the relation of the speaker to her speech-act is *necessary* and the relation of the musical composer/performer to her work is *contingent*; or more exactly: *that* the speech-act is grounded in the speaker is necessary even though *what* relation the speaker bears to the speech-act is contingent, indeed radically so. The speaker's intentions are never irrelevant in determining the meaning of the speech-act as the intentions of the musician are irrelevant to the music that she performs. Music is essentially *sundered* from the musician, from the whence of its performance. By contrast the speech-act, though also sundered from its sensuous particulars insofar as it, like music, points beyond itself, is also, and at the same time, essentially *bonded* to the concrete time and place of its enactment within the world and to the concrete speaker who enacts it before some other. Unlike the case in music, in which the "from" in its *from/to* semantic relation is perpetually nullified, in the speech-act, the "from" is, as it were, always taken (reflexively) into account.

The semantic dimension of the speech-act is reflexive thanks to its distinctive formal resources as a medium. When we speak, of necessity we express our ideas in some tense (past, present, or future), in some person (first, second or third), in some number (singular or plural), in some mood (indicative, imperative, or subjunctive), and in some voice (active or passive). Music, and for that matter aesthetic media in general, lacks these formal resources; music has no active voice, no past or future tense, no indicative mood, and so forth.

As W. H. Auden has remarked, because music lacks the resources of speech, it is unable to express even the simplest asseveration: "I love you." Auden says: "If I were a composer, I believe I could produce a piece of music which would express to a listener what I mean when I think of the word *love*, but it would be impossible for me to express it in such a way that he would know that this love was felt for *You* (not for God, or my mother, or the decimal system)."[17]

Auden's remark about music applies, for him, to all of the aesthetic media: it is simply impossible to say "I love you" in art. Yet he does make distinctions among the arts, especially the ones that have language as their medium (poetry, verse, etc.) and the ones that don't (music, painting, etc.) As music cannot express the 'you' in "I love you," because it is intransitive, so painting cannot express the 'I' in "I love you," because it lacks the active voice. Auden says:

> If I were a painter, I believe I could paint a portrait that would express to the onlooker what I mean when I think the word *You* (beautiful, lovable, etc.), but it would be impossible for me to paint it in such a way that he would know that *I* loved You. The language of painting lacks, as it were, the Active Voice, and it is just this objectivity which makes it meaningless for the onlooker to ask: "Is this really a portrait of N (not of a young boy, a judge or a locomotive in disguise)?" (DUW,36)

In poetry, or in any form of speech as art, or in any art form whose medium is language, we get closer to being able to say "I love you." Even though speech as art has resources lacking in music and painting—for example, three persons, three tenses, and an active and passive voice—it yet lacks the full resources of an existential speech-act. For one thing it lacks the indicative mood. Auden says: "As an artistic language, Speech has many advantages . . . but it has one serious defect: it lacks the Indicative Mood. All its statements are in the subjunctive and only possibly true

until verified (which is not always possible) by non-verbal evidence"
(DUW,36–37).

Although Auden is very helpful in calling attention to the differences
between the aesthetic media and the existential medium of the speech-act,
and although he nicely points out differences among the media in art—
for example, the differences between poetry on the one hand and painting
and music on the other, and between painting and music—he does not
make the distinction that I am taking to be critical: namely, the distinction
between the psychical/aesthetic and the pneumatic/aesthetic. He says at
one point that speech as art has three tenses and that music and painting
have only one tense, the present (DUW,36). The argument I am making
depends on making a distinction between the "present" of painting (and
sculpture and architecture) and the "present" of music. The former "present" is psychically qualified, that is, static, visual, and spatial; the latter
"present" is pneumatically qualified, that is, dynamic, auditory, and temporal.

But let us return to our effort to present the distinctive resources of the
pneumatically qualified, existential speech-act. Because of the fact that the
medium of speech has in its formal structure the resources I have mentioned, it allows us to take up various relations to our speech acts. This is
what I call the *personal backing* that we give to our words. This personal
backing is an essential element in the determination of the meaning of
what is said. The way we inhabit our words, the way that we are present
in them, or the way that we are absent from them, constitutes the tacit
dimension of our speech-acts. This dimension is not said, but shows itself
in and through what is said. In speech, I can own my words, fail to own
them, tentatively own them; I can speak assertively, tentatively, ironically,
hypothetically, authoritatively, jokingly, and so forth. As such, the tacit
dimension of my speech-act, that is, the relation that I bear to what I say
and to whom I say it, is critical in determining *what* is said. Or what is the
same thing, the meaning (ideas), of my speech-act, what is expressed
through it, can be determined only to the extent that my listener knows
not only *how* it is expressed but also something about my *intentions*, my
personal backing, the *who* of my expression. A critical element in determining the meaning of my words is what I mean by them.

This reflexive relation that a speaker bears to his words is absent in
music. Again, Auden is helpful in grasping this contrast. He says: "The
language of music is, as it were, intransitive, and it is just this intransitivity
which makes it meaningless for a listener to ask: "Does the composer really
mean what he says, or is he only pretending?" (DUW,36).

Central to the semantic and reflexive resources of speech are its pronouns. The pronominal resources of speech include the demonstratives
'this,' 'that,' 'these,' and 'those'; the possessives 'my,' 'mine,' 'yours,' 'ours,'
'his,' and 'hers'; the personals 'I,' 'you,' 'me,' 'we,' and 'us'; the relatives
and interrogatives 'who,' 'which,' 'what.' These pronouns are at the heart

of the reflexive resources of speech for *bonding* the speaker to his words, his words to the world, and himself to himself. *I* am able to speak freely and faithfully in my own voice, thanks to the fact that *I* can speak in the first person; *I* can make reference to items and features in, of, or about the world by representing them in words, or ostensively by pointing to them and saying, "Look at this," or "That is the point," and so forth. In addition, when I speak in my own voice I take up a stand in relation to the other to whom I speak and to the world about which I speak. Insofar as I speak in my own voice it is possible for me to claim what I say as my own.

Of the pronominal resources that are available in the speech-act, the most significant for the expression of self are the personals, especially 'I' and 'you.' Auden's comments on this are too rich to pass up:

> It is a grammatical convention of the English language that a speaker should refer to himself as "I" and to the person he is addressing as "You," but there are many situations in which a different convention would serve equally well. . . . There are many situations, that is to say, in which the use of the pronoun "I" and "You" is not accompanied by the I-feeling or the You-feeling. (DUW,42)

And going on to explain what the 'I' and 'You' feelings are, he says:

> The I-feeling: a feeling of being-responsible-for. (It cannot accompany a verb in the passive.) . . . The You-feeling: a feeling of attributing-responsi-bility-to. . . . Common to both the I- and the You-feeling: a feeling of being-in-the-middle-of-a-story. I cannot think *I love You* without including the thoughts *I have already loved You* (if only for a moment) and *I shall still love you* (if only for a moment). (DUW,42–43)

The personal pronouns 'I' and 'you' enable us to enter into covenantal relations with each other, to say, "I love you." The bonds of this relation form a mysterious but palpable hyphen between us; this *in-between* forms our world; and, as Auden tells us, this world is essentially historical, essentially a *world-story*.

Because of these distinctive resources as a medium, I, as embodied speaker, am able to speak in my own voice before you. In so doing, I am able to appear in the world before you as the unique "I" that I am called to be. (I must add, however, that I am empowered to speak in my own voice only because I have first been spoken to, addressed, called; in this sense all of my felicitous speaking is a kind of answering.) In speaking (answering) in my own voice before some other, I own my words commit-ally and reflexively, acknowledge that I am the free and responsible au-thor of their contingent utterance, and take my stand in and behind my words as the lively ground of their authority, weight, and power. As well, when I speak felicitously to you, I own up to my words as the responsible bearer of the largely unpredictable consequences of what I say. The words that I speak, insofar as I own and own up to them before you, are, in short, *mine*. Of course, I can own and own up to my words in this personal sense only to the extent that I am willing to allow my speech-act to be governed by the formal and informal conditions of felicitous speech, its surface rules of syntax, grammar, and semantics, and by its depth grammar that includes the horizon of the unsaid. It is by so owning my words and owning up to them before some other that I come to have a self and only in so owning my words before some other that I am able to appear in the world as simultaneously transcendent and immanent.[18]

Music lacks anything equivalent to these personal resources; in music there is no way for the musician to own or to own up to what is expressed in the music she performs or composes. Without these personal resources music turns out to be a semantic medium that is not reflexive. Lacking reflexive resources, music expresses its ideas by sundering them from the world, from historical time and place and from the musician who composes or performs the music. Without semantic resources that are reflexive, resources that are necessary for establishing bonds between the self and the world, the musician cannot *say* anything through her music; it is the music that expresses the ideas of restlessness, tumult, and storm, not the musician; the intentions, the personal backing, and so forth, of the musician are not at play in this expression. Music provides no space of appearance for the musician because, it, like every aesthetic work, has a life of its own, a life essentially detached from the existential situation of the musician. As essentially detached from the musician, music is left with no grounding, no reflexive *whence*, no connection to the world.

As a non-reflexive semantic medium, music is perfect for expressing the demonic. In nullifying the sensuous, it is perfectly suited to expressing the spirit of discarnate rebelliousness, the spirit of restless world-alienation, the transcendence of perpetual flux, the worldless transcendence of the immediate moment. Although music can certainly express other ideas, it finds its absolute subject in the fleeting immediacy of the perpetually vanishing moment.

The speech-act, on the other hand, is the perfect medium for expressing spirit in its positive existential sense, spirit as it was first posited by Christianity, spirit as essentially incarnate. Speech provides us with resources for situating ourselves within a world and with the resources for stabilizing our existence within historical continuity. And it is able to provide this stability within immanence without robbing us of our dynamic transcendence. Speech can also express other ideas; indeed, in the most perverse case, it can even express the demonic. Yet the speech-act finds its absolute subject in spirit as historical transcendence, *spirit as a transcendent presence within the historical continuity of the world, that is, spirit as self*.

These contrasts between music and speech, between spirit and the demonic, are at the very center of Kierkegaard's critique of the modern age;

it forms the very heart and soul of this book. So far, I have presented them in only their briefest outline; in the chapters that follow, I will elaborate and substantiate these contrasts with the aim of showing their value and power in providing a rich hermeneutical framework that can aid us not only in diagnosing the malaise of the modern age, but in prescribing a path of recovery as well.

II

DABHAR AND EXISTENTIAL IMMEDIACY

> If I have exhausted the justifications I have reached bedrock, and my spade is turned. Then I am inclined to say: "This is simply what I do."
>
> (Wittgenstein)

As Kierkegaard has remarked in *The Concept of Irony*, "actuality (the historical actuality) stands in a two-fold relation to the subject: partly as a gift that refuses to be rejected, partly as a task that wants to be fulfilled."[1] It is certainly possible to interpret Kierkegaard to mean by the term "historical actuality" something like the particular culture and tradition into which one is born. Without denying this interpretation, it is plausible to think that he may also mean something more fundamental. He may mean not just the particular cultural context of a particular human being, but the natural context of human being as well. On this reading, the historical actuality embraces both cultural and natural components. I will assume this second reading. Accordingly, I will interpret Kierkegaard to mean that we human beings find ourselves presented with both a natural and cultural *givenness* to our existence. We find, indeed, that these given facts will not admit to being ignored, even in the face of concerted efforts to do so. As well, I will interpret Kierkegaard to be asserting that we are not only presented with a natural and cultural *givenness* in our human being, but that we are confronted with a *task* of critically appropriating that givenness toward the end of being (fully) human.

The first section of this chapter will elaborate several basic premises that inform these reflections. I am assuming that we human beings find ourselves already in a world, already within existence, *prior* to our coming to any kind of self-conscious knowledge or appropriation of this actual presence-in-the-world. I will also assume that this actual existence is defined by what we do and are given to doing as humans, our actual practices. And finally my central premise is that the speech-act is the definitive human practice, that speaking is bedrock to our pre-reflective actual existence as persons among other persons in a world. What we find, in short, is that this *given* world, as well as the *givenness* of ourselves in it, is, on its most basic level, defined by the practice of speaking, hearing, and responding.

Although the form and content of our speech-acts, *what* we find ourselves saying, and *how* we find ourselves saying it, may be culturally relative, the fact remains *that* we find ourselves speaking and *that* we find ourselves placed in a human world that is defined by this human practice. The speech-act is the definitive element in the human form of life.

I realize that the idea that human beings exist in a common given world is notoriously fraught with difficulties. Cultural relativists warn us to be suspicious of the notion of a bedrock given, telling us that there may be no such common human world, no practice that is human per se. Even if there were a cross-cultural, transhistorical, bedrock human world as defined by a particular practice that is human as such, a cultural relativist might argue that it would be impossible to know how to identify it, since we would never be sure if or to what extent the practice we take as bedrock is a function of the culturally determined world-picture in which it is enacted.

In some ways I agree with the relativist on this point. Indeed, I have already asserted that there are no picture-neutral practices, that every human practice intends a world-picture and, moreover, that every practice is affected by the world-picture in which it is enacted. At the same time, however, I am convinced that we can productively *distinguish* the two elements; and that we can do this even though 'practice' and 'picture' are abstractions and the one never occurs apart from the other.

My claims *that* there is a bedrock human practice and *that* it is the practice of speaking/hearing/responding are, I must acknowledge, awkward to defend. Part of what makes the task of substantiating these claims so awkward is that their truth is, or at least ought to be, so embarrassingly obvious. For me to try meaningfully to assert that human beings ordinarily and as a matter of course speak is a little like me trying meaningfully to assert that I exist. The assertion presupposes itself. To formulate an articulated justification for the speech-act as our bedrock human practice would itself be a speech-act. Here justifications have come to an end, or better, here justifications begin.

Asserting that human beings ordinarily and as a matter of course speak is a bit like asserting that human beings ordinarily and naturally walk on two legs in an upright posture. Yet my claim is a stronger one than this. Human beings who do not or cannot walk are not handicapped in terms of their task of being human in the same way as those who do not or cannot speak. Speaking is definitive of human being in a way that walking on two legs in an upright posture is not. This stronger claim has yet to be established.

While I acknowledge the problems in assuming that there is a bedrock human actuality that is given, I also recognize that there are problems if we assume no such bedrock. This dilemma is as old as Plato. In Plato's language, 'human being' is a universal; if it is to have a meaning, it must refer to something, and moreover, the same, or at least similar, entities. The fact that we can speak meaningfully of human beings in bygone times and cultures and in other present but diverse cultures indicates that there is a bedrock meaning to the term, that there are criteria of its application, and therefore possible misuses of the term, etc. We need not adopt Plato's doctrine of forms to account for the meaningfulness of universals. It is possible to take Wittgenstein's alternative explanation of the meaningfulness of universals according to which there does not have to be one thing in common to which universal terms refer. Yet even Wittgenstein admits that the many things named by a universal term must themselves have a unifying family resemblance.[2] I suppose my claim is somewhere between Plato's and Wittgenstein's alternatives: there are many things human beings have in common and these many things bear a family resemblance to one another, but at the bedrock level there is this *one* fact: all of the many common things exist by virtue of the fact *that* we speak.

Despite this apparent difference between myself and Wittgenstein on the issue of universals I have to acknowledge that I have derived the metaphor 'bedrock' from his work. Consider the following remark:

> The mythology may change back into a state of flux, the river-bed of thought may shift. But I distinguish between the movement of the waters on the river-bed and the shift of the bed itself; though there is not a sharp division of the one from the other. . . . And the bank of that river consists partly of hard rock, subject to no alteration or only to an imperceptible one, partly of sand, which now in one place now in another gets washed away, or deposited. (OC,97)

Although I am making a slightly different use of the metaphor, it is at least consistent with the image presented here. The river's bedrock—for me, what is not subject to alteration, or only to an imperceptible one—is the fact that we as human beings ordinarily, and as a matter of course, speak.

Another crucial problem in denying the existence of a common human world and a common human being is that we are forced into a relativism that ultimately reduces the designation 'human being' to a matter of biological taxonomy and ultimately to a merely factual description. A strict relativism can only admit to a myriad of descriptive differences and similarities among human beings; it can never judge a people to be inhuman; it cannot accuse a people of falling short of what human beings ought to be or to do.

As I understand it, human being is a normative concept. It refers to a reality that is incipiently given and to a reality the full intention of which must be realized. Our given *human being* presents us with the task of *being human*. Human beings can succeed or fail at their task of being (fully) human.

If such a normative structure of human being is denied, then there can be no intelligible interpretation of Kierkegaard's claim that the given self can be separated from, as well as reconciled to, its *true* self, the self it is intended to be; or to Pascal's idea that man has fallen from his *true* place. I will elaborate this claim in the subsequent sections of this chapter.

Human being is a normative concept because it is essentially connected to a normative activity: what human beings *are* is defined by what they uniquely *do*, or more exactly, by what they are uniquely capable of doing; and what human beings are uniquely capable of doing is normative through and through. What is this? Following a long philosophic tradition, I will say that human beings are uniquely capable of *action*.[3] And following up on what I have already said, I will assert that the actions human beings are uniquely capable of are those that are enacted by means of speech. My claim, then, is that there is a bedrock normative practice that determines human being as a normative concept and distinguishes it in kind from all other kinds of being in the created order. This bedrock human practice is the *speech-act*.

The speech-act, as a normative concept, can succeed or fail for a number of reasons. Critical to the success or failure of a speech-act is the speaker/actor's relation to it. Although other elements are necessary for success, the reflexive authorization of the speech-act by the speaker, who addresses some other, is a pivotal factor for that success. It is in a human being's taking up, or failing to take up—in whatever degree of either— this reflexive relation to the speech-act, that the success or failure of being human is measured. That is, a person can succeed or fail at being fully human and this success or failure is essentially connected to the matter of whether and to what extent a human being takes up the task of reflexively owning and owning up to the words that he finds himself already speaking before he comes to reflective self-consciousness.

To set the discussion of these matters in the context of the previous chapter, let me assemble a few brief reminders. I am taking *dabhar* as the paradigm of the speech-act. On this model of speech, there is an intimate connection between speech and action, between words and deeds; as such, speech, on this model, is a dynamic phenomenon. To put it in Kierkegaard's language, speech as *dabhar* is a *pneumatically qualified medium*. The lively unfolding sensuous sounds of speech are constantly annulling themselves making way for the ideas they intend.

Yet, as I have already argued, the medium of speech must be distinguished from another pneumatically qualified medium, music. Speech as *dabhar* has within itself, as the medium of music does not, semantic and reflexive resources which enable the speaker to use his words to *say* something about the world. A speaker can not only take up a transcendent relation to the world in the dynamic movements of his speech, but, at the same time, he is enabled, because of the semantic and reflexive resources within the speech-act, to take a stand within the world, bonding himself to it, and to the other before whom he speaks, and before whom he is revealed—both to the other and to himself. No such reflexive resources are available in music.

As I argued in the last chapter, although speech and music are both semantic media—both "negate" the sensuous, though in different ways—only speech is an essentially reflexive medium. Its semantic and uniquely reflexive resources make speech the perfect medium for expressing spirit in all of its paradoxical transcendence *of*, and immanence *in*, the world. Apart from a medium that can express this paradoxical tension between spirit and the sensuous, spirit cannot come forth in all of its power and existential actuality.

This last point is crucial to my argument. The practice of the speech-act (as *dabhar*) intends a *dabhar*-centered world-picture. It was just this pneumatically qualified world-picture that Christianity posited concretely in the world as a world-historical force. Moreover, the appropriation of this *dabhar*-centered (Christian) world-picture is necessary for the speech-act to realize its telos, namely, the expression of spirit. Or to put this more paradoxically, spirit and the speech-act receive in Christianity a reciprocal vesting of rights, a co-realization, as it were. In Christianity, spirit and speech burst forth into their full existential power and reality *together*, and necessarily so.

Before developing this argument, I must defend my assertion that the bedrock human practice is the speech-act (*dabhar*). The last section of this chapter will begin to lay the groundwork for showing what I mean by saying that the practice of speaking must be appropriated within a *dabhar*-centered world-picture in which speech is accorded the ontological efficacy necessary for it to reach its telos of expressing spirit in all of its existential reality and power.

Speech and Human Being

Speaking, whatever else it may be, is a practice to which we, as human beings, are given; the fact that we speak is therefore not a function of a particular culture or tradition. As I said, it is almost as natural for us to speak as it is for us to walk on two legs in an upright posture. Again, however, although walking and speaking are equal in being given in our human nature, they are not equal in terms of their weight in defining the human. Speaking is definitive of human being in a way that walking, or for that matter, anything else, is not. I am assuming that we can legitimately *distinguish* a naturally determined fact about human beings from a culturally determined one (such as shaking hands as a greeting) without implying something that I think is not true, namely, that culture can be coherently *separated* from nature. Or what amounts to the same thing, I assume that we can distinguish between natural and cultural facts about us while at the same time maintaining that *nature and culture are encompassed by the historical actuality*—the actuality that Kierkegaard says presents itself to us as both gift and task.

But is the claim that speaking is the bedrock human practice as free of culturally determined assumptions as I have asserted? Doesn't this claim simply reflect the values of western culture, or perhaps, even more narrowly, the Judaeo-Christian tradition? In fact, isn't it simply one interpretation—indeed, one among many other possible ones? Couldn't we just as legitimately say that human beings are uniquely given to thinking, reasoning, making moral distinctions, greeting one another, remarking on the weather, telling stories and jokes, etc.? And what makes one of these practices bedrock and the others not? Isn't it the case that it is our world-pictures that establish whatever preeminence one practice has over another?

My reply is based on my assumption that pictures are either *made of words* or presuppose a context of speech. If this is true, it means that the fact *that* we speak must be more than merely a picture of human being; indeed, it must be the condition of the possibility of our having pictures at all. Our world-pictures may interpret this ontologically primitive fact that we speak and tell us, for instance, what kind of phenomenon speech is, its place in the scheme of things, its importance to human being, its ontological efficacy, etc. This makes the actual practice of speaking a bedrock fact about us in comparison to our pictures which interpret speech. Moreover, in any world-picture that interprets with words, or within the context of words, a particular human practice in which speech is the means for engaging in that practice, the fact that we speak will show itself as the antecedent presupposition of that picture. Again, and more generally, we can say that the fact that we have pictures at all is due to the antecedent fact that we are and must be speakers before we are enabled to reflect.[4]

What this establishes is that the practice of speaking is logically antecedent to pictures which are made of words, or made in the context of speech. But what makes speaking the bedrock practice in comparison to other human practices? I think a similar argument holds. Namely, those practices that are peculiarly human are precisely those practices that are conducted in and through speech; I mean the practices of making moral distinctions, of telling stories, of asking questions and responding to them, of describing things, of explaining things, of telling jokes, of praying, and so on and so forth. We of course engage in other activities—we eat and drink, we procreate, etc.—but these are activities that are not distinctively human. Indeed, even activities we share with the animal world are transformed in their human appropriation by the power of speech: we humans dine, an activity which is the occasion for conversation, and we human beings procreate, but, at least in some cultures, within the covenant of marriage, a covenant enacted by speech.

In some ways I suppose this justification for my claim that speaking is the bedrock practice among the myriad of human practices sounds a bit like begging the question. After all, I have simply asserted that the distinctively *human* practices are those which presuppose speaking. I agree that this is not quite an argument, not quite a justification, but again, we are dealing with a matter where justifications end and begin. I have no other justification to offer, my spade is turned. Again I feel that trying to justify the claim that speaking is definitive of human being, that it is our bedrock practice, is like trying to justify the claim that I exist, or that the law of non-contradiction is a correct logical principle.

As a bedrock fact about human beings, then, the practice of speaking is not culturally relative, nor is it merely conventional (that is, a matter of convenience); at the same time it is not, by any means, necessary or inevitable that every human being will speak any more than it is necessary that every human being will walk. It is certainly not physically or causally necessary—in the efficient or mechanical sense of causality—in the way that, say, certain chemicals cause certain determined reactions when combined with other chemicals in a given environment. Nor is it teleologically necessary in exactly the way that, for example, a healthy pear tree will bring forth pears as a matter of course in the maturation process and in the biological cycle. Human beings come to be able to speak only if they are called forth to do so by other speakers whose speech stands as an invitation to the initiates to participate. This too, we might say, is a matter of course, but not just a matter of biological maturation or natural cycle. The practice of speaking is a practice that has to be "entered into." Another way to put this is to say that the practice of speaking involves not only an intentional structure, but also a *consent* and ultimately, in the case of reflexively integral speech, a self-conscious, freely chosen *intention*.

While speaking is a natural practice to which we are given, it is not a *necessary* but a *contingent* fact that we speak. And what is it contingent on? Partly on physical and biological facts, on the health of the person, on the bodily mechanisms needed to speak and hear being in good working order, on maturation and environment, and on native abilities and skills, mental and physical, and so forth; but coming to be a speaker among other speakers is also contingent, and uniquely so, on what I have just called the consent and the intention of the would-be speaker to enter the world of the speakers who are buzzing around her in the dynamic sounds in which she intimates *meaning*. The speaker's act of consent and intent to enter into the world of speakers is a *free* act, though this does not imply that it is the product of an explicit deliberation and decision. I am assum-

ing that intentions and decisions can range over the whole gamut of consciousness, from the so-called unconscious to the conscious, or better,
from the tacit to the explicit.

After choosing to enter into speech, however, the speaker is presented
with another choice: will I, as a speaker, speak as myself? in my own
voice? Will I own my words before some other and own up to them? Will
I speak with *reflexive integrity*? If I elect not to speak, in the full-blown
sense of the term, this of course does not mean that I must stop talking.
This means that speaking in the fullest sense of the term is contingent on
the *will* of the would-be speaker, on her self-conscious *decision* to exist
among other speakers.

It is a contingent fact whether or not human beings enter into speech,
and equally a contingent fact whether or not human beings take up the
task of being human, of realizing the human potential which speaking
intends. However, there is a *necessary* connection between taking up speech
and taking up and realizing the telos of human being. If someone fails
for some reason to enter the world of speech, then we say of him that
something has gone wrong with his development, that he is handicapped
or impaired, that his human potential has been arrested or thwarted. To
put it differently, we can define the necessary connection between taking
up speech and realizing our human telos by saying that the former is
normatively required for the latter, which is tantamount to saying that it is
normal for human beings to speak and *abnormal* if they do not or cannot.

I realize that putting the matter in terms of normalcy raises our anxiety,
and rightly so. How easily this distinction between the normal and the
abnormal can lead us astray! Consider the following chilling remark by
Wittgenstein concerning a people whose children are learning to count.
He says:

> A certain tribe has a language of kind (2). [A language of kind (2) is es-
> sentially that of Par.1–2 of the *Investigations*: It contains "demonstrative
> teaching" of names of building blocks, and a series of numerals learnt by
> heart.] . . . The children of the tribe learn the numerals this way: They are
> taught the signs from 1–20 . . . and to count rows of beads of no more than
> 20 on being ordered, "Count these." When in counting the pupil arrives
> at the numeral 20, one makes a gesture suggestive of "Go on," upon which
> the child says (in most cases at any rate) "21." . . . If a child does not re-
> spond to the suggestive gesture, it is separated from the others and treated
> as a lunatic.[5]

This does seem like a hasty judgment to say the least. Many injustices,
of course, have been rendered on a similar basis. Yet does this mean that
nothing would count for us in determining that someone is, in the final
analysis, a lunatic? insane? pathological? or in some way outside the realm
of normal human being? And isn't this ultimately determined by us by

reference to the *refusal* or inability on the part of the impaired person to enter into the world of coherent speech-(action)? And yet don't we hold these impaired human beings to have intrinsic worth and value just because they are human beings and are, as such, the kind of beings which uniquely bear the potential for a fully personal existence as self and spirit? And don't we always hold out the hope that these human beings whose full human potential has been thwarted can nevertheless be called forth in the way that such a potential is called forth from our children into the actuality intended by that potential?

To make the distinction clearer between potential and realized potential, between gift and task, I will say that *human beings* are individuals who have the potential for *being (fully) human.* Individuals who have realized the human potential, to whatever degree, are human beings who have become human, to whatever degree. I continue to assert, with Kierkegaard, that spirit is the telos of human being and that becoming human is the same as becoming a self in self-conscious possession of self, and this is the same as being spirit and as existing personally. As such, I am contending that there is an essential connection between becoming human and speaking, insofar as I am, with Kierkegaard, taking speaking to be the perfect and normatively required medium for the full expression of spirit, as spirit.

One obvious obstacle to entering the speaking world and, if I am right, to taking up the task of being human, is found among human beings who are deaf or mute. Given that speaking is fundamentally an auditory, oral/aural, phenomenon and that it is the central human practice, am I forced to relegate the deaf/mute to a position of not being able fully to actualize the telos of their human being?

Let me first say that the deaf and the mute are handicapped when it comes to the practice of speaking insofar as speaking requires in its normal execution an ability to hear and an ability to articulate words audibly. Yet it is obviously possible for the deaf/mute to compensate for their loss of the sense of hearing with other senses, with sight, smell, taste, and touch. Sign languages compensate for the deficit in speaking by substituting visual signs for words and sentences allowing the signer to become a speaker, to engage in speech-acts. This is possible, however, only because the signs trade on the logic, syntax, grammar and the bodily ground of speech. What I mean by saying that sign-words trade on the bodily ground of speech is that they are rooted in the same gesticulations and bodily motility, sentience, and orientation in which articulated oral/aural speech is rooted. This common rootedness of the spoken word and the visual word-sign in the tonic ground of our rhythmic, sentient, motile, and oriented mindbodies makes it possible to substitute the word-sign for the word and hence for the deaf/mute to enter the human world of speech and action.

Yet if the deaf/mute person is born deaf, his entry into the world of speech is not simply a matter of substitution and it is certainly not simply a matter of course. The person born deaf faces extraordinary obstacles. It may be that because of this, we have come to have enormous respect for the deaf/mute "speaker" and "hearer." Our respect is a way of acknowledging our appreciation of and our amazement over the effort and will it took for the deaf/mute person to enter the speaking world—an effort and will much greater than is required by hearers, since, as we imagine it, the normal route into the speaking world is a routine matter of course. This appreciation, it seems to me, is well placed, even though it does harbor a possible misleading tendency to reduce the normal entrance into speech to a wholly unremarkable matter of course, which, obviously, it is not.

This respect for those who have overcome the obstacles of deafness is nowhere more profound than in our appreciation of Helen Keller. Not only did she become deaf shortly after her birth, she was also born blind. Until she was enabled, with the help of her teacher, Anne Sullivan, to enter the human practice of speaking, she had not become human to any significant degree, though she was a human being with that potential. Because she was not able to do as a matter of course what human beings normally do and are routinely given to doing, she behaved as a kind of animal responding immediately to its environment—though here, unlike the case with the animal, the environment in which Helen was trying to make her way was not a merely natural one; it was an environment whose inhabitants were speakers. This produced an extraordinary tension between Helen and her family and Helen and her teacher, a tension that perhaps more than anything provided the impetus for her famous breakthrough at the well with Miss Sullivan, in which Helen got the connection between the word-sign and the items and features of the world to which they semantically referred. This was a breakthrough, I would say, into the human world, the world defined by the speech-act. Walker Percy remarks on the significance of this event: "Eight-year-old Helen made her breakthrough from the good responding animal which behaviorists study so successfully to the strange name-giving and sentence-uttering creature who begins by naming shoes and ships and sealing wax, and later tells jokes, curses, reads the paper, writes *La sua volontade e nostra pace*, or becomes a Hegel and composes an entire system of philosophy."[6]

One of the reasons why sign language can compensate for the inability to speak and allow the deaf/mute to enter the speaking world and take up the task of being human is that both words and sign-words are rooted in the embodiment of the speakers which is the *common ground* of their speech. We all, hearers and non-hearers alike, live in and from a common ground of meaning because we are all mindbodies, alive, sentient, rhythmic, oriented, and motile.[7] The dynamic forms and patterns of meaning that we discern in the world and express in our speech have a common ground because these meanings originate in, and never completely leave, the primordial, pre-reflective intentional and dynamic structure which is our embodiment-in-the-world. Because of this common ground, human beings universally are enabled to recognize the dynamically unfolding motifs embodied in the visual gestalts of a smile, a gesture, a look of puzzlement, love, pity, etc. This fact accounts for our being able to get along remarkably well in a foreign country in which we do not speak a word of the native language. Both spoken words and sign-words trade on the fact of our common dynamic embodiment, and on the common patterns of meaning that embodiment affords.

It seems that I can still maintain that speech is the ultimate bedrock fact definitive of human being, even though I acknowledge that it is itself rooted in a more primitive ground, our sentient, rhythmic, oriented, and motile mindbodies. The reason that I say this is that the fact that we are mindbodies is not definitive of human being per se. Here we meet the common ground on which both humans and animals stand, and perhaps even the common ground that ties humans not only to animals but to rocks and trees, and all to cycle and season. We are part of the natural order, rooted in it, inescapably bound to it. In fact this primitive bond to nature is the source of our biological life, and the source of our sense of our kinship to nature, our feeling of being at home in a common natural world.

It may sound as if my emphasis on grounding speech in our deeply felt sense of rootedness in the natural order is a return to the dominant motif of the psychically qualified world-picture that we have previously discussed. It need not be so, however. Although the context of human being, as I have asserted, is the historical actuality, as opposed to natural cycle, this does not imply that human beings are separated from nature. On the contrary. This is so because the historical actuality encompasses both the natural and the cultural. What the positing of the historical actuality does effect is the introduction of a new possibility for defining the human relation to its natural ground.

The new possible relation to nature that a pneumatically qualified world-picture introduces to the human imagination is incipiently present in the practice of speaking, but in that practice, it is not posited concretely and fully. When the pneumatically qualified world-picture is posited, then the resources become available in which the practice of speaking can be authorized and ratified and speech can be vested with its rights. Once this occurs, the redefinition of the human relation to the natural order can be appropriated. This redefinition is in terms of the dialectical categories of sundering and bonding which only speech—speech fully vested with its rights—can express.

The point I am trying to make here is that even though our practice of speaking is bonded to a natural ground, the center of which is our own mindbodies, and even though it retains an essential relation to nature in the pneumatic redefinition of the self/world relation (a redefinition that dialectically sunders us from and rebonds us personally to the natural order) the practice of speaking, and not that ground, defines and is the bedrock criterion for human being per se.

Having said this, I must immediately double back and, from the perspective of this bedrock definition of the human being as speaker, say something about the human status of what I will for convenience sake call pre-speakers and post-speakers. Pre-speakers are of two sorts: (1) children who have not learned to speak; (2) and those who are so infirm that they are never able to be initiated into the practice of speaking. Post-speakers are those who once spoke but who have lost the ability to speak through illness or injury, mental or physical. By defining the bedrock human practice as speech, am I excluding them from the human? On the contrary.

Pre-speaking infants have a human status precisely because they are pre-speakers, because they are the kind of beings who, usually and normally, and as a matter of course, come to speak. What I mean by "kind of being" is that pre-speakers are mindbodies of a certain shape, namely, the shape that speakers have. As mindbodies, pre-speakers have an upright posture, a human face, limbs and features in the right place, and so forth. Dogs and cats, and even chimpanzees, who do not speak, are not regarded by us as pre-speakers, not only because they don't speak, but because they do not have the embodiment that speakers require. As Wittgenstein once put it, *"If a lion could talk we could not understand it" (PI,223)*.[8] Insofar as pre-speaking children are sentient, oriented, rhythmic, and motile mindbodies in human form, that is, in the form that speakers require to be speakers, they are rightly accorded human status. But again, our pre-speaking children receive their human status by reference to the bedrock human practice of speaking: they are potentially speakers, speakers in promise we might say.

Similar things can be said about those pre-speakers for whom speaking will not be a matter of course, indeed, for whom speaking with words or signs, or gestures, or any other substitute, will never be possible at all. Such a situation is tragic precisely because it is acknowledged that this pre-speaker who has the bodily form of a speaker will never realize so many of the riches of the human life that speech affords. We feel the deep tragedy of a baby born severely retarded or brain-damaged or autistic for we know that he will likely never be able to take part in human discourse of any sort and will have to be taken care of as an infant for his whole life. Yet in holding this a tragedy, we accord a human status to this pre-speaker and again we define this status in terms of speech. The tragedy is that this pre-speaker, and ultimately this non-speaker, shares the common ground of human speech by virtue of his human embodiment and yet cannot speak.

The human kinship of bodily form makes it possible to enter into some level of human relation with those unable to speak insofar as the dynamic intentional structures of the human mindbody pre-figure the dynamic intentional structures of speech. Looking into a human face that smiles or

frowns or is puzzled or sad, or responding to a gesture of the human
hand, we can discern motifs that are human precisely because they are
motifs that strain toward expression in speech. This makes our nonverbal
relation with an infirm pre-speaker fundamentally different than the corresponding relation we have to the animals we also care for, feed, and
love. The difference that the common form of our human embodiment
makes forms the basis for whatever humanness that can be achieved between speakers and those who are not able fully to enter the speaking
world.

If we grant the importance of the human form as the ground for the
human practice of speaking we are still faced with the problem of the
status of human zygotes and embryos, the stages of human gestation
where the human form is barely if at all discernible. Are we forced to say
that the zygote and the embryo are not human beings? The same logic
prevails. The zygote and the embryo are human by virtue of their potential for becoming human, by virtue of their potential to take up the human
practice of speaking and the task of being human. While this does not
settle any abortion issue, it blocks off any argument that would justify
abortion on the basis that the life that is terminated in an abortion is not
human.

The logic of the potential/actual dialectic can just as well apply to the
post-speaker—the one who once knew the richness of human speech but
who now, for whatever reason, is no longer able to speak. Certainly such
a post-speaker is accorded the status of human being not because he
someday may enter the speaking world again but because he was part of
it in the past. Even if he is in a coma and completely unable to respond
at any level to anyone and has therefore lost all traces, save his bodily
form, of an actual human presence, we nevertheless acknowledge his humanness on the basis of his past, and, if the prognosis allows, we hope for
his return to that former presence. It is because the ability to dwell in the
world of speech is so central to our human being that the tragedy here is
so deep. The tragedy is especially felt when the one who has lost his ability
to participate in the practice of speaking is aware of his loss. We are faced
with an agonizing choice when we are asked to chose which is worse, the
case of the one who cannot speak but who has no conception of the riches
of speech or the case of the one who knows these riches and has lost them.
The one advantage of the latter is that we have before us, even if there
is no promise of his return to health, the human form that evokes in us
the memory of a human life. Perhaps it is better to have lived and lost life
than never to have lived at all.

I bring this section to a close, but not with any conviction that I have
accomplished what I set out to do. Perhaps it is finally not possible to
justify what is at the bedrock of all of our justifications. I therefore will
be content with what I have said, and hope that one thing at least is clear,
namely, what I mean by asserting that the practice of speaking is the bed-

rock criterion definitive of human being as such. If I am right, this definition of human being is not only consistent with Kierkegaard's analysis
of the self but advances our understanding of that analysis.

Speech and Being Human

What I have been saying is that human being has a given intentional
structure and therefore a telos to be realized. That telos is the goal of
being (fully) human, a goal I am equating with the aim of becoming spirit
or self. I am attempting to make the case that the realization of that goal
of being human, to whatever degree it is realized, is directly correlated to
the realization of our human capacity for speech; or, to express it differently, that the call to be (fully) human, i.e., spirit, and the call to be a
speaker, in the full sense of that term, are but two sides of the same coin.
In this regard, I have claimed that entering the world of the speech-act
is a *normal* unfolding of the human telos; if we human beings don't or
somehow can't enter that world, then we—while remaining human beings—are handicapped in our capacity to respond to our calling to be
(fully) human.

I must now go on to elaborate my claim that the speech-act is a normative or intentional phenomenon. But before I turn to this more detailed
elaboration of the normative/intentional structure of the speech-act, I
want to reiterate my global aim in such an elaboration. What I want to
show is that the success of the speech-act is the sine qua non for reaching
the goal of being human. My ultimate claim, extrapolating from Kierkegaard, is that the call to be (fully) human, that is, to be spirit or self, is
not a call simply to utter words, but a call to *speak* in the fullest sense of
that term. To realize the telos of the speech-act is to realize the telos of
human being, that is, to be human in the fullest sense.

The speech-act is an intentional phenomenon simply because speaking,
as J. L. Austin has reminded us in his *How to Do Things with Words*,[9] is a
performance. To speak, Austin points out, is to act. Austin's seemingly
new discovery that the speaking of words is an essential component in the
doing of deeds, is actually the rediscovery, unacknowledged by Austin—
most likely because he did not explicitly realize it himself—of the ancient
Hebraic understanding of speech as *dabhar*. Austin's "discovery" appeared
new to the philosophic community only because the dynamic understanding of speech as *dabhar* had long been eclipsed by the dominance of the
more static conception of speech as *logos*.

One exception to the modern tendency to eclipse speech as *dabhar* is
found in Hannah Arendt's important book *The Human Condition*. Arendt
"discovered" the correlation of words and deeds in the pre-Socratic praxis
of the Greek polis and in early Greek epic poetry where political practice
was definitive of human life; she does not acknowledge finding it (even

though she is herself a Jew—perhaps in a deeper sense than she realized) in the biblical narratives where *dabhar* is embraced not only in the life of the Hebrews but in their accounts of the real. That Arendt was able to dis-(re?)cover speech as *dabhar*, speech as a dynamic, temporally unfolding activity, speech, in other words, as act, in a world—the Greek world—that ultimately moved in its accounts of the real in the direction of eternity, stasis, and repose, and in the direction therefore of developing a more static and visual model of speech, namely, a model of speech as *logos*, shows the stubborn persistance of *dabhar* even in the face of cultural pressures to suppress it. Or to put this differently, if *dabhar* is the bedrock meaning of speech, as I am claiming, then it is not surprising that *dabhar* is discernible at the base of every account of speech, even accounts that seek to transform speech into a static, visual phenomenon.

But let us return to Austin's contribution to our rediscovery of speech as *dabhar*. That contribution is found in his careful linguistic phenomenology of our ordinary practices. This phenomenology shows in no uncertain terms just how closely our words and deeds are connected in our actual practice of speaking, and just, therefore, how much speech is a lively and dynamic performance. In example after example Austin shows that the lived practice of speaking/hearing/responding will not fit into an account of speech where words are descriptive reports on our acts and therefore essentially removed from them. For Austin our words are not *about* our deeds, as if our deeds were inward, silent, private acts, but the tools necessary for the performance of them. "I promise" is not a report on my inward act of promising; rather saying those words, or some appropriate substitute, is the way that I engage in the act of promising. It is not that the saying *is* the doing, for other factors are relevant, but the saying is the *means* necessary for the doing to be accomplished.

Because acts are essentially intentional, to claim that speaking is the necessary means for engaging in an act is to place speech in an intentional framework as well. To say that acts are essentially intentional is just to say that acts embody a telos which can be realized in varying degrees. Actions can be performed well, so-so, or poorly, etc. Criteria define what the telos of the act is and critical assessments by competent judges determine the relative success or failure of the performance. I am thinking here about such ordinary assessments as the ones used by judges in the Olympic Games who appraise the dive or the skating routine, or the everyday assessments we make when, upon watching our child attempt a forward roll on the gymnastic floor, we say that it was well executed, or that it needs work; or on the tennis court when we say, "good shot."

A moment's reflection shows that we treat our ordinary practice of speaking in a way similar to the way that we treat any performance or act. Indeed we quite routinely and unproblematically submit what we say to judgments of success or failure, or, as Austin has put it, to the judgments of being either happy or unhappy, felicitous or infelicitous. Our sayings as much as our doings are rule-governed and can go wrong or succeed; what we say as much as what we do involves intentions, goals, and purposes which can be realized fully or in part and what we say, like what we do, is always liable to failure.

What we say is governed on the most superficial level by the rules of syntax. In order to say something the words uttered must have a coherent order. Merely uttering a random string of words does not constitute a felicitous speech-act. Words could not add up to sentences without rules of syntax that govern the proper relations among its elements, the verbs, nouns, adverbs, articles, etc. The sentence, "Bring ball the please me" is not coherent despite the fact that one may get the sense of it by tacitly translating the proper order of the words into "Please bring me the ball," or something more primitive like "Ball," while pointing to the ball. Such incoherencies can easily be overlooked if the circumstances warrant, for example, if the speaker is just learning the English language, has had a hard day, and so forth.

Our speech is also governed by rules of grammar. As competent speakers we know that our sentences must be constructed so that subjects and verbs agree, so that our modifiers don't dangle, so that our infinitives don't split, so that our verbs are properly conjugated, so that we have not confused predicate nominatives with direct objects, and so forth. Even the most careful, however, is liable to mistakes on these matters. Usually these mistakes can be overlooked and, with the patience and forbearance of our interlocutor, the sense and meaning of our words comes through. Sometimes this overlooking of grammatical errors can sediment into accepted usage. "Is it them?" instead of the correct "Is it they?" can come to *sound right*; this may lead us to think that grammatical rules are unimportant. Those who denigrate the significance of correct grammar might argue that such rules are designed to serve sense and meaning and not the other way around. We can imagine someone of this bent saying "It really don't matter how you say something so long as we know what somebody means and so long as we get the point across."

On the other side of this, however, rules of grammar and syntax do in fact serve sense and meaning. There is a rather significant difference between the sentence "Give the prize to a child," and "Give a prize to the child." The meaning and sense of the two sentences is different just by virtue of the selection and placement of the articles. If the speaker wants to say something clearly, a minimum condition for the success of this effort is that the speaker follow the rules of grammar and syntax.

This much is perhaps more than obvious. But there are other dimensions to the intentional structure of the speech-act. One such dimension is what Wittgenstein called "depth grammar."[10] The depth of the intentional structure of the speech-act is liable to go unnoticed since "saying something" is so often taken to be equivalent to uttering a grammatically and syntactically coherent sentence. For example the sentence "I have a rock in my shoe but I don't feel it" is as syntactically and grammatically sound as the sentence "I have a pain in my leg but I don't feel it"; and yet the former sentence makes sense and the latter does not. The reason for this is that the meaning of 'pain' is such that it is the kind of thing that we feel if it is our pain; the claim that we have an unfelt pain is ungrammatical in the depth grammatical sense.

But what accounts for depth grammar? For Wittgenstein, and for me, depth grammar is defined in and by our bedrock practices, what we do and say and what we are given to doing and saying. The bedrock practice of speaking which is the ground of what is explicitly said in the speech-act goes way beyond the words. The depth grammar of the speech-act is rooted in informal felicity conditions which play a decisive part in determining the success or failure of the practice. These felicity conditions, which are often referred to as "extralinguistic,"[11] include the circumstances of the speech-act, the intentions of the speaker and the uptake of those intentions by the hearer, the tacit backing of what is said, the body language of gesture, glance, smile, and grimace, which do not merely accompany speech but constitute the necessary ground in relation to which our words come to have the meanings that they have.

It is a commonplace that it is possible for the attentive listener to pick up on discrepancies between the speaker's words that are spoken and the body language, tone of voice, look, and so forth which form the tacit ground of the words. Here what is not said is speaking louder than the words. Indeed I will say that in the speech-act what is not said is more important than what is said, even though this tacit ground of what is said is not said but shows itself *through* what is said. To put this in a familiar Kierkegaardian idiom it is not what you say but how you say it. And to expand this: it is not only what is said and how it is said that is critical in determining meaning, it is also *who* says it. What is of enormous importance in the speech-act is the intention of the speaker, an element of the speech-act that is not said but shows itself. In fact it is a logical impossibility for the tacit backing of the speech-act to be made explicit. When I say something and then say that I meant it, the question arises as to whether I was serious when I said that I meant it, and so forth in an infinite regress. Ultimately the ground of the speech-act, then, is in its tacit backing and the center of this is the speaker himself.

I could continue to point out the various elements within the complex network of felicity conditions for the success of the speech-act. However, I will assume that the point of the intentional structure of the speech-act has been amply argued, if not by me here, then in the works of those to whom I have referred.

The issue that I am interested in, and to which I would now like to turn, is one that assumes all of the foregoing claims, but carries the idea of the intentional structure of the speech-act and the correlate idea that the speech-act is subject to felicity conditions further than linguistic philosophy is usually willing to. With Kierkegaard I want to claim that the ultimate telos of the speech-act is the expression of the full reality of spirit; that is, I want to claim that a person can be a self and come to herself only within the context of the speech-act and that the speech-act aims at self-realization, self-revelation, and self-possession. Beyond this I want to claim that world-pictures play an essential role in the realization of the intention of a given speech-act. My claim, with which I think Kierkegaard would agree, at least by implication, is that the world-picture in which the speech-act is enacted is crucial as a felicity condition in determining whether the ultimate intention of the speech-act is realized or not. In this regard our world-pictures can either thwart or enable spirit to come forth into its own.

While it may be true that in our practice we are given to speaking, none of our practices, including speaking, are picture-neutral: there are no pure practices. Every speech-act is enacted within a theater of reflection in which the speech-actor is conscious, at whatever level, and has a conception, however ill-defined, of what she takes herself to be doing. Any world-picture which does not accord a central place and an ontological efficacy to the speech-act would of necessity produce for us a conceptual-existential discrepancy and render ourselves problematic to ourselves, calling our place in reality into serious question. Our human practice of speaking, to which we are given, requires for the full realization of its intention—the intention of expressing spirit or, as we might put it, self-expression—a world-picture which vests the practice with an efficacy appropriate to that expression.

Word and Spirit

Before Christianity, the psychical world-picture that the Greeks had and lived in and from was one that attempted to thwart what was to their imaginations the order-destroying and meaning-destroying flux of temporality and contingency. That temporality and contingency were so stringently denied any positive status in the Greek world-picture testifies to the fact that they form an ineluctable dimension of the human experience; a *given* dimension that cannot be ignored; a dimension that impinges on our lives and demands to be reckoned with. To the extent that temporality and contingency were incipiently and negatively present in the lives of the Greeks, so was the incipient presence of spirit; spirit lives and moves and has its reality within temporality and contingency. The Greeks sensed this presence of spirit in the place where it most normally appears, namely, in the dynamic and lively practice of speaking to one another in the course of their everyday lives. And this sense of the presence of spirit on the level of the speech-act was perhaps all the stronger by virtue of the fact that speech was so central to Greek life. Perhaps this explains why the Greek philosophic community felt such an urgent need to address the issue of the relation between time and eternity and the Greek tragic poets were led to address the agony of the conflict between the exigencies of a temporal and contingent life and a cosmology where temporality and contingency are denied any positive ontological status.

Spirit, then, was intimated by the Greeks—as it has been in every human community since man's origin—in their actual practice of *presenting* themselves to one another in their words and deeds. Yet without a pneumatically qualified world-picture the Greeks were not able to acknowledge or embrace this incipient presence of spirit. Lacking such a picture, temporality and contingency were terrifying; indeed it is no wonder that the Greeks sought to flee into eternity, necessity, fate, stasis, and silent contemplation. Unable to appropriate the incipiently present spirit and ultimately their own concrete, historical, and contingent existence, the Greeks repressed spirit by defining it as psyche and substituted a timeless eternity for the temporality they lived within and fate and necessity for the contingency they could not face.

In the end the Greek flight from spirit led to the rejection of speech itself in favor of the silent (visual) contemplation of the eternal. As Hannah Arendt has remarked:

> The philosopher's experience of the eternal, which to Plato was *arrheton* ("unspeakable"), and to Aristotle *aneu logou* ("without word"), and which later was conceptualized in the paradoxical *nunc stans* ("the standing now"), can occur only outside the reality of human affairs and outside the plurality of men, as we know from the Cave parable in Plato's *Republic*, where the philosopher, having liberated himself from the fetters that bound him to his fellow men, leaves the cave in perfect "singularity," as it were, neither accompanied nor followed by others. Politically speaking, if to die is the same as "to cease to be among men," experience of the eternal is a kind of death, and the only thing that separates it from real death is that it is not final because no living creature can endure it for any length of time. (HC,20)

The modern age has it in common with the Greek age that its dominant world-picture denies spirit its full reality. The important difference between the Greek age and the modern age, however, is this: the Greek cosmos provided no world-picture in which spirit could come forth into its full reality; rather it remained only incipiently present as psyche. Because of the formative influence of Christianity, modern culture has been ruled by the pneumatically qualified world-picture—a picture in which spirit was vested with its rights and so burst forth into the world *as spirit*. This means that the modern denial of reality to spirit takes a different form than the Greek denial. To put this in the way that Kierkegaard does, we can say that Greek culture was unable to let spirit come forth and so was *spirit-less* in this sense; whereas modernity represses, avoids, supplants, destroys, or otherwise denies spirit after it has been posited in the world and so is *spirit-less* in this sense.

This difference is not that mysterious, indeed, not more so than the difference between being spouse-less as one is who has never been married, and being spouse-less as one is who has been married and is now divorced or widowed. The latter condition of being spouse-less is, I would say, somehow more agonizing, the former, more innocent; in the former, the reality of having a spouse is only intimated, in the latter, the reality of having a spouse has been irreversibly actualized. Because of the irreversible actualization of spirit in modernity, its spiritlessness is staggeringly ironic, for its rejection of spirit is a spiritually qualified rejection, the rejection itself gaining its traction from the very reality it seeks to reject.

I want now to turn to a discussion of my claim that an essential felicity condition required for the speech-act to realize its ultimate telos of expressing spirit in the world is that the speech-act be enacted within a pneumatically qualified world-picture. I will focus, in the following two subsections, on showing how two elements of the pneumatically qualified world-picture are central to the speech-act. These two elements are temporality and contingency. Because these are essential elements within the speech-act, I will claim that the efficacy of and hence the place of the speech-act as medium will be directly determined by the ontological place that is accorded to temporality and contingency.

Freedom and Temporality

What, for Kierkegaard, is the mark and test of the realization of the telos of human being? Or, what is the same question, what is the mark and test of the realization of spirit in the world? My claim is that this mark and test is found in *the relation that the speaker bears to his words* in the speech-act. Or to put this in a more familiar Kierkegaardian idiom, the stages on the self's way to itself, often exclusively interpreted as modalities of *existence*—i.e., the aesthetic, the ethical, and the religious—are ultimately modalities of *saying*. In other words, my claim that what Kierkegaard is getting at in his analysis of the self is that the self comes to or flees from itself by taking up a certain relation to his words, for example, an aesthetic, ethical, or religious relation. For Kierkegaard, spirit is realized concretely and existentially when someone takes up a religious modality of existence (religiousness B). For a person to take up this modality of existence is just for him to take up a reflexively integral relation to his words, which is the same as *speaking faithfully*. That is, the mark and test of the realization of a self is the extent to which a speaker *owns his words, owns up to them, is present in them*, and *present in them before some other*.[12] *The mark and test of the life of faith—the life where spirit is realized—is, in short, faithful speech*. Alternatively put, I will say of a speaker who owns and owns up to his words before some other person that he speaks with *reflexive integrity*; and that it is in reflexive integrity that spirit finds its decisive expression.

This claim needs some elaboration and clarification. In the first place I must issue a caveat. This caveat has to do with an oft-made criticism of Kierkegaard's putative individualism. The charge against Kierkegaard is that he is so concerned with the individual self that he provides no essential place for community in his analysis of the self. This seems to be a mistake if we attend to the importance of speech for the expression of spirit, or self. Indeed if the expression of spirit or self is the aim of the speech-act, then spirit can be realized only in the context of *relation*, or, to put it more biblically, in the context of *covenant*. By its very nature, a speech-act requires the *presence* of *both* speaker and hearer. That is, the speech-act requires as a felicity condition the presence of at least a minimum *com-munity*. While we often talk to ourselves (and this may be a sign of health or mental illness) this is a derivative practice that trades on the primary condition of plurality basic to the speech-act. Arendt has made this point central to her argument in *The Human Condition*. She says that human plurality is the basic condition of speech and action (HC,188).

My claim and, if I am right, Kierkegaard's claim as well, that faithful speech is the decisive mark and test of a self having come to itself, is not a claim—indeed far from it—that the self as spirit can be fully realized in isolation from the presence of others. Presently I will also say that reflexive integrity cannot be realized apart from *a world* whose structures of fact, value, and meaning determine the parameters of what we can say and of what we can mean by what we say. Reflexive integrity is not simply an matter of *sincerity*. For now, however, let me focus on the subjective side of this dialectic and say more of what it means for a person to own his words, to own up to them, and to be present in them. I can make this point by contrasting two possible relations a speaker may bear to his words: an aesthetic and an existential (religious) relation.

A paradigmatic aesthetic relation to words is found in the stage actor's relation to the words that he "says." The words of the actor do not originate in his own freely chosen intention to speak "his own mind," but with the intention to speak the words of the playwright. When Richard Burton says, *as Hamlet*, "To be or not to be," he, *as himself*, says nothing. That is, Burton means his words as a good actor is supposed to mean them, namely, as the character he is playing. When a person speaks *as himself* the speaker says what *he*—not the character he is portraying—means. In reflexive integrity there is no deception, not even the harmless and playful deception of the stage, for now words bear an existential weight of responsibility and seriousness.

It is, of course, possible to speak aesthetically and not be "acting" on stage in a play. Such an aesthetic "speaker" knows that by speaking this way he can avoid responsibility for his words. And this aesthetic characterization is true of anyone who imagines that his expressions in the world are externally imposed by his social "role." Such a "speaker" is subtly mute, at least *as himself*, and lacks reflexive integrity, or, what is the same thing, lacks a self.

The contrast between aesthetic "speech" and reflexive integrity is obvious when we consider Kierkegaard's paradigm for the latter, namely the words of Christ. He remarks:

> Christ himself declares: "I am the way, the truth, and the life," and as for the apostles' view of him, it was palpable—not just an ingenious work of art. "That which we have heard, which we have seen with our eyes, which we have looked upon, and our hands have handled" (I John 1:1). *As for what he [Christ] said, one could always take him at his word; his words were life and spirit.* (CI,14, italics added)

I take a person at her word only if I believe, and I am of course often mistaken, that the words are *her* words, that they issue from her own intentions, that they are owned by her, that she is *present* in them. Ultimately, her words are her own, in the requisite sense, only when they are spoken in covenant before some other particular person with a proper name. This stands in opposition to the actress who speaks the words of the character she is playing—intentionally of course—to another character or characters in the play; or perhaps to *anyone and everyone* in the audience.

Now the condition of the possibility of words being owned is that the speaker have the power and capacity to own them. The capacity for reflexively integral speech is grounded, therefore, in the *freedom* of the speaker. Indeed the act of owing one's words in the presence of some other, the act of speaking in the first person, may just be definitive of human freedom. W. H. Poteat has thought so and remarked as follows: "Our freedom is our reflexive power to speak in our own names—to answer, when addressed: *It is I*—even though notwithstanding we are finally opaque to ourselves" (PM,128).

It is clear that Kierkegaard associates freedom with spirit and argues that the realization of spirit comes with the taking up of the religious modality of existence—a modality of existence that he identifies as the life of faith. I am claiming that the mark and test of this life of faith is *faithful speech* or *reflexive integrity*. It is commonplace to note that Kierkegaard draws essential connections among freedom, spirit, and faith; but that he connects all of these to faithful speech is a claim less often made.

The freedom of the speaker is, I assert, an essential felicity condition for a successful speech-act, for reflexive integrity. How I stand to my words, whether ironically, seriously, playfully, prayerfully, somberly, sarcastically, fatherly, etc., is an essential element in the determination of the meaning of the speech-act. In other words, *what* is said can be comprehended fully only if *how* it is said is taken into account; and how something is said can be comprehended only by constantly taking into account *who* said it; that is, the speaker herself, her intentions, and the tacit backing that forms the extended body of what is said. That a speaker has the freedom to stand to her words in this way or that is what makes the words *her own*. Freedom is at the very heart of reflexive integrity.

Temporality is the necessary context of freedom. In order for me to take up a relation to the words that I speak that could properly be called free, I must be able to choose that relation from a field of *possible* such relations. The choice is only as real as the possibilities. A field of possibilities (a future) can be real, however, only in a context of temporal succession. Apart from such a succession, the future is only apparently not-yet; in its static reality it already is; indeed it is the moving image of eternity.

Moreover, when I must choose and take up a relation to my words, I of necessity do so *from* some standpoint. The necessary context for this is a field of *actuality*, a past; that is, a world, a context, a tradition. A past, however, like a future is real only within the context of real temporal succession. In the psychical context of eternal cycle, the past is not really past; it will be again.

If the temporal distinctions between past and future were not real, that is, if temporal succession were not real, then the possible/actual distinction would itself become an illusion; therefore, so would freedom. This was precisely the case with Aristotle and so it is with any psychically qualified world-picture. For Aristotle, actuality is prior to potentiality (possibility) and the latter is simply a "temporal" unwinding of what *is*, that is, of what is already eternally actual.[13] This is why Aristotle, who made such a close observation of natural changes, did not notice the radical dimensions of natural changes that Darwin noticed. For Aristotle the idea of a *new* species emerging was unthinkable. In Aristotle's psychically qualified world-picture wherein reality is a cosmos there is no room for novelty, the radically new, for any radical sense of possibility and contingency. The Darwinian theory of evolution had to wait for the Christian era, for the pneumatically qualified world-picture wherein temporality was accorded a positive ontological status.[14] For Aristotle, as for Plato, time was not accorded this positive ontological status; it remained ultimately nothing more than the unreal image of eternity. Within the Greek cosmos freedom is reckoned as chaos and the self's task is not imagined to be that of freely taking up itself and realizing its telos; rather the "task" of the self is simply that of enduring and giving way to changes in the way that an acorn evolves into the oak tree that eventually and in the natural course of things it becomes.

The upshot here is that freedom and hence reflexive integrity are possible only under certain ontological conditions, only in a certain ontological context. Among the most important of these conditions are the following: reality must unfold in time; it must therefore be incomplete, that is, not exhausted in actuality; it must be composed, therefore, of both possibilities and actualities; moreover, possibility must be ontologically and temporally prior to actuality. This ontological context is the absolute requirement for a speaker to take a stand in the world, to author and own his words before some other. Only within such a world-picture does it make sense to accredit himself with freedom, with the capacity to actualize a freely chosen possibility; and only within such a picture does it make sense to picture actuality as that which is brought into being from the array of real possibilities presented in the ever opening and expanding horizon of the future.

Within a psychically qualified world-picture, there can be no reflexive integrity, no faithful speech. This is so because temporality is not vested with its rights. As such freedom is absent; and because of this the speaker cannot come forth as the owner of her words; and so cannot come forth as spirit. In the absence of the reality of possibilities and the reality of the capacity to actualize them there is literally no *place* for the speaker as the *author* and *owner* of the words she speaks; and so no place for the self.

Moreover, in a psychically qualified world-picture actuality is not dependent for its establishment upon being brought into being by some person, some speaker. In the psychical cosmos there is no way to make sense of the biblical notion of creation, of the idea that Yahweh brought the world into being from nothing (potentiality) and sustains it with his word. Rather in a cosmos what is real is what is eternally and impersonally actual; here the real is in no need of being established at all; were it in such need this would make reality historical and mutable, not eternal and immutable.

On psychical assumptions, the most that a speaker could be imagined as doing when he speaks is *reading* the eternal and immutable text of the cosmos (*logos*). In this world Oedipus could not say with reflexive integrity, "I will not kill my father." Indeed everything that can be "truly said" is already determined and, strictly speaking, can only be *read off* the long and immutable *logos* of reality; and the most that any "speaker" can do is "faithfully" to read the lines that have been assigned to him from eternity.

Let me expand a bit on this claim that in the psychical world-picture the account of speaking that issues out of that picture is one in which speaking is understood as a kind of reading. Reading is primarily a visual phenomenon in which the text is before the reader in a static space in which all of its parts are simultaneously co-present in a timeless eternity. If reality is an eternally actual *logos*, a text that is finite and complete, closed and fixed, then what can be said in truth is only what can be read off of the text of the cosmos. If the time of the cosmos is like the time of the solar system (psychically construed), if the succession of moments is like the succession of this closed and finite system, then it would be possible in principle to read off the exact positions of every part of the system at any given time and to predict with absolute accuracy any "future" event. If reality were like this, if all of our lives were like the life of Oedipus, or the movements of the planets and stars (again, psychically construed), then there would be no openness to the future, no genuine temporal succession, and hence no possibility for freedom.

Not until the pneumatic world-picture is posited does the present come into its own as the dynamic dimension where possibilities are actualized. In this picture the self is given an indispensable *place* in the establishment of the world—a place that is analogous to Yahweh's place as its creator. This is an anthropocentric world precisely because it is a historical world. In the pneumatic world-picture, persons are imagined as existing in the mysterious and dynamic present; and this present is imagined as being the very center of the creative process. Possibilities would forever remain only that if they did not become actual; but without persons such an actualization would never occur. Persons are at the center of historical actuality precisely because, on the pneumatic world-picture, persons are charged with exercising a responsible creative freedom, a freedom that draws from and relies on a past that persons have established and persons sustain, and reaches forward into the indeterminate future in order to establish and sustain ever new realities.

I can think of no better model for the pneumatic world-picture than that of a conversation. The future in a conversation is predictable in many ways, depending on how well we know the other and he or she us, and on the mutual attentiveness of both hearer and speaker so that whatever is said in novel acts of speaking and hearing is bound in its surprising appearance by the mutual fidelity and moral commitment of each with and to the other. Moreover there is structural order to this conventional bonding and to the unfolding of the conversation within these bonds, namely, the unfolding of the conversation is governed by the rules of grammar, syntax, and semantics. This however does not make the conversation a rigid contract or a prescribed script: genuine conversation remains radically open, forever unfolding toward, and revealing new, possibilities. But precisely because of this movement in a conversation toward the unknown and the uncertain, conversations, like existence, produce anxiety and can exist in any full sense only within the context of faith, covenant, and mutuality. Conversations exist in this full existential sense only when their participant speakers and listeners freely own and own up to their words. Such faithful speaking in mutual trust and covenant brings forth the courage necessary to embrace a radically open future. The essential openness and contingency of a conversation is the absolutely necessary condition for human freedom. It is precisely because of conversation's essential historical openness and freedom, and precisely because of its demand for order and faithfulness, that it serves as the dominant model of the self/God relation and of the self/world relation in the biblical narratives.

When we speak with reflexive integrity, we are involved in giving our word to some other. Speaking with reflexive integrity then is subject to the same felicity conditions of any promise, of any covenant. Consider, for example, the felicity conditions that the ordinary act of getting married requires in order to gain the traction necessary for its successful accomplishment. In order for a man and woman to be able to exchange wedding vows with reflexive integrity and in order for the mutual commitments these vows entail to be entered into in good faith, the vows must be made in full recognition of the openness of the future—a double edged openness to sickness and health, riches and poverty, etc.—and in full recognition of the freedom of each to own and own up to responsibilities these commitments imply. Marriage, as such an exchange, as such a covenant of mutually acknowledged and owned responsibility, is quite literally impossible apart from a picture of the world in which time, contingency, and freedom are real. Having this world-picture is, we might say, a felicity condition for the act of getting married to succeed. Both parties in the ceremony must be able to picture themselves as freely intending what they say; and they must be able to picture the world as the sort of place in which promises make sense, and themselves as having the capacity responsibly to back up, come what may, what they have vowed. If these and other felicity conditions are met a new reality comes into being in this exchange of vows: what did not previously exist now has come into determinate actuality. This bond of marriage that is freely entered establishes a reality as palpable as anything can be. Yet this bond could have been brought forth as real only on condition that reality is not complete; only on the condition that it is in the process of unfolding. In such a picture, reality is not timelessly eternal; rather it shows itself in its determinate actuality within time. And in this picture persons are more than passive observers of the real; here they are vested with the freedom and the power to bring possibilities into their determinate actualities.

Without a world-picture in which temporality and freedom have a place, that is, without a pneumatic world-picture, reflexive integrity cannot be realized, and so neither can spirit. Kierkegaard's claim is that Christianity introduced the world to this pneumatic picture. In so doing Christianity vested spirit and speech with their rights. This claim is consistent with at least one New Testament image of Jesus according to which what impressed those who encountered him was not so much what he said but the fact that he spoke with *authority*. If Kierkegaard is correct it may just be that Jesus was the first person to *speak* in the fullest sense of that term, and the one therefore, who—by decisively modeling faithful speech—first incarnates spirit in its full reality and power. "His words were life and spirit."

Efficacy and Contingency

What I have just been claiming is that a world-picture in which freedom and temporality are accorded a positive ontological standing is a necessary felicity condition for the ratification of the speech-act, necessary, that is, for the speech-act to reach its telos of realizing spirit in its fully determinate actuality. I am claiming that reflexive integrity is the mark and test of that realization—and I am careful to say 'realization' instead of 'achievement' since, as I have already suggested, there is an essential dialectic of gift (grace) and task involved here.[15] Reflexive integrity is realized only to the extent that the speaker *appears before some other in the first person as the transcendent owner of his words, and hence, as the ground of them.*[16] Or, what is the same thing, reflexive integrity (spirit or self) is realized only to the extent that a speaker *appears in his words as himself*. Only a world-picture which accords a positive ontological place to freedom can provide the conceptual space for reflexive integrity to be realized and consequently for human beings to realize the telos of being fully human, a telos the realization of which is just the appearance of spirit in its fully determinate actuality. By the same token, only a world-picture which accords a positive ontological status to temporality can vest freedom with its full reality.

When freedom is realized in the dynamic speech-act, speech has reached its telos and spirit or self comes forth in its fully determinate actuality. This can happen thanks only to the resources of the speech-act for reflexive self-reference. In reflexively integral speech the speaker's words not only point beyond themselves (and hence beyond the sensuous medium they jointly constitute) but also and always reflexively *back to the self*—the indispensable *whence* on which the force and meaning of the speech-act hinges. This *from/to* dialectic is what makes the speech-act essentially semantic and reflexive. This semantic/reflexive dimension of speech makes it the perfect medium for expressing not only the dynamic, temporal transcendence of spirit but its dynamic immanence in the world as well. To speak with reflexive integrity, that is, to speak *as oneself*, is to mediate oneself to oneself and to others and to take up one's stand, one's place, in the world. This sundered/bonded self/world relation is just the relation spirit (self) requires for its full existential realization.

To freedom and temporality I now want to add another felicity condition vital for the realization of the telos of the speech-act; or, more precisely, I want to explore freedom and temporality from another direction. I assert that the telos of the speech-act cannot be realized unless it is enacted within a world-picture in which words are accorded their full *ontological efficacy*; and that the only such world-picture is one in which *contingency* is accorded its ontological rights.

The speech-act cannot be accorded its full ontological efficacy unless one very important condition is met. The goal of efficacy cannot be realized if the speech-act is not pictured as *referential act*. When speaking is pictured in this way, then it is not only pictured as reflexive, that is, as grounded in the *whence* of the speaker, it also gets endowed with an ontologically significant outreach. Speech as reflexive act situates the speaker within the given actuality; as referential act, it highlights the place of the speaker as a *doer*, as a contributor to actuality itself. In the felicitious speech-act, the speaker brings new realities into existence; and he is called on to bear the responsibility of sustaining those realities with his steadfast continued endorsement of them.

It seems rather obvious that if words are accorded no power to refer to anything outside of themselves, then the speech-act will be crippled in its primary aim, namely, the aim of saying something *about* something, *to* some other. To empty words of their power of reference is to empty them of their essential power. Such a picture of words is incoherent if applied across the board to everything that is said. If no words could be used to say something, then it would be impossible to say even this, and indeed, such a picture of words would make it impossible to say anything, and would bring rationality itself to an end. For this reason this picture of words has rarely been applied across the board to all words, or categories of words.[17] The more usual move is to say that certain categories of terms have an ontological reference while others do not; for example, it might be held that while factual terms have an ontological reference, other categories of terms, for example, value terms, or theological or metaphysical terms, do not.[18]

The classical philosophical debate about ontological reference is the ancient debate about the ontological reference of a specific category of words, namely, universals or class names. But I want to suggest that this debate is not only about ontological reference, but also about the power of speech to bring something about, to effect the determinate actuality of something, to make something happen. In other words, I think the debate is not only about the question of the ontological reference of a class name, the proverbial question: What's in a name? It is also about another question, the question of the ontological impact of *the act of naming*, the slightly different question about what effect giving a name to something has on what is named.

The position of the realist regarding class names—names like cats, dogs, persons, tables, justice, goodness, and beauty—is that such names are labels that refer to eternal essences whose reality is not dependent on being given that name, or on any other relation to a subject who gives it that name. On the first issue in the question "What's in a name?" the issue of reference, the realist says there *is something* in a name; he accords names a positive ontological reference.

On the second issue in the question "What's in a name?" namely, the issue of what there is to the act of naming, the realist takes up the position that *nothing happens in the act of naming*. Here names are simply read off from the eternal text of the cosmos. Words are labels with no constitutive effect on the reality that they name. This is the Greek or Platonic position in the controversy, what we might call the psychically qualified position: class names have no ontologically constitutive relation to the eternal essences whose reality is immutable and impersonal. Again the visualism that dominates in this psychically qualified world-picture is obvious, for

speaking is pictured as a kind of reading where the speaker is not author-
ing the words as a speaker does within the dynamic and radically contingent context of a conversation but reading off the words of a text that is
statically and determinately before the eyes of the reader in the silent
space of the immutable text. As Poteat has put it, Plato is "ruled by this
picture of a very large but finite text all of the particulars of which are at
every moment equally accessible" (PM,114).

To put this in Austin's terminology the realist has a constative interpretation of naming.[19] On the constative interpretation, names intend, indic-
atively refer to, that is, name, what *is the case*—some fact or state of affairs.
The success or failure of this intention of naming can easily be judged in
terms of the categories of truth and falsity. This constative interpretation
of naming is reminiscent of the theory of language that Wittgenstein at-
tributes to St. Augustine (PI,par.1).

Both Wittgenstein and Austin work against the grain of this word-object
picture of language (a picture implicit in realism and in the Greek view
of language as *logos*) and attempt to introduce a new picture, a picture
that emphasizes performance and use, a picture of language as *dabhar*.
Naming in this more dynamic picture of language markedly contrasts to
the constative, realist, Platonic position as far as the way the relation between what a thing is and what it is called is conceived. Naming as *dabhar*
is given an ontological efficacy in the sense that what something is, is dependent upon what it is called; and the calling of something by its name
brings what is called into its determinate actuality. In other words, both
Austin and Wittgenstein are trying to give a positive answer to the question of what is involved in the act of naming. Does this mean that they
have taken the nominalist point of view? Or, to put this in terms of our
previous discussion, is a picture of language as *dabhar* a picture that entails
nominalism in the way that a picture of language as *logos* certainly seems
to entail realism?

To set the stage for answering this, I must say something more about
what I mean by saying that the full ontological efficacy of the speech-act
requires that the process of naming (and more generally speaking) be accorded a power that enables a speaker to bring something about, to bring
something to its determinate actuality, to make something happen. In
making this point I will show that it is only within a world-picture in which
contingency is accorded a positive ontological status that speech can come
into its own as *act*; only within such a context that a speaker can come
forth as spirit, as self; only within such a context that a human being can
come to be fully human.

If we pay close attention to our actual practice of speaking, as Austin
has done in a systematic way, we notice that we rather routinely and unproblematically accredit our speech-acts with an ontologically constitutive
efficacy. Let me again take recourse to the example of the common human practice of getting married. This practice (ritual) is essentially con-

nected to the felicitous saying of certain words, which culminates in the pronouncement that the two are husband and wife, a pronouncement that brings into existence a new reality: two people who were not married before the ceremony now are. The exchange of vows and the authoritative pronouncement of the officiant brings about at a particular time and place a palpable bond that was not *present* before, a bond as real as anything can be, a bond that can only be dissolved at some future time by an equally potent saying of another sort.

Other examples abound. The act of placing a bet brings something about that did not exist before, an obligation, a bond. The same is true of any promise. Indeed, almost all forms of felicitous speech—describing, telling, praying, warning, discussing, arguing, courting, planning, reminiscing, and so forth—involve the giving of one's word, and so are acts of promising and bring novel bonds into existence.

The bonds that felicitous speech-acts bring forth, the bonds of commitment and responsibility that are entailed in reflexively integral speech, constitute the fabric of human culture and tradition. These bonds form a web of human affairs that Hannah Arendt identifies with the human world (HC,181ff). No doubt it is this ontological efficacy to which Auden was referring when he said, "A sentence uttered makes a world appear."[20]

In saying these things about the ontological efficacy of saying, I am not espousing a doctrine of linguistic determinism.[21] Rather I simply want to point out what I would call the dialectical interpenetration of words and world. If we think of language as primarily consisting of nouns, this dialectical relation is likely to be eclipsed. As Hannah Pitkin has remarked:

> If our example is a noun used primarily as a label for a simple physical object, we are most likely to find that what "it" is, is independent of what we call it. But if our example is a concept shaped in many complex language games, then we are more likely to feel that "it" is not "given" in the world but constructed or picked out by our conceptual scheme. . . . It is difficult seriously to imagine human beings lacking such concepts one day "happening upon" a stepsister or a mistake and giving the phenomenon a name. (WJ,114)

While Pitkin may be right in her claim that things (physical objects) in the world seem to have an independent existence and a determinate actuality apart from the naming of them, she seems to ignore in this passage what may be a more fundamental interpenetration of words and things. Perhaps Pitkin has failed to take seriously enough the distinction that her mentor, Stanley Cavell, goes to such pains to make. This distinction, of which Pitkin is aware, is between the Austinian and the Wittgensteinian criteria for naming. Cavell asserts that for Austin the issue of naming is focused on the following sort of non-grammatical question: "What kind of object is this?" The way to answer it, according to Austin, is to point out certain markings by which we tell not only that this object is such and such, but that all objects of this kind are such and such. For Wittgenstein the issue has a different focus. As Cavell puts it, "The Austinian 'kind of object' is a class object, a species of some well-known kind of (generic) object, whereas the Wittgensteinian 'kind' of object is something like a natural kind or a metaphysical category of objects (mind, matter, sense-data, meanings, colors, etc.)" (CR,77).

And further, and more to the point of establishing the fundamental dialectical interpenetration of words and world, of the ontological efficacy of words, Cavell remarks that if you lack the grammar of "objects" in this more basic ontological (Wittgensteinian) sense of the term, then "you cannot be told the name of that object, because there is as yet no *object* of that kind for you to attach a forthcoming name to: the possibility of finding out what it is officially called is not yet open to you" (CR,77). Not knowing that this chair is of a certain style and period is one thing; not knowing what a chair is or what sitting in a chair is, is quite another. Without this latter sort of grammatical knowledge we cannot function as speakers in a world. If someone does not have this sort of knowledge, it is not, as Cavell notes, because he has neglected these matters in his studies, "but because he is for some reason incapable of (or has been given up on as a candidate for) maturing into, or initiation into, full membership in the culture" (CR,77).

As I have said, in our practice of speaking we routinely and unproblematically take our speech-acts to be ontologically efficacious. We make promises, name things, make pronouncements, and so forth, and we take it as a matter of course that our words bring possibilities into actuality. We cannot imagine a human community in which it would not be possible to make a promise. Yet in reflection we may wonder if our practices can be effective in the way we think that they are: we may wonder if we have the power to bring the bond of a promise into existence; we may wonder if there is room in the world for such a novelty. Indeed if we cannot find a place for such novelties within our picture of the real we will be forced to deny that picture or reinterpret our practice. Such a discrepancy, as I have already mentioned, lies at the heart of Greek tragedy.

If speaking is to be vested with the ontological efficacy it seems to be accorded in our unreflected practices it must be set within a world-picture in which that efficacy has a place. The roots of this picture of speech as ontologically efficacious, as world-creating, as I have already noted, are in the Hebraic doctrine of creation wherein the picture of speech as *dabhar* is introduced into the human imagination as a thematized picture of speech.

According to the biblical account of creation, God spoke the world into existence: "He spoke and the world stood forth." And beyond this, He named things: "He *called* the light day" and this is what it became. The reality of everything, in this picture, is conferred by a name and every such reality is brought forth into existence by an act, or, more precisely, a speech-act. Or as Kierkegaard would put it, reality is essentially *historical*. For him, "Everything that has come into existence is *eo ipso* historical. For even if it accepts no further historical predicate, it nevertheless accepts the one decisive historical predicate: it has come into existence."[22] On this account everything that *is*, is grounded transparently in the power which constituted it; the power that brought it into existence in its determinate actuality. That power has its locus in the lively, dynamic, ontologically efficacious, and absolutely faithful *dabhar* of Yahweh.

In the biblical story of the creation man is created in God's image. This means at least that man has an analogous creative power of naming. Indeed man is given the task of naming the animals: what he called them is what they were. So on this account human beings are pictured as participants with God in the creative process; and herein may be the heart of the human imago dei: the human likeness to God is found in the human capacity to hear God's address and to answer it, in the capacity to call realities forth into their determinate actuality; in the capacity to own and to own up one's words—a capacity that enables humans to sustain and to stabilize what they have brought forth, a capacity that enables them to transform the dynamic flux of temporality into the order of historical continuity.

Only from within a historical world-picture does it make sense to think of actuality as coming into existence (from possibility). In such a historical picture reality is *radically contingent*; here reality is open, incomplete, in process, unfolding, on the way, dynamic, and evolving. In the historical framework, what *is* is that which has come into existence; in such a framework then—indeed only in such a framework—is speech (as *dabhar*) installed in its rights. In the historical world-picture, possibilities need some means to be transposed into historical actualities. It is just at this point that speech is granted its full ontological efficacy. Now the speaker is granted the power to bring something about, to make something happen. As such, in the historical world-picture, not only does actuality receive a *subjective grounding* in the speech-act and ultimately in the speaker, the speaker himself comes forth in all of his determinate actuality. The very same speaker that is charged with the responsibility for establishing actuality also, and paradoxically, "comes into existence" himself—indeed, comes into actuality as a self in the very act of establishing the actuality of the world. Here the ground of the historical actuality is itself historical. This is radical contingency.

Yet the historical world-picture does not leave us without sources of stability. Indeed, in the Judaeo-Christian version of the historical world-picture there is one absolute source of stability, the *dabhar* of God, and myriad sources of relative stability in the words of human beings whose speech is modeled on God's faithful word. On the one hand, this is all there is to stand upon in the historical world-picture; on the other, it is, perhaps, quite enough.

Back to the question of whether Austin and Wittgenstein are nominalists and to whether my support of their interpretation of language is a support for nominalism. The answer is a qualified "yes." Against the realist, I deny that the real is fixed and fully actual and thus ahistorical and that words simply refer, as labels, to these static independently existing realities. The mistake, however, that I think the modern day nominalists make is that they assume a *logos* interpretation of language and at the same time deny the Platonic ontology with which that interpretation is perfectly matched.[23] This produces a view that names have no ontological efficacy. If we were to assume a *dabhar* interpretation of language, then a qualified nominalism becomes plausible. Here there are no realities independent of their names, no sense in which realities exist in any determinate way prior to the naming process. At the same time, on this interpretation, names refer to realities in a much closer ontological sense than in realism, for here the naming context is essential in the process of bringing the real forth into its determinate actuality. And so, on this *dabhar* interpretation, the interpretation of language that I think is at the heart of Kierkegaard's analysis of it as the perfect medium for the expression of spirit, the long and the short of the answer to the question "What's in a name?" is an unequivocal "Everything!"

If it is true that speech aims at ontological efficacy, if it is only then vested fully with its rights, then the essential felicity condition that must be met in order for this to happen is that speech be enacted within a world picture in which the reality of the world and the self are radically contingent and temporally successive. Only in such a picture are the resources available for making sense of the speech-act as the ground of the existence of the external world and of the self: only in a world that is open and temporally unfolding can any sense be made of the dependency of the real on being called forth into its determinate actuality; only here can the real be consistently understood as essentially personal.

A world-picture which accords a positive ontological efficacy to speech must be a picture which also accords a positive ontological status to contingency. Outside of the context of openness, novelty, and possibility, there would be no need for, and no consistent place for, a medium whose telos is to call forth and to establish the real. Ontological efficacy is precisely the *bonding* power of speech to establish the real; in a world-picture in which reality is eternally and impersonally established there is no place for this power of speech to be realized; and in this vacuum, there is no place for a speaker. Moreover, if speech is the perfect medium for the expression of spirit (self) then the impotence of speech is necessarily matched by the disappearance of the self. On the other hand, a world-picture that enables the realization of the power of speech also enables the spirit to find its incarnate expression and allows spirit (self) to appear within the world.

I realize, and mention again, that this analysis may sound as if I am claiming that only a world-picture that authorizes linguistic determinism can serve as a proper context for the realization of the telos of the speech-act. I do not intend this. What I do intend is the claim that reality is fundamentally relational; and further that the only world-picture where relation can be ontologically primitive, where self and world can be pictured as coming into their determinate reality together, is a picture where the speech-act is accorded ontological efficacy. In such a picture the self is not prior to the world in any temporal way; there is not first a self that later calls a world into existence; rather in this picture self and world dialectically interpenetrate as do words and world.

And one last point on this matter of linguistic determinism. I do not intend to imply that as speakers we are "free" to create the world and ourselves in whatever manner we may like. Rather, and on the contrary, I intend to say that the ontological efficacy of speech bonds us in responsibility to the given actuality of the world and others. The condition of our having come to be speakers and, as speakers, radical initiators and world-creators, is that we were first addressed within a *world* by some *other* before whom we stand. I take this to mean, in contrast to a linguistic determinism wherein one can make the world into whatever he wants it to be, that an essential felicity condition for the full ratification of the speech-act is that it be enacted within a world-picture in which there is a given otherness, a given world. Such a context of givenness defines my place in the world prior to my being called to take up that place as my own. Kierkegaard does not think that we are called to create the actuality of either the world or of ourselves out of nothing; rather he thinks our task is to *actualize actuality*, a *task* that makes sense only on the condition that actuality is also *given* to us.

I hope that I have made it clear that a crucial felicity condition for the realization of the speech-act is the requirement that the speaker take up his practice of speaking from within a world-picture within which that bedrock human practice can be thematically appropriated, authorized, ratified and made his own. As I have interpreted Kierkegaard, the self (spirit) can be fully realized only when the self that is incipiently present within our actual practice of speech is able to relate itself to itself; this it can do only by virtue of a world-picture; and the only such world-picture that makes this appropriation possible is one that is not only not discrepant with that practice but that provides the traction that practice requires for its full realization.

As I interpret Kierkegaard, the only world-picture that is not discrepant with the personal within our actual practices is the picture introduced into the human imagination by Christianity. I will continue to develop that picture as these meditations continue to unfold. For now, I shall turn to a discussion of the world-picture that is the modern derangement of this basic Christian picture. I will show how the modern world-picture leads to our uniquely modern forms of spiritlessness (selflessness) by showing the discrepancy between the modern world-picture and our actual existence, the bedrock and definitive practice of which is the speech-act.

III

DON GIOVANNI, MUSIC, AND THE DEMONIC IMMEDIACY OF SENSUALITY

> Don Giovanni is absolutely musical. . . .
> Words, lines, are not suitable for him. . . .
> He does not have that kind of continu-
> ance at all but hurries on in an eternal
> vanishing, just like the music.
>
> (S. K.)

As I have been reading it in the foregoing, Author A's claim in *Either/Or I* that Christianity brought sensuality into the world expresses the interpretation of Kierkegaard himself about the nature of the impact of Christianity on the human imagination. While A celebrates the advent of sensuality, Kierkegaard is working behind the scenes, in his usual indirect method of communication, to establish a philosophical premise that is the key to his work as a whole: that Christianity brought into the world a world-picture in which spirit, that is, self, is represented as being at once dialectically sundered from, and at the same time bonded to, the sensuous.

When Christianity introduced this picture of spirit as being in radical tension with its sensuous embodiment, it ipso facto introduced liabilities heretofore not conceivable. Christianity's introduction of this picture of spirit as sundered/bonded had the effect of uprooting spirit from its domicile within the psychical world—of rupturing spirit from its organic submersion within the cosmos. Yet Christianity introduced this spiritual break with the world in order to establish a dynamic personal self/world relation; a relation that can be maintained only to the extent that it is stabilized and transhistorically grounded in faith. When such a faith collapses, when no such ground is available, the self/world relation that Christianity intended to establish disintegrates into a mis-relation. In this mis-relation the tension that both sunders self and world *and* bonds them together is broken, and the two elements of the relation (self and world) fly off in their own separate directions. Kierkegaard describes this disintegration of the sundered/bonded spirit/sensuous relation as follows:

> As spirit, qualified solely as spirit, renounces this world, feels that the world not only is not its home but is not even its stage, and withdraws into the higher realms, it leaves the worldly behind as the playground for the power with which it has always been in conflict and to which it now yields ground. Then, as spirit disengages itself from the earth, the sensuous shows itself in all its power. It has no objection to the change; indeed, it perceives the advantage in being separated and is happy that the Church does not induce them to remain together but cuts in two the band that binds them. (E/O I,89)

This, I assert, is a perfect description of the modern age. The predominant picture of the self/world relation in modernity is one in which self is pictured as dynamically *sundered* from the world, and in which the world is depicted as perpetually vanishing and as utterly devoid of spirit. At first the modern age found this liberation of spirit intoxicating; it was exhilarated over its new-found freedom from the bonds of worldly existence.

To keep itself "free"—so it thinks—the modern spirit has to renounce the world and every entanglement in it. Accordingly the speech-act is the chief enemy of the modern age. To its credit, the modern age indirectly recognizes that to speak felicitously is to situate oneself in the world, to feel the bonds of responsibility before the other, to take a stand. For the sake of its newly discovered, unbridled, "freedom," and in an intoxicated celebration of its sense that spirit has been finally liberated from the world, the modern age retreats from speech and takes up its abode in a medium with which it feels a deeper kinship. That medium is music. From the Kierkegaardian (Christian) perspective the modern uprooting of spirit from the world and its transmutation of the world into perpetual self-nullification turns the sensuous into demonic sensuality and spirit into demonic spirituality. This demonic spirit/sensuous relation finds no more perfect expression than in music; moreover, in music, the immediate dawning of this demonic relation finds no more perfect expression than in Mozart's *Don Giovanni*.

Before we turn to a more extended discussion of the figure of Don Giovanni as the perfect expression of the perversion of the Christian spirit/sensuous relation, as the perfect expression of the demonic spirit of modernity, let me take a moment to state again the positive self/world relation that Christianity posited and which modernity perverted. Even though Christianity made the modern perversion of the spirit/sensuous relation possible, its sundering of spirit from the sensuous was only one dimension of its world-picture. Christianity did effect a sundering of spirit from the world, but this sundering was always for the sake of introducing a new sense of bonding to it, namely, a personal sense of bonding. Without this bonding, spirit and the sensuous become demonic. Let me try to explain.

The innovative world-picture that Christianity first posited in the world was a radicalized version of the self/world relation that it inherited from its Hebraic, *dabhar*-centered ancestry. Insofar as Christianity made this new world-picture a world-historical force, it effected a cultural shift of momentous proportions. In this shift, the stable, static, eternal, and impersonal *logos*-centered world-picture crumbled and gave way to a dynamic, historical, personal, *dabhar*-centered world-picture. The pneumatically qualified world-picture represented spirit as sundered from its psychical repose within the harmony and accord of the cosmos, but the aim of this sundering was to give to spirit a new, pneumatic bond to the sensuous actuality from which it was sundered. This new bond was a personal one, a bond analogous to the bond that Yahweh paradigmatically established to the world as its creator and redeemer; a bond analogous to the self/world relation that Jesus exemplified in his life and teaching.

The radical apocalyptic message of Jesus—a message he both lived and taught—was that in order for the Kingdom of God to come the world must first come to an end. In Kierkegaard's language this means that spirit can be fully posited only to the extent that it is absolutely related to the Absolute (God) and only relatively related to the relative (the world). That is, what Jesus was preaching was that spirit can only become spirit in its fullest sense when it is sundered from every idolatrous absolutization of the relative. Spirit comes to be spirit, self comes to itself, only insofar as it exists as an 'I' *before God.*

For me to exist as a self before God, as spirit, I must be grounded transparently in the power that constitutes me—that is, I must be addressed by God and answer him; I must take up the *place* to which I have been called as my own. To put this differently, my place before God, my identity as a self, is my *vocation.* Paradoxically, the process of being placed before God is dialectically preceded by a radical dis-placement of the self in relation to the world. In order for me to respond positively to God's call to faith, I must sunder myself from every idolatrous attachment to the world; I must be uprooted from my primordial home—as Abraham was uprooted from Ur.

This radical dis-placement of self from its psychical bonds to the world however aims at a pneumatic re-placement; only by virtue of the transcendence of the pneumatic disruption of spirit from the world is it possible for the world to become *my own.* In this dialectic of psychical dis-placement/pneumatic re-placement, spirit is posited as spirit, as transcendent and immanent. To put this in Kierkegaard's idiom: the knight of faith— the one who lives as a self before God—is absolutely bonded to God in a covenantal relation (a promise); this absolute relation to God sunders the knight from every absolute relation to the world. This first movement of faith, however, is not all that faith is—far from it. Faith is incomplete apart from its second movement: in this movement of faith the knight is covenantally bonded (of his own volition) to the world and to others; in this movement the world is given back from the hands of the Eternal, every inch.

The dialectical task of Christianity (and Kierkegaard) in all of this is to make sense of how spirit can at once exclude and "negate" the sensuous and, at the same time, remain incarnate within it. The Christian existential stratagem is to live *in* the world without being *of* it; yet in order to live this dialectic, it must be possible to understand how spirit's exclusion and negation of the sensuous does not entail its *separation* from the world. Moreover, without a model of the positive (Christian) self/world dialectic that makes sense of it, it is impossible to recognize the modern picture of that relation as a perversion. Do we have an intelligible model of such a dialectical sundered/bonded relation of spirit to the sensuous? I think that we do.

I propose that the sundered/bonded relation of spirit to the sensuous finds no better analogue than to an epistemological distinction/relation that Michael Polanyi has drawn between what he calls subsidiary and focal awareness.[1] Since my understanding of the sundered/bonded relation of spirit to the sensuous is so crucial to my interpretation of Kierkegaard, and since it is so thoroughly informed by Polanyi's epistemology, I must divert our discussion at this point in order to present a brief account of Polanyi's view of the *from/to* structure of focal and subsidiary awareness.

In Polanyi's view, all consciousness is normally directed *from* our sentient, oriented, motile mindbodies *to* something outside ourselves in the world. As is the case with all instruments, the use of our mindbodies is a skillful activity in which perceptual, motor, intellectual, and many other clues are integrated into some comprehensive focus. We can successfully rely on our own mindbodies as the instruments of knowing only insofar as we do not attend *to* them. Consider, for example, a pair of glasses as an instrument for clearer sight. If I focus on my glasses, then they cease to function instrumentally for me. Only when I attend *from* them do they serve the purpose for which they were designed. We are surely aware of our glasses while they are in use, but not *focally* aware of them.[2] My mindbody, then, is the active subject of my experience of the world—the proximal pole in the dialectical *from/to* stretch of consciousness from which I attend to distal objects in the world.

This theory of tacit knowing helps us to frame our knowledge not only of our own mindbodies, but of others as well. When I comprehend some other person, I do so by attending *from* my own bodily situation in time and place, and *from* the immediate sensuous presence of bodily clues in the person before me, *to* what they jointly mean, that is, *to* the comprehensive entity that the person is. Or, to put this in Kierkegaard's terminology, I encounter the other as the self or spirit that he is only when I am able "to depress the sensuous to the level of a mere instrumentality."

If I were to attend to my own attending or to the wagging tongue of the person who is speaking to me or to the sweat droplets on his brow or the movements of his adam's apple, I would miss the person that is expressed in and through his sensuous, embodied presence.

Nowhere is the dialectical distinction/relation between the subsidiary and the focal more decisively present than in the auditory phenomenon of the spoken word. If we say a word over and over we notice that it becomes meaningless, a mere sound.[3] This is because we normally attend not *to* the sounds of words but *to* their meaning. This feat of attending to the meaning of the spoken word would be impossible, however, were we not also, and at the same time, aware of the sensuous particulars that constitute the *whence* of the production of the speech-act. Indeed, attending *to* the sounds of speech themselves, instead of *from* them, would be an obstacle to hearing what ought to be heard, the meaning; yet that meaning can only come forth to the extent that it retains its vital relation to its whence. In summary: the meaning of a speech-act can only "come through" the sensuous particulars that constitute its whence to the extent that they are being constantly annulled (focally) and yet constantly (albeit dialectically) "taken into account" (subsidiarily) as excluded.

It is this *from/to* dialectic that is guiding my attempt to make sense of the Christian conception of spirit as sundered *from* and bonded *to* the sensuous world; and it is in terms of this from/to dialectic that I am attempting to characterize the modern perversion of the spirit/sensuous relation.

Let us return then to the issue at hand, namely, the modern *demonic perversion* of the dialectical sundered/bonded self/world relation. To do this we must turn our discussion to the figure of Don Giovanni and to the perfect medium for his expression, music.

Music, Worldlessness, and Anxiety

The Christian proclamation of the incarnation faith, a proclamation that posited in the world for the first time a world-picture in which spirit is understood as dialectically sundered from and at the same time essentially bonded to the sensuous, produced an ironic conceptual and existential possibility. This novel possibility that Christianity indirectly posited was the plausibility of a world-picture in which the self could be depicted as completely sundered from its sensuous embodiment and correlatively a world-picture in which the sensuous could be depicted as completely sundered from every trace of spirit. This way of depicting the spirit/sensuous, self/world relation exclusively in terms of radical disjunction is ultimately, as I see it, a demonic perversion of the Christian world-picture. Yet it is precisely this perverted, demonic, world-picture that dominates the modern age; indeed, it dominates to such an extent that it has become virtually beyond the reach of criticism. To understand this picture, we must turn our attention to Kierkegaard's discussion of Don Giovanni as the perfect expression of the immediate stages of the dawning of this modern demonic perversion.

Don Giovanni is the figure that perfectly expresses, Kierkegaard says, the worldly spirit of the sensuous. The worldly spirit of the sensuous is the sensuous insofar as it has been completely abandoned by spirit. In its state of abandonment by spirit, as Kierkegaard says, "the sensuous now awakens in all its profusion, in all its rapture and exultation . . . so it was that the whole world on all sides became a reverberating abode for the worldly spirit of sensuousness, whereas spirit had forsaken the world" (E/O I,89).

Kierkegaard likens the kingdom of the de-spirited sensuous world of sensuality to the popular Middle Ages myth of the mountain of Venus—a mountain not found on any map—a mountain perhaps not in the world at all. It is here, he says, that the "sensuous has its home" and here that "it has its wild pleasures, for it is a kingdom, a state. In this kingdom language has no home, nor the collectedness of thought, nor the laborious achievements of reflection" (E/O I,90).

What then is this kingdom of sensuality like? Kierkegaard's reply is as follows: "there is heard only the elemental voice of passion, the play of desires, the wild noise of intoxication. There everything is only one giddy round of pleasure" (E/O I,90). Don Giovanni, he goes on to say, is the first born of this kingdom of sensuality. Because the Don's sensuality completely *excludes spirit*, Kierkegaard says that he is the paradigmatic "expression for the demonic qualified as the sensuous" (E/O I,90).

The demonic character of Don Giovanni, however, is not yet an ethical determination of him; the kingdom of sensuality is not yet the kingdom of sin. Kierkegaard's contention is that the appearance of Don Giovanni is one of "aesthetic indifference." When sin or ethics is of concern, reflection must enter the picture. As I just noted, the worldly kingdom of sensuality, in all of its momentary immediacy, is dialectically prior to the advent of reflection. Kierkegaard says: "When sensuousness manifests itself as that which must be excluded, as that with which the spirit does not wish to be involved, but when spirit has not as yet convicted it or condemned it, sensuousness takes this form, is the demonic in [a]esthetic indifference. It is a matter of only a moment" (E/O I,90).

The key to understanding what Kierkegaard means in all of this is the distinction he makes between the psychical and the pneumatic qualification of the sensuous. Following Kierkegaard's lead, I have claimed that the sensuous, that is, what is immediately present to the senses, within the psychical world-picture, is not pictured as constantly annulling itself, but as constantly being taken into account. The paradigmatic model of this psychical relation of the sensuous to psyche, a relation of harmony and accord, is found in the Greek understanding of the sensuous—an understanding that is derived exclusively from the concept of vision. In contrast, the pneumatically qualified sensuous/spirit relation is one of opposition, exclusion, and negation, and finds its paradigmatic model in the dynamic structure of sound.

It is only from within a concept of the sensuous as dynamically qualified that it makes sense to conceive of spirit as constantly disengaging itself from the sensuous. When *this* element of temporal transcendence—an essential element within the dynamic dialectical succession of sounds in any sonic phenomenon—is exclusively emphasized, that is, when the *bonding* of spirit to the sensuous is without play, the result is a picture of the sensuous in which it is not only depicted as perpetually vanishing, but this vanishing has become an end in itself. In other words, when the perpetual vanishing of the pneumatically qualified sensuous becomes completely emptied of every trace of spirit, or as we might say, de-spirited, then it has become demonic sensuality. When this occurs the sensuous is no longer depicted as annulling itself in the service of expressing spirit in its essential transcendence, but now stands on its own as a power and self-contained principle: now the perpetual vanishing is a reality and power in and of itself. The pneumatically qualified sensuous, when it has been completely de-spirited, is simply the sensuous in the vanishing moment, the sensuous without stability or continuity, the sensuous in perpetual self-destruction.

This pneumatically qualified sensuality finds its perfect medium of expression in music. The reason for this, again, is that the ideas that music's sonic tones express are constantly disengaging themselves from the sensuous. Music breaks every bond with finitude. As a semantic medium, music is always pointing beyond the sensuous, always "negating" the sensuous. Strangely enough, however, the absolute musical idea to which music points is the very idea that the music as sound is, that is, sensuality in its dynamic, restless tumult and immediacy, the sensuous as perpetually vanishing.

Don Giovanni is, in Kierkegaard's analysis, a perpetually vanishing sensuous moment wholly disconnected from the world of here and now, the world of historical continuity, the world of place and spatial orientation, the world that is the horizon of our tonic mindbodies, the palpable world of flesh and blood. His existence is one of hovering; at most, his connection to the world is like that of a stone to the water over which it skips. As Kierkegaard remarks: "When one throws a pebble in such a way that it skims the surface of the water, it can for a time skip over the water in light hops, but it sinks down to the bottom as soon as it stops skipping; in the same way [Don Giovanni] dances over the abyss, jubilating during his brief span" (E/O I,129–130).

As I interpret Kierkegaard, the Don's hovering is the *transcendence* of musical tone; or more accurately, the Don just *is* the musical. The spirit of the Don, as captured in Mozart's opera, the transcendent, demonic spirit that Author A celebrates and admires, is, from Kierkegaard's perspective, the spirit that is the enemy of Christianity. While A, the aesthete, celebrates the freedom of Don Giovanni's hovering, the freedom of infinite possibility, of 1,003 in Spain, Kierkegaard subtly and indirectly has A insert into the essay on the musical erotic a "note" to which A, more often than not, turns a deaf ear. This "note" is *dread (anxiety)*. A, of course, is not completely unaware of this dark side of transcendence, this dark side of Don Giovanni's infinity, it is just that his attention to the dread of freedom is averted thanks to his steadfast intoxication with the power of music to break the bonds of finitude.

Author A writes, commenting on the opening of Mozart's opera, that it begins with deep notes that compare in nature with the anxiety-generating rumble of thunder and flash of lightening in a threatening storm on the horizon. His description is too vivid a characterization of the darkness of Don Giovanni's dread not to quote at length:

> The overture begins with a few deep, earnest, even notes; then for the first time we hear infinitely far away an intimation that is nevertheless instantly recalled, as if it were premature, until later we hear again and again, bolder and bolder, more and more clamorous, that voice which at first subtly, demurely, and yet seemingly in anxiety, slipped in but could not press through. So it is in nature that one sometimes sees the horizon dark and clouded; too heavy to support itself, it rests upon the earth and hides everything in its obscure night; a few hollow sounds are heard, not yet in motion but like a deep mumbling to itself. Then in the most distant heavens, far off on the horizon, one sees a flash; it speeds away swiftly along the earth, is gone in an instant. But soon it appears again. . . . There is anxiety in that flash; it is as if in that deep darkness it were born in anxiety—just so is Don Giovanni's life. There is anxiety in him, but this anxiety is his energy. In him, it is not a subjectively reflected anxiety; it is a substantial anxiety. In the overture there is not what is commonly called—without knowing what one is saying—despair. Don Giovanni's life is not despair; it is, however, the full force of the sensuous, which is born in anxiety; and Don Giovanni himself is this anxiety, but this anxiety is precisely the demonic zest for life. (E/O I,129)

The modern age, like Don Giovanni, was born in the dawning consciousness of infinite possibility. And like Don Giovanni the modern age became intoxicated with this yet unreflected upon consciousness and the liberation it portended—a liberation from the bonds of worldly existence. But, also like Don Giovanni, the modern age felt, however inchoately, the darkness such a discovery of infinite possibility also inevitably portended.

This discovery, unique to the modern age, was made possible indirectly by Christianity. As we have said, it was Christianity that effected a major shift in world-pictures, a shift from the psychical to the pneumatic. The pneumatic world-picture brought spirit forth into its full transcendent and infinite reality and power. Modernity was born in the wake of another conceptual shift; this time it was a shift *within* the pneumatic world-picture.

The Christian, pneumatic world-picture represents spirit as dialectically sundered from and bonded to the sensuous world. Modernity was born when spirit came to be represented as completely sundered from all worldly bonds. This conceptual shift was effected thanks to the fact that the authority of biblical faith was, for whatever reason, crumbling. The collapse of the authority of this faith meant the collapse of the Christian world-picture that it supported and, however inadequately, tried to maintain.

Only within the context of the authority of the Christian world-picture—that mythological picture of the self and the world as grounded in God's paradigmatic speech-act—is spirit allowed its transcendence within its essentially incarnate bonds to the world. With the modern undermining of the authority of biblical faith and the correlate undermining of the Christian world-picture all bonds to the world were broken and possibility in its absolute infinity burst forth. This is the modern age; this is Don Giovanni.

Within the Christian world-picture, the sensuous world is pictured as dynamic and contingent. Whatever stability there is to be found in this pneumatic world-process is to be found in nothing firmer and more stable than the covenants that are established between God and man and between man and man. The authority and legitimacy of these covenants are grounded in the Christian myth of the creation, according to which the words of Yahweh brought the world into reality. Within this world-picture it is the speech-act that keeps the transcendent self tied essentially to the world; within this pneumatic picture *our word is our only bond*. The breakdown of this picture spells the breakdown of every bond to the world; and with this, the full force of a pneumatically qualified—but perverted—modern sensuality (and spirituality) emerges.

In short, the modern age burst forth celebrating the absolute transcendence of the human spirit—a spirit with no essential connections to the world, with no place to stand, with no place at all. The modern awakening to the radical contingency of the world, coupled with the modern loss of faith, produced a situation in which all sources of stability, continuity, and constancy had vanished into thin air. The Christian picture of the world as unfolding in historical continuity and stabilized by the faithful covenants between man and God and man and man—covenants authorized and legitimized only from within the Christian world-picture—gave way to the uniquely modern world-picture according to which the world is represented as perpetually slipping out from under our feet. In this modern celebration of transcendence, there are no resources for establishing a stable, enduring world and hence there is no suitable place for a human being to actualize his telos of being fully human. In this new modern situation of groundlessness, there is no *logos* and, in the wake of the modern loss of faith, no *dabhar* either. There is nothing left that can give life its point of reference, its orientation, its direction—every such absolute has become relative and every ground perpetually vanishes into a radically contingent universe.

While there may be in all of this some cause for glee, the celebration will be short-lived. When the hazards of a pneumatic existence, no longer in the hands of a providential God, are encountered, an existence in which anything is possible, the security of a closed cosmos will seem a preferable alternative. Anxiety is a permanent companion of spirit; and when spirit loses its resources for grounding and for stabilization, when it loses its basis for continuity and coherence, a pneumatic existence becomes terrifying. Modern man knows, all too painfully well, just how infinitely frightening such an existence is.

If the bonds of a pneumatically sundered spirit are not reestablished to the world, there can be no full appearance of the self. Without a world there is no place for a human being to become fully human, to appear as spirit, as the self that relates itself to itself, as the self it is called to be. But apart from the accreditation of the full ontological efficacy of the speech act, an accreditation that is itself virtually identical to faith in Yahweh as the source of that accreditation, there can be no way to establish the dynamic stability of historical continuity. Recall that, for Kierkegaard, only language (speech) can express historical continuity.

Don Giovanni is the perfect expression of the immediate dawning of the modern demonic spirit of disembodiment, the demonic spirit of a sensuous immediacy emptied of idea, the demonic spirit of perpetual self-destruction. His lightness, his giddiness, his joy, his retreat from the world, however, show up finally as equivocal goods. It does not take too long for any individual who tries to live out the Don's hovering "freedom," his breaking of every shackle of commitment, his absence from, his retreat from his own words, to discover the dark and equivocal nature of an existence that is lived wholly within the immediate moment of the temporal flux. An existence that completely lacks a tie to the world, an existence that is completely severed from historical continuity, an existence wholly within possibility—infinite possibility—is an existence without any source of stability. When the darkness of such an existence comes to reflection, the inevitable consequence is despair.

Kierkegaard sees so clearly and with such precision this darkness, this anxiety, this madness of Don Giovanni's musical hovering. And again, like his predecessor Pascal, Kierkegaard feels the terror of the madness of Don Giovanni's carefree worldlessness. Pascal's familiar description of the modern world perfectly captures Don Giovanni's "world" and the dread and the terror that are always lurking in it just beneath the surface. As Pascal puts it, the modern world, and, as Kierkegaard might well say, Don Giovanni's "world," "is an infinite sphere, the center of which is everywhere, the circumference nowhere" (PP,par.72). And further, in recoil from such a centerlessness, he says in horror: "The eternal silence of these infinite spaces frightens me" (PP,par.206). Surely it is the placelessness of the musical hovering that Pascal is describing when he says: "I am frightened, and am astonished at being here rather than there; for there is no reason why here rather than there, why now rather than then" (PP,par.205).

To explore further this dark, demonic side of Don Giovanni's musical hovering, I want to turn now to consider the effects of that hovering on speech. Especially I want to focus on what seems to be a necessary, but negative, connection between demonic dread and speech. I want to assert that an inextricable correlate to demonic worldlessness is a demonic retreat from speech, a demonic dread of the good.

The Demonic Retreat from the Word

For Kierkegaard, the demonic spirit is the exact opposite of the Christian spirit, for the demonic individual is absolutely *faithless*, while the individual who appropriates the Christian spirit exists in radical and absolute *faith*. As Kierkegaard understands it, to exist in faith before God—to the limited extent that this is ever fully realized—is to actualize the telos of human being, the telos of being fully human. This realization finds its most concrete expression in what I have been calling the reflexive integrity of the felicitous speech-act. I have been trying to substantiate the thesis that being fully human and existing in faith before God (being a Christian in its most radical sense) are the same thing; further I have been attempting to show that the realization and incarnation of such a faithful existence before God is co-extensive with the reflexive integrity of the felicitous speech-act.

I acknowledge that I am placing an emphasis on the speech-act that is not always clearly at the focus of Kierkegaard's words. I will not admit, however, that I am forcing my interpretation on him. The undeniable textual fact is that he does actually make a number of remarks that suggest an essential connection between word and spirit. One example of this, which is the key text for this inquiry, is what he says in *Either/Or I*. Indeed, the claims that he makes here and in other places stand at the base of my claim that what Kierkegaard means by 'spirit' can only be made fully intelligible when its essential connection to the speech-act is made explicit.

It might be granted that Kierkegaard does make some explicit remarks that could be construed as drawing an essential connection between word and spirit and as giving to the speech-act a central place in the life of faith. Yet these remarks are so few and so far between and so wrapped in the tangle of pseudonymous authorship and irony, the question arises as to whether they are sufficient to warrant my attempt to put the speech-act at the very center of Kierkegaard's analysis of spirit and self. My response to this is simply to assert that Kierkegaard's analysis of faith, self, and spirit relies, in ways that were not always clear even to Kierkegaard himself, on the biblical model of faithfulness. That model is God (Yahweh), the paradigmatic faithful self, the one who speaks the words, "I am that I am," the one whose words are absolutely reliable. Insofar as Kierkegaard is a Christian, this model of the absolutely faithful self found its decisive historical expression in Jesus of Nazareth whose words were life and spirit.

Even if I am bringing out something that is not explicitly central in Kierkegaard's analysis of self and spirit, it may be that the justification for doing this, for making the speech-act central to faith, is that such a move serves the positive hermeneutical purpose of bringing forward the operative biblical basis of Kierkegaard's analysis of faith. If indeed this biblical model of faithfulness, the faithfulness of Yahweh's eternal word, is the operative model of faithfulness in Kierkegaard's interpretation of faith, then making this explicit is essential if we are to gain a viable exegesis of what he does say and so obtain a felicitous interpretation of his analysis of spirit and self.

As well, if faithful speech is as central to Kierkegaardian faith, spirit, and self, as it is in the biblical narratives, if Kierkegaard accordingly assumes an essential connection between a faithful existence and faithful speech, this is perhaps enough to save his analysis of the self from what I believe to be an unfounded charge, namely, the charge that a faithful existence for him is an existence that is fully actualized only by the radically isolated individual, the individual that is radically isolated from the world and from a community of others, the individual who lives out his faith in absolute silence before God. It is just such a charge that offers to us an occasion for exploring further the contrast between demonic faithlessness and authentic Christian faith; and the negative and positive connections the two bear, respectively, to reflexively integral speech.

Mark Taylor has accused Kierkegaard of providing no essential place for community or speech in his analysis of the self.[4] He has suggested that Kierkegaard's unbridled praise for the individual, coupled with his disdain for "the crowd," drove him too far in the direction of an individualism that finally lacks the resources to place faith within a community of speech and within the world. For Taylor, this is a critical mistake. The reason he thinks so is that for him the individual self can be constituted as such only in relation to others, only from within a community of other selves. For Taylor relations and hence community are ontologically definitive of the individual self. He says: "Relations are ontologically definitive—to be is to be related. In terms of human being selfhood is essentially social, spirit fundamentally intersubjective. Concrete individuality can arise *only* in community, with other free subjects. Apart from such interrelation, the self remains totally abstract, utterly indefinite, and completely incomprehensible" (JS,274).

Taylor does not want to deny the importance of the individual and so agrees with Kierkegaard to this extent; but he claims that *to be*, that is, to be a distinctively *human* being, *is to be related*, and that for Kierkegaard *to be is to be isolated* from others and in retreat from the world. As Taylor puts the point: life in community is for Kierkegaard a "concession to the human weakness of being unable to bear the isolation of spiritual individuality" (JS,180). And further he claims that for Kierkegaard, "[T]he birth of such spiritual individuality requires severing the umbilical cord of sociality through the difficult labor of differentiating self and other. The one who understands this spiritual pilgrimage ever remains a lonely wayfarer" (JS,180).

Of course Taylor recognizes that Kierkegaard is attacking "the crowd" when he speaks of society and agrees with him that the faithful self cannot exist in such thoughtless and mechanical associations. What Taylor thinks, however, is that Kierkegaard did not distinguish between genuine community and the "the crowd" and that, hence, when Kierkegaard rejects the latter he also rejects the former. Taylor remarks: "A major problem with Kierkegaard's argument at this point is his refusal to acknowledge the possibility of a form of human community that enhances and does not abolish responsible individuality" (KPA,253–254). I want to defend Kierkegaard against this charge and at the same time explore the contrast between the demonic retreat from speech as the essential expression of faithfulness and the felicitous speech-act as the essential expression of authentic faithfulness.

The starting point for this venture is a small section of Kierkegaard's *The Concept of Anxiety* entitled "Anxiety about the Good (the Demonic)."⁵ A close examination of this section of text reveals that Taylor is mistaken in his charge that Kierkegaard failed to give an essential place to the communal component in the life of faith. The key to Taylor's mistake is his failure to recognize the central role that Kierkegaard gives to the *speech-act* in the life of faith. Because speaking presupposes a social and communal context, if I can show that Kierkegaard allocates an essential place in the life of faith to speech, this would show that Kierkegaard allocates an essential place in the life of faith to the communal component. My claim is that this text on the anxiety of the demonic over the good shows decisively that Kierkegaard does give an essential place to the speech-act in his analysis of the life of faith.

As I read this text, I find that Taylor's charge against Kierkegaard is not only mistaken but also profoundly ironical. The irony lies in the fact that Taylor has confused Kierkegaard's understanding of the life of faith and the demonic life of faithlessness. In fact, it seems that what Taylor takes Kierkegaard's conception of the life of faith to be is actually the opposite, namely, the demonic. The key to perceiving this mistaken interpretation is found when we recognize that Kierkegaard thinks that faithful speech plays a positive role in the life of the faithful self and a negative role in the demonic life.

In a telling passage, Taylor summarizes his criticism of Kierkegaard and discloses the heart of its irony. I have italicized the phrases that indicate that what Taylor understands as the life of faith is actually closer to what Kierkegaard himself understands as the demonic life. He says:

> Since he sees faith as lying within the inwardness of the self, Kierkegaard must contend that at the deepest level, the level of one's faith, *persons cannot communicate with one another.* Each individual is *locked up* within the inwardness of his own subjectivity. Selves are discrete and isolated, and where the most profound issue of the self's life is concerned, there is no possibility of relating to other selves. This is the point of his repeated emphasis on *silence.* (KPA,350)

In *The Concept of Anxiety* the Danish word that Kierkegaard uses to characterize demonic existence is *indesluttede*. Thomte has translated this word into the English phrase *inclosing reserve* (CA,123) while the earlier translation by Lowrie— a translation that rendered 'angst' as 'dread' instead of 'anxiety'—translates 'indesluttede' as the awkward English word '*shut up ness.*'[6] One interesting feature of both of these renderings is that 'indesluttede' is clearly connected to the absence of freedom. Although I will follow Thomte's translation, there is a suggestive element in Lowrie's notion of '*shut-upness.*' 'Shut up' connotes both the sense of unfreedom of the sort involved when someone is locked up or incarcerated and so is externally restrained from doing as he wills; and also the sense of unfreedom where someone is, for perhaps some more inward reason, unable to speak or to be present in what he says, and so is unfreely *silent* or *absent.* The command "Shut up!" is a familiar enough command for silence; it is a command designed to get someone to *stop speaking.* The irony here, in relation to Taylor's criticism of him, is that Kierkegaard is implicitly and surprisingly connecting unfreedom—the most radical form of which is the demonic—to silence; and by further implication, freedom (spirit) to (faithful) speech.

Kierkegaard begins the section called "Anxiety about the Good (The Demonic)" by charging that his generation has either not reflected at all on the demonic or that its reflections have been superficial. Most reflections on the demonic, he says, get arrested on "one or another unnatural sin," in which there is an "ascendancy of the bestial" over the human (CA,118). The explanation given for this ascendancy is usually in terms of what Kierkegaard calls "the bondage of sin," that is, the demonic life is claimed to be a manifestation of that bondage.

What is important for this discussion is that Kierkegaard characterizes the bondage of sin in terms of the relation a speaker bears to the words he speaks. He likens the person who is in the bondage of sin to a game in which two people are concealed under a cloak, *appearing to be one person.* In this game, "one speaks and the other gesticulates arbitrarily without any relation to what is said" (CA,119). A life in the bondage of sin, therefore, is a life abstracted from itself, a life *lacking reflexive integrity*. A decisive manifestation of such a bondage of sin is the discrepancy between what is said and the inward life of the one who speaks.

Like the bondage of sin the demonic is also characterized by a *lack of reflexive integrity*. Despite this similarity, however, the two are radically different. Kierkegaard puts it this way: "The bondage of sin is an unfree relation to the evil, but the demonic is an unfree relation to the good" (CA,119). For Kierkegaard *the good* "signifies the restoration of freedom, redemption, salvation, or whatever one would call it" (CA,119). And we can imagine filling in the 'whatever' here with such words as spirit, faith, transcendence, self, and so forth. For our purposes, I am focusing on the good as freedom. The dialectical consequence of this focus is that evil or the demonic gets identified with unfreedom. To say then that the individual who is in the bondage of sin is anxious about evil is just to say that he is anxious about unfreedom, while the demonic individual is anxious about the good, that is, about freedom.

Freedom, as I have argued, is a prerequisite for reflexive integrity since a speaker's words can be owned and owned up to only to the extent that she freely and inwardly appropriates them as her own, stands behind them in responsibility, and bodies them forth in her life. The individual in the bondage of sin desires the freedom of reflexive integrity; she would like to be able to will to break the bondage of her sin, but she cannot; she is anxious in the face of unfreedom. As unfree the individual in the bondage of sin exists in reflexive dis-integration and her anxiety is about a deeper unfreedom and a deeper dis-integration. As Kierkegaard puts it, the individual in the bondage of sin knows that "No matter how deep an individual has sunk, he can still sink deeper, and this 'can' is the object of his anxiety" (CA,113).

In contrast to the individual in the bondage of sin, the demonic individual is more radically evil; indeed the former is good in comparison to the latter. Again the reason for this difference in character is that the individual in the bondage of sin is anxious about the proper enemy of the good, unfreedom. The demonic individual on the contrary is anxious about the good, about freedom. Being *in* sin the demonic individual is unfree and reflexively dis-integrated, yet, at the same time, she is anxious about and flees from the good, from freedom, and does not want, nor does she seek, reflexive integrity.

The anxieties felt by the individual in the bondage of sin and by the demonic individual are both different from the anxiety felt in innocence. Anxiety about unfreedom and anxiety about freedom are both anxieties *in sin*, not the anxiety of innocence, which is the anxiety *before sin*. The innocent individual exists in unfreedom but of a different sort than that possible after freedom is existentially posited, that is, after it has become actual and concrete. In innocence, anxiety is produced when freedom appears before itself in possibility. In the biblical fall, freedom is concretely actualized but lost in the same act. Hence, after the fall, when freedom is no longer a mere possibility but an actuality, its opposite, unfreedom, also actually exists. The individual *in sin* has lost his freedom and is unfree in this sense; the individual *in innocence* has never been free and is unfree in this sense.

Recognizing the different senses of unfreedom in the demonic life and in the innocent life will help us to see the difference in the objects of their anxieties. This distinction is important because on the surface the demonic individual and the innocent individual appear to be anxious over the *same thing*, namely the good, freedom. Both then seem to be different from the individual who is in the bondage of sin and is anxious about evil, unfreedom. The principle at work in Kierkegaard's analysis seems to be something like this: the innocent individual is anxious about the good, about a freedom he has never concretely actualized, whereas the demonic individual is anxious about the good in another sense—the freedom he has concretely actualized and lost at the same time.

The demonic individual knows something about the good, freedom, that the innocent individual is ignorant of: it entails responsibility and it can be misused and lost. What he knows is that freedom is an equivocal good. While freedom may offer the extraordinary advantage of a reflexively integrated existence, its concrete actualization brings with it an awareness of responsibility, guilt, and death. Because freedom is ambiguous, because it can be misused and lost, the demonic individual flees from it like someone who anxiously flees a love relation because he knows of its implied bonds of responsibility, of how easily such relations can be broken and how devastating that can be. Because the demonic individual knows of the ambiguities of freedom, and because he does not have the resources to face these ambiguities, he is anxious in the face of freedom, in the face of the good. In this anxiety over freedom he flees into a false "freedom"—a worldless transcendence.

The defining characteristic of the demonic, Kierkegaard claims, is what he calls "inclosing reserve" or "shut-upness." He says: "The demonic individual is anxious, is *inclosing reserve.* . . . The demonic is *inclosing reserve and the unfreely disclosed.* . . . inclosing reserve is precisely the mute and when it is to express itself, this must take place contrary to its will" (CA,123). Notice again how speech is connected to freedom and muteness is connected to unfreedom in this definition of the demonic. For Kierkegaard "freedom is precisely the expansive" (CA,123); it is what reaches out to the world as speech does. Inclosing reserve is the very opposite of the expansive for it withdraws within itself, into the silence, the muteness, the shut-upness, of unfreedom.

We must be careful at this point not to think that the demonic "muteness" that Kierkegaard identifies with the demonic is a *literal silence.* The demonic individual can and does use words even though he does not speak in any felicitous sense. Demonic speech "takes place contrary to its will." The muteness, the silence, of the demonic individual is subtle and deceptive. It is a silence that "lies" behind unfree expression. Here there is no reflexive integrity between what the demonic individual says and what he does because there is no reflexive integrity between the speaker and what he says and does. His words are full of sound and fury but signify nothing.

The opposite of the demonic life is the life of freedom; this is the life of reflexive integrity, the life of speech. As Kierkegaard remarks: "Freedom is always communicating. . . . unfreedom becomes more and more inclosed and does not want communication" (CA,124). And further: Inclosing reserve is precisely muteness. Language, the word, *is precisely what saves*, what saves the individual from the empty abstraction of inclosing reserve . . . For language does indeed imply communication" (CA,124; italics added).

What may easily be missed in Kierkegaard is the distinction that he makes between the silence of demonic inclosing reserve and the lofty silence of faith (CA,126). This distinction makes sense, however, only when we recognize that, for Kierkegaard, freedom is essentially connected to speech. The distinction between a stage actor's expression, an *aesthetic expression*, and a reflexively integral expression of a concrete individual who claims the expression as his own, an *existential expression*, again becomes relevant. Consider first aesthetic expression of the demonic type and its relation to freedom. If one speaks aesthetically and demonically the words issue out of unfreedom—they are imposed externally and do not arise out of the will of the speaker except to the extent that he has suspended it in order to play the part of someone else other than himself. As such these words are not owned by the speaker and are like the words spoken by the play actor; they are not self-expressions. That my expression is not integrally related to my inward self *shows* that I am not free in relation to my words. This is expected in a drama. If I adopt this relation to my words in life, however, then I do not speak, at least *as myself*; as such I am silent in the demonic sense of inclosing reserve. In existential expression, what shows decisively through is the speaker's freedom, for such reflexive integrity presupposes that the speaker's expressions originate in, and arise from, his own will. Such existential expression is to the life of spirit and faith what aesthetic silence is to the demonic life.

Yet silence also has a place in faithful existential expression. The difference between demonic, aesthetic silence and the silence of faith is subtle. In demonic silence—the silence wherein the speaker does not speak as himself—what shows is that the speaker is unfree in relation to his words. When I say that the demonic individual is unfree in relation to his words, I mean that he is either unable to or defiantly will not own or own up to his words. In lofty silence—the silence of existential expression—the speaker is absolutely free in relation to his words. This is shown in the fact that the existential speaker is absolutely *able to be silent*, as well as speak as himself. Reflexively integral silence is a silence that is freely and responsibly chosen. Since words are owned in reflexively integral speech and because these words originate within the will and intention of the speaker, the speaker is the absolute proprietor of his words. As absolute proprietors, we are both absolutely free and absolutely responsible in relation to what we own. In fear and trembling we are aware that we always say more than we know, and that the consequences of what we say go far beyond what we can imagine; yet we know that these are our words and that we must responsibly own up to them as our own. Yet there is a radical freedom in this, for to the extent that we are the responsible proprietors of our words, that is, to the extent that we speak with reflexive integrity, we are at least aware of our power to withdraw from our words, to shut-up, to stop speaking. In this awareness we realize that the words we speak require our personal backing; in this awareness we also realize our power to take up various such backings, from the very earnest to the ironic and the flippant; but most importantly we realize that this power is the very center of our radical freedom.

Why does the demonic individual flee from freedom into the existential muteness of unfree expression? Kierkegaard's answer is that the demonic individual lacks the faith to extricate himself from the anxieties generated by the recognition of freedom's equivocal and ambiguous nature. Because he is not able to meet and take up in a positive appropriation the anxieties attendant to a life of freedom, he seeks at all costs to flee from integral expression, from reflexive integrity; he knows this would bring with it the concrete realization of what he cannot bear, namely, freedom—in the fully equivocal sense of the term.

The demonic individual flees from reflexive integrity, from speaking *as himself*, because he recognizes that the speech-act is just as equivocal as the freedom that it concretely actualizes. Even though the speech-act, in its fully felicitous enactment, is "precisely what saves," it is vulnerable and fragile insofar as words themselves have a rich open texture and so are ever liable to be misunderstood and misinterpreted; and this entails that the speaker of those words is equally vulnerable and fragile in that the words spoken always reflexively retrotend back to the speaker. This reflexivity of the speech-act opens the speaker to attack, to abuse, to scorn. Moreover the semantic outreach of the speech-act to the world establishes bonds to the world, bonds of responsibility that are difficult to bear, bonds the roots of which reach far beyond what the speaker can possibly be explicitly aware of and extend into an open future far beyond what can be predicted. To utter a sentence is not only to make a world appear; it is at the same time to place oneself in that world as one among a community of speakers who in the covenants they mutually establish become the

responsible agents in and through whom the world's continuity and stability are grounded. For the demonic individual, this is just too fragile,
just too heavy; he must avoid felicitous speech at all costs.

The demonic individual is clever and insidious in her evasions of the
reflexive integrity of faithful speech. The cleverest of these aesthetic techniques for fleeing from the speech-act is her "use" of speech itself. Since
the demonic individual knows or at least intimates that the speech-act is
the means of freedom's positive historical appropriation, she conspires to
take this means to precisely the opposite end, the end of avoiding reflexive integrity. Given that the speech-act is precisely what saves and that its
felicitous use is the concrete occasion for the positive actualization of freedom, we can see how insidious and how ironic the demonic individual's
clever use of precisely what saves to forward her demonic project of evad-
ing freedom, spirit, and ultimately her own self.

Kierkegaard's discussion of the 'sudden' sheds light on the demonic
project of evasion. He claims that "*the demonic is the sudden*" when the
relation of the demonic to time is at issue. As he puts it: "when the content
is reflected upon, the demonic is defined as enclosing reserve; when time
is reflected upon, it is defined as the sudden" (CA,129). "The sudden,"
he goes on to say, "like the demonic, is anxiety about the good. The good
signifies continuity, for the first expression of salvation is continuity"
(CA,130).

When Kierkegaard speaks of the good as continuity he is talking about
the continuity of historical time, the continuity of a temporal orientation
within a past, a present, and a future. His claim is that faithful existence
can be realized only insofar as it is concretely integrated into and actualized within historical time. The reason that the self can come to itself only
from within the continuity of the dynamic tensions of historical past, present, and future is that this historical continuity alone provides the ontological space essential for the full appearance of the self as a synthesis of
the finite and the infinite, freedom and necessity, eternity and time. The
radical contingency and unpredictability of the future of historical time
opens the self to eternity, to the infinite possibilities of spirit, of transcendence, and such a radical appearance of possibility before the self is absolutely essential for freedom's positive actualization. The irreversibility of
the past likewise provides a component absolutely essential for freedom's
full actualization. That component is the stability of the finite, temporal
world—a stability that rests in an established past, including the anonymous past of our own mindbodies, the given established traditions into
which we were born, religious and secular, and the established cultural
facts and values we inherited by virtue of the time and place of our birth.
Without the stability of the worldly conditions of historical time and place,
the present would lack any connections to anything other than itself—it
would simply pass away in immediacy. When the present is set within the
historical continuity of past and future, when the past becomes really past,

really over and done with all of the pathos and relief that such a real past implies, and when the future really becomes open, i.e., really not-yet, with all of the hope and dread such and openness to possibility entails, then and only then can the historical present come into its own as the center of historical concrete existence.

Kierkegaard clearly recognizes that it is speech that is the perfect medium for expressing historical continuity, just as "the sudden" is the negation of continuity. He says: "The words and the speaking, no matter how short when regarded *in abstracto*, always have a certain continuity for the reason that they are heard in time. But the sudden is a complete abstraction from continuity, from the past and from the future" (CA,132).

Because of the essential connection between speaking and continuity, the negation of continuity in the sudden is most often correlated with the negation of speech. An ideal representation of "demonic suddeness" can thus be found in the *demonic silence* of mime. This demonic silence implies not the absence of sound, but rather only the absence of speech. If this demonic suddeness/silence is to be properly represented on the stage, e.g., as Mephistopheles, words must be avoided altogether. The sudden is captured in the leap of Mephistopheles through the window and in his silent stationary position in the attitude of the leap. A walk would suggest continuity. He must leap and move with sudden, detached, and abrupt action.

Although the demonic negation of continuity in the sudden can be represented aesthetically through the abrupt and silent gestures of the mimic art of the stage actor, its most insidious and cleverest manifestation is *the appearance of continuity*. In the following I will show just how the sudden in its appearance of continuity is found in the reflective immediacy of Johannes the Seducer. But before I turn to Johannes, I must say a bit more about his predecessor Don Giovanni. Johannes and the Don live in pneumatic, aesthetic immediacy—one reflective, one sensuous—but both represent a demonic retreat from the world and from the word.

Music and Sensuous Immediacy

As Kierkegaard has author A point out, Mozart's *Don Giovanni* presents us with a picture of a seducer in the sensuously immediate sense of the term. This qualification is crucial, and so Kierkegaard says: "Provided that it is more urgent for one to say something correct than to say anything whatsoever, one must apply the word 'seducer' to Don Giovanni very cautiously" (E/O I,98). He is not a seducer in the sense that Johannes of "The Seducer's Diary" is, for the latter's seduction requires reflection, consciousness, cunning, craftiness, and so forth. Don Giovanni does not seduce in this sense; he lacks this reflective consciousness; rather, "He desires, and this desire acts seductively. To this extent he does seduce. He enjoys the satisfaction of desire; as soon as he has enjoyed it, he seeks a new object, and so on indefinitely" (E/O I,98–99).

As a seducer in the immediacy of the sensuous moment, Don Giovanni is not an individual; he is, as Kierkegaard puts it, a force of nature. He hovers between being an idea and being pure energy. He is always in the process of being formed, never complete; he is without a history; he seduces endlessly and as little tires of seducing as the wind tires of blowing, the waves of crashing onto the shore, the waterfall of plunging down from the heights (E/O I,93). Accordingly, the list of the seduced, 1,003 in Spain, is also a number constantly increasing; it is odd and accidental, never finished. As A remarks, "We almost feel sorry for Leporello, who not only, as he himself says, must hold watch outside the door but, in addition, must keep account books so complex that they would give an experienced office secretary enough to do" (E/O I,93).

Don Giovanni is not an individual but neither are the objects of his desiring. He desires woman in general even though he pursues her not in the immediate abstraction of reflection but in the immediate abstraction of the sensuous moment. He is after no particular woman, but all women; and as he loves one, he thinks of the next. Who, how, when, and so forth are absolutely insignificant. This can be seen in the seduction of Zerlina, the common peasant girl. She is as insignificant as is possible but this is her significance. Although she is young and pretty this is a quality she has in common with hundreds of others and it is precisely this commonness, this generality, that Don Giovanni desires. As Kierkegaard imagines it, Don Giovanni might well say: "I am no husband who needs an unusual girl to make me happy; every girl makes me happy, and therefore I take them all" (E/O I,97).

Immediate sensuous seduction takes place in the fugitive moment. It is a pure spontaneity of sense perception; a spontaneity in which the senses run rampantly from one moment to the next drinking in every passing sensation, every passing desire, every passing emotion. This immediacy of the senses is absolutely dynamic; it is the perpetually vanishing moment of appetite and erotic desire. This sensuous immediacy is without continuity (that is, existential immediacy, that is, historical presence) for each moment in its dynamic movement is absolutely discrete; absolutely disconnected from what went before and from what is to come after; absolutely momentary. Don Giovanni perfectly expresses this sensuous immediacy. He is always hurrying along like the music that expresses his sensuality. The Don is animated with an energy as effervescent as the intoxicating wine he drinks at the joyous feast of life.

> He needs no preparation, no plan, no time, for he is always ready; that is, the power is always in him, and the desire also, and only when he desires is he properly in his element. He sits down to dinner; happy as a god he flourishes his goblet—he rises with the napkin in his hand, ready for the attack. If Leporello awakens him in the middle of the night, he always wakes up sure of his victory. But this power, this force, cannot be expressed

in words, only music can give us a notion of it; for reflection and thought it is inexpressible. (E/O I,101)

This energy and power of Don Giovanni, Kierkegaard claims, cannot find expression in speech, for speech involves reflection, idea, concept, thought. Indeed the Don does not speak, he does not think, he does not plan, he does not remember; rather, he sings, and we need not be confused by the fact that his songs contain words; his medium is music and his words are lyrical; they are—like musical notes—perpetually passing away; his "words," like the musical sounds that perfectly express his demonic life, vanish into thin air; they leave no trace in the world.

Why can't the power and the energy of Don Giovanni be expressed in words? Again, because of his dynamic *sensuous immediacy*. Don Giovanni is absolutely without a hint of reflection. If Zerlina were asked about the captivating power of Don Giovanni she would probably say that she didn't know. And as Kierkegaard remarks this would be quite correct for, as [sensuously] immediate, the power and energy of Don Giovanni are indeterminate, obscure, beyond the reach of reflection. Only music can express this sensuous immediacy. Don Giovanni's immediacy is the sensuous immediacy of sound and it can only be *heard* in the dynamic immediacy of music. Kierkegaard says: "Don Giovanni is not to be seen, but is to be heard. . . . Listen to Don Giovanni—that is, if you cannot get an idea of Don Giovanni by hearing him, then you never will. . . . Hear his wild flight; he speeds past himself, ever faster, never pausing. Hear the unrestrained craving of passion, hear the sighing of erotic love, hear the whisper of temptation, hear the vortex of seduction, hear the stillness of the moment—hear, hear, hear Mozart's *Don Giovanni*" (E/O I,103).

Music is much like speech: both are dynamic; in both what is to be expressed is constantly disengaging itself from the sensuous; both address themselves to the ear; both are spiritually qualified media. But as I have also said, there is a great gulf between music and speech. In a key passage in *Either/Or I*, Kierkegaard recognizes that nothing could be farther from music than the language of *prose*. And yet Kierkegaard knows that even the language of prose, with its own temporal, rhythmic, tonic dimensions, can easily collapse into music. He says: "If I assume that prose is the language form that is most remote from music, I already detect in the oration, in the sonorous construction of its periods, an echo of the musical, which emerges ever more strongly at various stages in the poetic declamation, in the metrical construction, in the rhyme, until finally the musical element has developed so strongly that language leaves off and everything becomes music" (E/O I,69).

In relation to the prose of language—the everyday speech-act, the language of first person discourse—music is an impoverished medium. Its impoverishment is in its incapacity to serve as a medium in which something can be *said*. The musician does not assert anything or name anything in his music; rather, he "presents" his music in all of its sonorous, sensuous, immediacy. The speech-act on the other hand is a medium that involves concept, thought, determination, distinction, assertion. These features of speech—inherent in it as a medium—make it a *reflective medium*, a medium of the idea. Reflection, Kierkegaard has remarked, is fatal to the immediate (E/O I,70). But is it fatal to all forms of immediacy?

In order to make sense of the various forms of *immediacy* that are at play in Kierkegaard's thinking, I have emphasized the distinction between psychical (static/spatial) and pneumatic (dynamic/auditory) immediacy and the distinction within the pneumatic between the aesthetic immediacy of music and the existential/historical, immediacy/continuity of speech. When Kierkegaard says that reflection—and hence speech as a reflective medium—"is fatal to the immediate," I take him to be talking about a pneumatically qualified sensuous immediacy, that is, the fleeting sensuous moment, the indeterminate, the nameless. This seems plausible, since he also thinks that reflection is often not only not fatal to some forms of immediacy, but essential to them. Clearly the Greeks were reflective, but their reflection was not fatal to the psychical immediacy that characterized their culture and philosophy; quite to the contrary. And clearly Faust is a thinker, an intellectual, who lives wholly within the idea; Faust's reflection does not, however, destroy every form of immediacy; again, quite to the contrary, since his reflection is a form of immediacy, namely, the immediacy of spirituality, the immediacy of the idea. But just as reflective immediacy is fatal to sensuous immediacy, and vice versa, both are fatal to existential immediacy, the immediacy of the *historical present*, and vice versa.

Spirit, in its incarnate, Christian sense, is the immediacy of historical continuity. Although it is not the immediacy of reflective spirituality (Faust), it is an immediacy within reflection. Spirit in this sense, therefore requires language for its expression. It is music, not language, that is impoverished when it comes to expressing spirit in its incarnate, historical presence. Music simply has no resources for expressing this immediacy. Only speech (the word as *dabhar*) can give expression to the *dynamic presence* of spirit in its positive existential and historical continuity. As Kierkegaard has Author A point out: "But that which religious fervor wants to have expressed is spirit; therefore it requires language, which is the spirit's proper medium, and rejects music, which for it is a sensuous medium and thus always an imperfect medium with which to express spirit" (E/O I,73).

The speech-act is Don Giovanni's deadly enemy. But this is so not because speaking in good faith sunders us from the world—in one sense, speech certainly effects such a sundering; rather, the Don flees speech because he is anxious about being situated within the world, about the responsibility of being bonded to it and to others. And what better refuge for the Don than the abstract medium of music? In music there is no place for commitment, no place for responsibility, no resources for binding the

musician to the world, to others; in it, there are no resources for establishing a reflexive *whence*. Music takes us out of the world; suspends us in
an infinity of negative freedom; loses us in a dynamic sensuous immediacy
so intensified that every hint of continuity is eclipsed. Don Giovanni is this
dynamic, demonic, sensuous immediacy.

Lyricism and Reflective Immediacy

If speech is in fact the perfect medium for expressing spirit in its historical immediacy and continuity, then whenever anyone "speaks," that is,
utters words, there is at least the *appearance* of such a dynamic historical
presence. Yet this may be only and merely an appearance. Indeed when
this "use" of words is undertaken in a conscious attempt to deceive, when
the medium unique to human beings—the medium in and through which
human beings mutually appear to each other in the world—is used as the
vehicle for disappearance, then speaking is transformed into an insidious
and demonically perverted act.

To grasp this, we must remember that a speaker's words, in their full
reflexive integrity, are the very means by which a person establishes her
immediate (historical) presence *within* historical continuity. When granted
its rights, the speech-act, in its reflexively integral use, disrupts the self
from its organic, static, psychical immediacy of harmony and accord within the cosmos and posits a pneumatic immediacy of strife and exclusion.
But this pneumatic historical immediacy established in speech also establishes historical continuity. The reason that the reflexively integral speech-
act can establish this historical immediacy/continuity is that it embodies
within itself a *from/to dialectic*: in the first moment of this dialectic the
dynamic succession of word-sounds annuls the sensuous, thereby enabling
them to point beyond themselves *to* the ideas they are used to express; in
the second moment of the dialectic the speech-act, because of its distinctive formal properties as a medium, establishes the sensuous as the *from*
of the expression, as its ground, as its stability, its continuity. This grounding of the speech-act in its *from*, that is, in the speaker, and in the time,
place, and context of its enactment, is exactly what makes the dynamic
self/world relation it establishes *personal*.

In a self/world relation that is personal, words are the very center of
the real. Yet words cannot be granted this status, this creative power, without being granted as well a negative power of destruction. When words
are used to this latter end, they become demonically and ironically perverted. When words become the means of avoiding all worldly bonds, indeed, the means for destroying these bonds, this use of "speech" ironically
destroys spirit (self) in its historical immediacy and continuity, replacing
this presence with an aesthetic absence, or better with a pneumatic/aes-
thetic, musical presence that is forever absenting itself.

Because the demonic individual is anxious in the face of the worldly bonds of real historical continuity—bonds that are implied in reflexively integral speech—he seeks at all costs to avoid reflexive integrity. One clever way to avoid reflexive integrity is to turn speech into its opposite, namely, silence; or, what is the same thing, the existential presence of speech into an aesthetic absence. Kierkegaard remarks on one form of this, what he calls the *contentless* and the *boring* (CA,132). Here the demonic individual avoids worldly bonds by turning the very resource for establishing those bonds, namely words themselves, into empty talk. Such empty talk, such prattle, conceals rather than reveals, dis-integrates rather than integrates; in this empty talk—this incessant talk—an ironic and deeper *silence* is revealed. Here there is a retreat from the world by means of a subtle retreat from words, a retreat accomplished by a constant detachment and absence of the "speaker" from the words he utters. Here the demonic individual gushes forth with words, he waxes eloquent in poetry and lyricism, and his rhapsody is as seductive as music; indeed this is because *his words have become music*! But in all of this sound and fury, nothing is said; here the "speaker" flees from himself, from freedom, from integrity, from presence, from continuity, from every worldly bond, by flirting with the very means through which these find their concrete actualization, namely, speech itself. Such a perverted "use" of speech may just be the most insidious demonic deception possible; in the end, however, it will, Kierkegaard asserts, finally show itself as a tragicomic attempt to conceal an infinite emptiness and a demonic anxiety about the good.

When "speaking" has become empty talk, when it has become music, words lose their grounding in the speaker, in the world. As such, the "speech-act" becomes not the means of appearance but the means of (perpetual) disappearance. When words are used to cloak the true intentions of the speaker, we meet with the lie; when the lie becomes the means for seduction, we meet with a version of the demonic somehow even more twisted than Don Giovanni. Indeed, in comparison to this reflective seduction, the Don seems almost innocent. When a seducer transforms speech into a means of deception the effect is to transform words into a means of perpetual vanishing; and this, in the end, is to transform speech into music, or, more precisely, it is to transform speech into speech-as-music. Speech-as-music, speech as the means of perpetual vanishing, provides the appearance of presence, while serving as the very means of absence.

The demonic flight from the world in reflective immediacy, however, is accomplished at a great price. The demonic individual knows that words, as lies, have the power to "free" us from any commitment, to "free" us from the world; what he may also come to realize is that his lies "free" him from the world only insofar as they effect its perpetual destruction. The demonic lie is not only the instrument of world-alienation, it will inevitably become the brutal instrument of world-destruction. The demonic individual reasons as follows: to be "free" the confining bonds of worldly existence must be perpetually destroyed, perpetually overturned; this is possible only to the extent that the world itself is kept under the absolute control of "freedom." And no better sign of this absolute "freedom" can be found than in the power to destroy the world at will—always, of course, for the sake of a newer, better one. This is a demonic perversion of God's creative *dabhar*, the power of spirit in its positive form to make the world appear; in the demonic lie, the ultimate effect is world-destruction.

The demonic retreat from the word finds one of its expressions in Johannes the Seducer (E/O I,301–445), its other, indeed, its absolute expression, in Faust. Johannes is more insidious than the Don, but more innocent than Faust. Johannes aims at fleeing from the world, from its confining bonds of commitment; Faust moves a step beyond this taking the logic of this flight to its disastrous final conclusion. That is, he sees clearly that we can only "free" ourselves from the world by destroying it, or more precisely, by perpetually destroying it. Don Giovanni is not nearly as destructive as this—he is not out to destroy the world; he has no plan to ensure his "freedom"; he is too busy for these matters; they require a reflection he does not have; besides, he is too caught up in the intoxication of the moment, in the celebration of his liberation from the world.

The Don is to Johannes and Faust as spiritless sensuality is to sensuousless spirit. Or what comes to the same thing, Don Giovanni is the worldlessness of immediate passion without reflection and Johannes and Faust are the worldlessness of immediate reflection without passion. Because of their reflection, Johannes and Faust cannot find their medium of expression in music; both require language. Yet as demonic, both figures express a spirituality outside the spirit expressed in reflexively integral speech. The only way to have it both ways is to transform speech into a medium of deception, a medium of disappearance. To do this, both Johannes and Faust—especially Faust—retreat from reflexively integral speech, and yet both continue to "use" words. It is in their perverted "use" of speech that language is subtly transmuted into lyricism and ultimately into music.

Because their medium is speech—even though it is a perverted form of it—Johannes and Faust are enabled to become seducers in a more complete sense of the term than was possible in Don Giovanni. A seducer, in the fullest sense of the term, is someone who is clever, cunning, crafty, someone who is a deceiver and a liar. A deceiver lays a plan and so has to have time and forethought, precisely the time and forethought that Don Giovanni, in his sensuous immediacy, has no need of. Don Giovanni is absolute spontaneity, a force of nature, always new, always fresh, always on the move, never in need of a plan, never in need of thinking out his strategy; it is just this immediate sensuous energy that is his attraction, just this energy that is his power of "seduction."

Unlike the Don, Johannes and Faust are not interested in sensuous immediacy; rather they are interested in the interesting, in the idea of the object of their seduction; they desire the absolutely immediate moment of reflection, the immediacy of spirituality. What Louis Mackey says about

Johannes could equally be said of Faust: "Seduction, as Johannes understands it, is not the act of defloration, nor does it presuppose an excessive concern with sex. To seduce a woman means: with no force but with much art to secure the free capitulation of her mind to yours. That sexuality will be the normal context for such an enterprise is obvious; but it is strictly incidental to the real objective, which is the conquest of the spirit and not the conquest of the flesh."[7]

Because the seduction project for Johannes, the seduction of Cordelia Wahl, is wholly an intellectual matter, a matter of reflection, of cleverness, of method, it is a project that can only be carried out within the medium of reflection, language itself. Yet in this project words cannot be used to establish a world between the two, a stable, lasting matrix of constancy, commitment, promise, and faith; rather Johannes' words must become the instruments of trickery, cunning, deceit, and faithlessness, the weapons of conquest, indeed the weapons that will keep Cordelia at bay and his own "freedom" intact. The words Johannes "speaks" do not reveal to Cordelia his intentions; quite to the contrary. Johannes lures Cordelia by cleverly transforming his own intentions into hers, by poetically turning his own desire for her "spirit" into her desire for him. His insidious end, which he finally accomplishes, is to trick her into surrendering her "spirit" to him without himself incurring any cost, any responsibility, any loss of his own "freedom."

The details of Johannes's seduction of Cordelia are too familiar to repeat here. I want only to observe that Johannes' aesthetic flight from the world and from any faithful relation with some other represents the other side of Don Giovanni: the latter is the perfect expression of a perpetually vanishing sensuality, that is, sensuous immediacy; the former is the perfect expression of perpetually vanishing reflection, that is, reflective immediacy. Both exist in a condition of being *sundered* from the world. Don Giovanni is sundered from the world insofar as the sensuous immediacy which he is, is completely and absolutely devoid of stability and continuity. His sensuality is the immediacy of musical sound. A world that is perpetually vanishing, that is perpetually disappearing like the sounds of a musical performance, leaves us hovering in mid air; such a "world" is no world at all. Johannes is also sundered from the world, but in a different direction. His reflection excludes any trace of the sensuous, of body, of worldly space and time. As such the immediacy of reflection, which he is, is ultimately worldless; Johannes is pure idea, idea as it is when completely disengaged from the sensuous. As Don Giovanni is the sensuous immediacy of perpetually vanishing sound, Johannes is the reflective immediacy of the perpetually disengaging idea; idea without a durable, stable, and tangible ground. The net effect in both cases is worldlessness.

With Johannes we move ever closer to the formulation of the outlines of the modern world-picture, a picture that, as we will see in the next chapter, overlaps with the world-picture that is embodied in the legend of Faust. But as I shall argue, Faust formulates more decisively than Johannes this modern world-picture, for Faust advances the essence of Johannes to an infinite, an absolute, level: Johannes is demonic, Faust is absolutely demonic. The essential demonic quality that Johannes exemplifies and that Faust absolutizes is the quality that Kierkegaard calls *romantic irony*. For Kierkegaard "romantic irony" is a sickness of the spirit, a demonic, nihilistic madness; it is the sickness at the heart of the modern age; it is a sickness unto death.

IV

FAUST, ROMANTIC IRONY, AND THE DEMONIC IMMEDIACY OF SPIRITUALITY

> All fixed, fast-frozen relations, with their train of ancient and venerable prejudices and opinions, are swept away, all new-formed ones become antiquated before they can ossify. All that is solid melts into air, all that is holy is profaned.
>
> (Karl Marx)

Goethe's *Faust* perfectly expresses, from Kierkegaard's point of view, the demonic spirituality of the modern age; as much so as Mozart's *Don Giovanni* expresses its counterpart—demonic sensuality. Modern spirituality is demonic through and through, even though, ironically, it was posited as a possibility by Christianity. Faust and Don Giovanni, like Christ, are pneumatically qualified figures; they all express a self/world relation in which spirit is pictured as dynamically and perpetually disengaging itself from the sensuous. Yet for Kierkegaard, Faust and Don Giovanni are demonic expressions of spirit and stand as such in absolute opposition to Christ. The opposition of the demonic spirituality/sensuality of Faust and Don Giovanni to the spirit of Christ is correlated to the contrast between music and the speech-act; between a self/world relation pictured as perpetual vanishing, and a self/world relation in which self and world are co-constituted in the speech-act; between a picture of the self/world relation in which the self is imagined as completely *sundered* from the world and a picture of the self/world relation in which the self is imagined as dialectically *sundered from and bonded to* the world.

In his usual indirect way, Kierkegaard asserts that the legendary figures of Faust and Don Giovanni are the perfect expressions of the two primary forms that aestheticism takes in the modern age. The aesthetic differences between Faust and Don Giovanni can best be understood by reference to the idea/medium relation. For Kierkegaard, the figure of Faust is the perfect expression of "idea" (reflection, intellectuality) as this is understood in a pneumatically qualified, but demonic, picture of the idea/medium relation. Faust is reflection (idea) in and of itself, in its absolute transcendence of the world. Don Giovanni is the perfect expression of "medium" as this is understood in a pneumatically qualified, but demonic, picture of the idea/medium relation. Don Giovanni is music (sensuous immediacy, passion) in and of itself, in its absolute momentariness, in its absolute transcendence of historical continuity. Don Giovanni, who floats between being an individual and being a force of nature, tirelessly and endlessly enjoys, without a hint of reflection, the intoxication of this disengagement; and this is so in spite of the momentary intrusions into his enjoyment of an immediately sensed dread, an immediate musical trembling above the abyss over which he hovers. Faust, on the other hand, appears closer to being an individual—at least insofar as he does not live within the flux of sensuous immediacy and insofar as he does live within the sobriety of thought, of reflection. Yet Faust is idea without any essential connection to the sensuous world; Faust is an "individual" completely disengaged from the world. As such, he is not yet an individual in any full-fledged sense of the term. Faust lacks the concreteness of historical continuity. Faust simply trades the sensuous immediacy of Don Giovanni for another immediacy, the immediacy of spirituality, of reflection, both of which deny historical continuity.

Obviously the immediacy of spirituality seems closer to spirit in its existential, historical, immediacy than does the immediacy of sensuality. Spirit, after all, *is idea*—indeed, man's basic concept; or to put it differently, the immediacy of reflection entails a certain kind of *self*-consciousness. In the awareness that reflection provides, Faust is forced to face—as Don Giovanni is not—some dreadful, sobering, questions: In the perpetually vanishing flux, in an essentially musical world in which all that is solid melts into air, where and how do I, in my pneumatically qualified existence, find my place? How can I find my feet in a "world" that is forever slipping into nothingness? How will I find meaning, stability, coherence? How will spirit avoid the abyss of despair when the effects of the intoxication have passed?

Unlike Don Giovanni, Faust cannot have music, in any straightforward sense of this term, as his medium because, as Kierkegaard puts it, "Music always expresses the immediate in its [sensuous] immediacy" (E/O I,70). Faust, who is pure reflection, must have language, in some sense of this term, as his medium, for again, as Kierkegaard has remarked: "Reflection is implicit in language" (E/O I,70). Yet Faust's medium cannot be the speech-act in any felicitous sense of this term for this would express spirit in the Christian sense and not spirituality in its intellectually qualified demonic sense. The medium of Faust then is "language"; or more exactly, language-as-music; language demonically twisted and distorted and ironically turned into "sound and fury signifying nothing." Speech is Faust's instrument of flight, his vehicle of perpetual vanishing; or as Kierkegaard has put it, Faust uses language to deceive; the method of his deception is *the lie*: "Faust, who reproduces [Don Giovanni], seduces only one girl, whereas Don Giovanni seduces by the hundreds; but in its intensity this one girl is seduced and destroyed in an entirely different way than all those Don Giovanni deceived—precisely because Faust as a reproduction has an intellectual-spiritual quality. The power of a seducer like that is speech, that is, the lie" (E/O I,99).

The deep irony in Faust's use of speech is this: speech is the perfect medium for the expression of man's essential idea, i.e., spirit in its uniquely Christian sense, spirit in its historical immediacy/continuity; yet in Faust's hands, words are used to express spirit in its complete disengagement from the historical continuity of the given actuality. Such a worldless spirit lies completely outside of spirit in the positive Christian sense of the term. As such, the idea that Faust expresses is the idea of spiritlessness; moreover, the medium in which it is expressed is the medium whose absolute subject is spirit. The result here is that we find in Faust an ironic and demonic use of speech: the medium that is perfectly suited to expressing spirit, when employed by Faust, expresses its opposite, a spiritless spirituality.

In the last chapter, we saw how Johannes the Seducer employed speech in this demonic, twisted sense. In Part I of *Faust*, we find this demonic use of speech appearing again. I want to explore this further and claim that in Faust (as in Johannes) there is a deeply ironic use of speech and that this irony is at the very center of modern sensibility and constitutes its demonic and deadly sickness. With Kierkegaard, I will call this Faustian species of irony *romantic irony*. In what follows I will discuss romantic irony in the context of Faust's seduction of Margaret. My claim will be that the modern age is so dominated by the musical picture of the self/world relation that it turns the very thing that can save it into the instrument of its destruction. That is, modernity ironically transforms the very resource necessary for establishing a space of appearance for spirit, namely, the world-constituting speech-act, into music—the perfect instrument for world-destruction.

In the discussion of romantic irony, I will be setting the stage for a discussion of Faust in his more demonic stage, his absolute demonic stage, found in the much neglected Part II of Goethe's play.[1] Here I will claim that Faust has come to depict perfectly the demonic spirit of the modern age in its fullest and most devastating expression. In Part II Faust finally gives up on speech, even speech as the lie, and turns his attention to what he had discovered earlier (Scene 3, Part I) but not fully pursued, namely, the deep inadequacy of speech. He has long since become dissatisfied with books, with scholarship; now that dissatisfaction becomes focused while he is reading the Prologue to the Gospel of John. While reading, he becomes profoundly dissatisfied with the word 'Word' in the famous lines that begin that Prologue, "In the beginning was the Word." After thinking about it for a while, and after thinking of replacing 'Word' with 'Thought,' he hits upon the insight to replace 'Word' with 'Act.' The reason for this is that Faust thinks that the word 'Act' captures, as the word 'Word' does not, the importance of activity, or more precisely, the specific activity at focus in the Prologue, namely, *creation*. It is not until the second part of the play that this insight is fully realized and the full demonic power of Faust is felt; not until here, that modern spirituality, in all of its demonic obsession with *creation*, with progress, with perpetual renewal, with perpetual striving for a better world, and so forth, is seen in its full irony as a demonic spirituality of *world-destruction*.

Before turning to these matters, I must take a brief detour. Since I want to characterize Faust and the modern age as suffering from an advanced case of romantic irony, I must present very briefly Kierkegaard's understanding of this concept, or better, my understanding of Kierkegaard's master's thesis where this concept is elaborated.

In his master's thesis, *The Concept of Irony*, Kierkegaard says, in his usual cryptic and indirect manner: "Irony is a healthiness insofar as it rescues the soul from the snares of relativity; it is a sickness insofar as it cannot bear the absolute except in the form of nothing" (CI,77).

In its broadest outline, Kierkegaard's argument is a critique of Hegel's view of irony, according to which irony is always a sickness (CI,265). While Kierkegaard agrees with Hegel that modern romantic irony is a sickness, he disagrees with Hegel's attempt to put Socratic irony in the same camp. For Kierkegaard, Socratic irony is a form of irony's healthiness and a key to understanding the essential place of irony in a healthy life. The main difference between the two forms of irony, Socratic and romantic, has to do with the relation that each bears to what he calls subjectivity—a term that is for him virtually synonymous with spirit. We can say then that, for Kierkegaard, both forms of irony are negative determinations of subjectivity or spirit, but in radically different ways.

In keeping with the preceding argument, I will take the concept of irony to designate a relation that a speaker bears to his own words, and as such, a manifestation of his relation to himself, others, and the world. Irony is the name of *a way of being* as manifest in *a way of saying*. Kierkegaard describes the ironic figure of speech as follows: "In oratory, for example, there frequently appears a figure of speech with the name of irony and the characteristic of saying the opposite of what is meant. Already here we have a quality that permeates all irony—namely, the phenomenon is not the essence but the opposite of the essence. When I am speaking, the thought, the meaning, is the essence, and the word is the phenomenon" (CI,247).

The distinction between the immediate phenomenon (the sign) and its mediated meaning (the signification) correspond to what we might call the "what" of the speech-act and the "how" of its intention. In irony, the distinction is inordinately "pronounced" for "what" is said (the phenomenon) is the opposite of "how" it is intended (the meaning). Irony produces thus a tension between the immediate and the mediate, between the phenomenon and the idea. Kierkegaard remarks on two common forms of this ironic tension: "It is the most common form of irony to say something earnestly that is not meant in earnest. The second form of irony, to say as a jest, jestingly, something that is meant in earnest, is more rare" (CI,248).

If an ironic speech-act is to be understood, the immediate phenomenon must be negated (*aufgehoben*) so that what is said and how it is said can be jointly comprehended. When this happens, when the listener realizes that the speaker's "earnestness is not in earnest" (CI,248), a decisive element of the speech-act indirectly emerges. Beyond the "what" and the "how," the "who" of the speech-act indirectly appears as the ground of the speech-act itself. The "who" is the subject of the speech-act and it is impossible to understand the full irony of a speech-act without meeting the subject who is behind it as the ground of its meaning. It is in this sense then that irony is a qualification of subjectivity (spirit): it provides the reflexive context of opposition and tension in which the subject can transcend the immediately given phenomenon and appear as the ground and authority of what is said.

Yet irony is a *negative* qualification of spirit. Irony shows the freedom and transcendence of the speaker insofar as it manifests the power speakers have to choose how they will stand to their words, and thus to themselves, the world, and others. In irony, ironists do not appear positively in their words; indeed, the opposite. In irony, the speaker "appears" negatively, as absent from his words; in the ironic saying, ironists are *present as absent*. Through the technique of withholding commitment from their words ironists avoid bonding themselves to others and to the world on which their words putatively have an effectual bearing. As we might put it, in ironic speech-acts ironists negatively appear as not owning their words. Here ironists do not speak to some other from within the boundary of a world; rather, they hover above the world, others, and even themselves in the negative freedom of noncommitment.

Because the ironist knows (however tacitly) that he is the ultimate ground of the meaning and authority of what he says (a positive awareness), he also recognizes how to become negatively free. Being unable, or somehow unwilling, to appear as himself, as the owner of his words, he appears only negatively as not owning them. As such, the ironist uses speech as a means of expressing his noncommitment and gains thereby a negative freedom from the responsibility he implicitly recognizes as entailed by being present in his words. The ironist's negative freedom shows itself in the clever techniques by which he isolates himself, by his refusal to present himself, as himself, to others within the boundary of a world. The ironist aesthetically cloaks his real (present) self by first appearing as this and then as that, but never appearing as himself; indeed qua ironist, he is or has no self in any positive sense.

The ironic mode of speech is very different from what I have called faithful speech. In reflexively integral, faithful speech, the speaker appears in the first person as present in what is said, as ready to assume responsibility for the speech-act. Kierkegaard puts this as follows: "When I am aware as I speak that what I am saying is what I mean and that what I have said adequately expresses my meaning, and I assume that the person to whom I am talking grasps my meaning completely, then I am *bound* in what has been said—that is, *I am positively free therein* (CI,247, italics added).

To be positively free, speakers must own their words before others; each must speak in the first person singular as integral 'I'; each must own up to his relation to his words, and to the effectual bearing of these words on the world. In positive freedom the speaker freely decides, however tacitly, and from within the boundary of the syntax, semantics, and grammar of her language, the how of their expression. In addition to this, the faithful speaker must take up in commitment and fidelity the worldly responsibility entailed by what she says despite the obvious fact that it often leads, because of its grounding in the contingency of history, beyond what the speaker can explicitly predict. To speak in good faith, then, a speaker must say what she means and mean what she says.

This positive freedom is, for Kierkegaard, decisively modeled for us by Christ. Again I quote a decisive text that ironically appears in Kierkegaard's Thesis as a footnote: "As for what he [Christ] said, one could always take him at his word; his words were life and spirit" (CI,14). In the appearance of Christ—the incarnate *dabhar* of Yahweh—we find the most positive qualification of spirit; here Jesus appears, through the mediation of the word, as himself; here we have the model of what it is to bond oneself in responsibility, before God, to the world and to others.

Given that the standard of health is the positive qualification of spirit as that appears in faithful speech, that is, serious speech, where the "who" is present as the one who owns her words before an other, how can irony be seen as a healthiness? For the answer to this, we must turn to Kierkegaard's treatment of Socratic irony.

The modality of Socrates' being is negative. His irony is a negative qualification of subjectivity; his freedom is negative. All that Socrates knows is that he knows nothing. He "appears" as one who is wise even though he is actually ignorant.

What Socrates had come to believe, Kierkegaard contends, was that the prevailing Greek picture of the world (what we have called the psychically qualified world-picture) was invalid. He says of Socrates:

> [T]hat the whole substantial life of Greek culture had lost its validity for
> him, which means that to him the established actuality was unactual, not in

> this or that particular aspect but in its totality as such; that with regard to
> this invalid actuality he let the established order of things appear to remain
> established and thereby brought about its downfall; that in the process Soc-
> rates became lighter and lighter, more and more negatively free. . . . But it
> was not actuality in general that he negated; it was the . . . substantial actu-
> ality as it was in Greece, and what his irony was demanding was the actu-
> ality of subjectivity. (CI,270–271)

To put this disillusionment of Socrates in the terms of this discussion,
we can say that the psychically qualified world-picture had lost its validity
for him. Accordingly, Socrates took refuge in irony and used it to withhold his commitment from that picture. In a "standpoint" of noncommitment he hovered in the clouds in negative freedom from the implications
of a world-picture he could no longer endorse.

Socrates adopts the negative "standpoint" of irony by disguising himself
as still guided by that world-picture that he could no longer support. He
feigns his allegiance to that picture and seeks to expose its inadequacy.
The method he uses, of course, is the method of questioning.

Socrates asks questions, but not like the Sophists who see questions as
only an occasion for gushing forth with answers. If one really questions it
must be out of genuine ignorance—Socrates is genuinely ignorant. But
the gods have told him that he is wise in his ignorance, for, unlike those
who pretend knowledge and yet are ignorant, Socrates is aware of his
relation to his own pretension to know; that is, he knows that they are
merely pretensions. He also suspects that this is true for others and sets
out to expose the pretensions of his fellow Athenians for what they are.

The object of the questioning is to see if those who pretend to know
can back up their claims with their own embodied justifications. That is,
Socrates is trying to get his fellow Athenians to own their words before
him, or to speak with integrity. What he finds is that they cannot. But this
is necessarily so, for the given world-picture in which they dwell makes no
room for this positive subjective move. Having then brought his interlocutors to a confession of ignorance, by getting them to recognize their own
failure to stand behind their words with integrity, Socrates sets into motion
the destruction of the given world-picture within which the issue of the
knower's relation to what he claims to know never comes up.

Why is this Socratic irony a healthiness? Again, we must keep in mind
that, for Kierkegaard, the sign of healthiness, the positive qualification of
subjectivity, is the radically free and hence radically transcendent and contingent act of owning one's words before some other in faithful speech.
In order for speech to be faithful speech, it must not only have an effectual semantic bearing on the world, it must establish a ligament between
speaker and the world, her own body, and others. This reflexive requirement demands that the speaker be present in her words as their ground
and authority. The acknowledgement, however tacit and indirect, of this

reflexive relation between speaker and her words, even if wholly negative, may be a step toward healthiness. This is, according to Kierkegaard, exactly the step Socrates made. By consciously refusing to be present in his words and by exposing the lack of presence his fellow Athenians bore to their words, Socrates demonstrated, via negativa, that words without personal, reflexive backing are empty. In fact, the prevailing self/world picture among the Greeks was one according to which the speaker's words had no effectual bearing on the world precisely because the world was imagined to be already, indeed from all eternity, determinately and impersonally constituted. In such a world-picture, words could not be vested with their rights and as a result subjectivity could not positively appear. Socrates' irony, however, moved as close as is possible, in the Greek, *logos*-centered, world-picture, to the positive appearance of subjectivity. It achieved this only negatively and at the expense of crumbling the Greek imagination.

Socrates was never able to move beyond the negative acknowledgement of subjectivity. But he moved close to the possibility of its positive appearance, for the ultimate effect of his words, his questioning, was to destroy the given world-picture which inhibited positive subjectivity. Ironically, in his noncommitment, Socrates disclosed the inadequacy of a picture of the world according to which the speaking subject has no essential part to play in that world's constitution.

But why couldn't Socrates move beyond this negative hovering freedom to a positive qualification of subjectivity? The reason is that Socrates was truly ignorant. He had no picture of what it would be to own his words, to be present in them as the ultimate ground of their meaning, authority, and integrity; he had no picture according to which speech could be vested with its world-constituting rights; he had no picture of positive subjectivity.

Kierkegaard thinks that the only world-picture which can adequately serve as the ground of the positive qualification of subjectivity is provided by the biblical narratives. As I have already pointed out, in the biblical world-picture Yahweh, who speaks the world into existence, is the model of faithful speech (*dabhar*), the model of the positive qualification of subjectivity. In this biblical picture, mankind is created in God's image. Here, the self is depicted as actively participating in the ongoing historical process of creation—a process in which the actuality of the world is called forth out of radically contingent possibility and subjectively grounded and sustained.

The key difference between the Greek and biblical pictures of the world is that, in the latter, the actuality of the world is established historically and in relation to a speaking subject and in the former the actuality of the world is eternally and impersonally grounded. The biblical picture is thoroughly personal; it alone offers an understanding of the world wherein positive subjectivity can fully appear. In this picture, what something is, is its vocation; ontological status is conferred here in relation to a speaker—a speaker who, by giving something a name, calls it forth into its full and positive qualification as real. In the Greek picture, what something is, it is eternally and impersonally and its ontological status is essentially independent of a relation to some speaking subject. In the biblical picture, reality is at bedrock subject/object in structure; in the Greek picture, reality is wholly objective. In a cosmos, there is no essential place for a subject to appear fully and positively as spirit.

To speak with integrity in the first person, to own one's words before another, is to bind oneself to the world and to others in responsibility. In this binding, both self and world dialectically appear in their positive fullness. This binding is, however, preceded by a movement of transcendence. Without this transcendence, the binding would be less than free; less than personal.

In the Greek world-picture, the notion of the self's transcendence of its own words and the world was absent, at least until Socrates. In the Greek imagination, words were thought to have no effectual relation to the real; at best words were thought of as felicitous if they "matched" the eternal objects they "named." Because reality was in no need of being realized in relation to a speaking subject, words were thought to stand in no need of being owned as the effectual authorization of the real. In the Greek picture, the only "relation" a "self" could have to the real was passive and silent: one could, on the one hand, contemplate, *sub specie aeternitatis*, the eternal forms (Plato) or, on the other, submit to one's lot in a wholly determined world (Sophocles).

In contrast to the health of Socratic irony, Kierkegaard regards romantic irony, that unique modern species of irony, as a sickness. Although the sources from which this modern romantic sickness emerged are complex, we can say, at least, that a key factor in this phenomenon is the erosion of the authority of biblical faith. The irony here is that it is the world-picture of biblical faith (the pneumatically qualified picture in which spirit was first posited as spirit) that provides the conceptual space for the appearance of romantic irony.

Modernity, especially in the Enlightenment, welcomed the appearance of subjectivity, indeed, it gloried in it. Yet this positive appearance of spirit was made possible only insofar as it was provided with a space of appearance—a world. The biblical doctrine of creation provided this. In this doctrine, the world was conceived as created, as radically contingent, as grounded in a subject who brought it into being by calling it forth. Such a historical conception of reality was inconceivable within Greek ontological premises (the real does not come into nor does it go out of being). In the biblical picture, God's *dabhar*, and not the ahistorical Greek *logos*, serves as the historical absolute and the transhistorical ground of the real. Even though the world is radically contingent in the biblical picture, it is given a transhistorical stability and solidity insofar as it is thought to be in the safe keeping of God's absolutely faithful word; it is this word that *provides* a transhistorical *ground* to the historical. Again, this is not the ahistorical ground of the Greek *logos*, but the temporally unfolding intentional and subjective ground of *dabhar*; here the real is grounded in a speaker whose words bring the world forth and whose steadfast fidelity holds it together through time.

In this biblical picture, human beings, created in the image of God, are vested with the power of the speech-act and hence with the power to call the world forth into its full actuality and to sustain it as such. In this picture what something is in its fully determinant actuality can appear only when it is called forth into what it is intended to be; this is its vocation, and in bestowing this vocation, human beings fulfill their own vocations and so become fully human.

Even though the world is called forth and owned by the human spirit, that world and that spirit must already be present as given, as the incipient ground for this positive appearance of spirit. That is, human beings are not called to create actuality from nothing, rather, they are called to actualize actuality. This presupposes a given; such a given makes sense, however, only if the Hebraic mythology of creation does. In this mythology, the solidity of the world rests securely in the steadfast word of an absolutely faithful Speaker. The loss of faith in this mythology is tantamount to a loss of the given. Yet this loss of faith is at the very heart of the modern age.

Modernity began by trying to fashion a world-picture in which there is no given actuality. In short, modernity tried to eliminate God and retain a secularized biblical image of the self. Lacking God as an ultimate ground of actuality, and yet retaining the idea that actuality must be called forth and given a subjective grounding, the self, in modernity, becomes god.

Unlike the Greek predicament where spirit is completely domiciled within the immediacy of harmony, order, and form, modern man is faced with the prospect of trying to be a self without a world. In the former, self and world were not yet separated out of their immediate psychical embranglement; in the latter, the self is without a ground, sundered from its own body, the world, and others. In such a state, the dis-covenanted self cannot own its own words. Without the space of the world there is no way for words to have an effectual bearing on anything outside of themselves; indeed, words, and so the world, become like musical notes perpetually vanishing. But the "self" remains in this picture. It remains in absolute "freedom" and transcendence. Now the self is free from its bonding to the world and to others: this is the heart of romantic irony.

The romantic ironist finds herself thrust into a radically contingent but godless universe in which she has no place to stand. She lacks this place because she no longer is able to be called to it by God, having lost faith in him, and no longer able to return to the serene immediacy of a Greek (psychically qualified) "place" in the substantial order of the cosmos, hav-

ing been irreversibly awakened, at least since the first appearance of subjectivity in Socrates, to her own transcendence. Without a God who calls
the world into being (that is, in the silent infinite spaces in the face of
which Pascal shudders) the "world"—now reduced to particles in motion—is no longer a fit place for human beings to inhabit. The space necessary for a self to appear before some other has vanished into
nothingness.

The romantic ironist then is a self without a world, but in need of one
to be a self. She therefore sets out to poetize her own private "world" over
which she can exercise absolute god-like power. As Kierkegaard puts it,
in romantic irony: "It was not an element of the given actuality that must
be negated and superseded by a new element [as in Socrates], but it was
all of historical actuality that it negated in order to make room for a self-
created actuality" (CI,275). In this irony, subjectivity does not negatively
appear in any healthy sense, as it did in Socrates; rather we have here "an
exaggerated subjectivity, a subjectivity raised to the second power"
(CI,275), or, as I have put it, a self unbounded by a given historical world
and others. This irony, Kierkegaard says, agreeing with Hegel, is "unjustified" (CI,275), or, in the language of Kierkegaard's earlier remark, "a
sickness."

The unbounded power of romantic irony is at the heart of Kierkegaard's condemnation of it as a sickness. He says:

> Irony now functioned as that for which nothing was established, as that
> which was finished with everything, and also as that which had the absolute
> power to do everything. If it allowed something to remain established, it
> knew that it had the power to destroy it, knew it at the very same moment
> it let it continue. If it posited something, it knew it had the authority to
> annul it, knew it at the very same moment it posited it. It knew that in
> general it possessed the absolute power to bind and to unbind. It was lord
> over the idea just as much as over the phenomenon and it destroyed the
> one with the other. (CI,275–276)

For Kierkegaard, an essential condition for the positive appearance of
subjectivity (spirit, self) is a historical actuality—a world in the sense presupposed by the Judaeo-Christian doctrine of creation, namely a world
grounded in the *dabhar* of Yahweh, who calls it forth and sustains it
through his faithfulness. Insofar as this world is not eternally grounded
in an impersonal *logos* but in the personal act of *dabhar*, it is essentially
historical, essentially contingent. The romantic ironist, having lost her
footing, that is, having lost faith in God and hence in the stabilizing power
of *dabhar*—the transhistorical ground of historical continuity—can have
nothing to do with the historical actuality any longer; it has become merely contingent, without continuity or stability. As Kierkegaard puts it: "The
actual history, however, in which the authentic individual has his positive

freedom because therein he possesses his premises, had to be set aside" (CI,277). In setting the historical actuality aside, the romantic ironist also sets aside positive freedom, that is, spirit and self.

In order to remain free from the world and the bonds of responsibility entailed by owning our words before some other (in order, that is, to remain in noncommittal hovering) the ironist must transform all actuality into possibility. The "world," for the ironist, is "*his* actuality," that is, finally only in his fantasy, in his own head, and as such his words are empty of any bearing on anything outside themselves. Kierkegaard writes:

> just as irony managed to defeat the historical actuality by placing it in suspension, so irony itself has become suspended. Its actuality is only possibility. In order for the acting individual to be able to accomplish his task by fulfilling actuality, he must feel himself integrated in a larger context, must feel the earnestness of responsibility. . . . Irony is free from all this. It knows it has the power to start all over again if it so pleases; anything that happened before is not binding. . . . Irony is indeed free, free from the sorrows of actuality, but also free from its joys, from its blessings. (CI,279)

In the biblical picture of the world, subjectivity (spirit, self) can positively appear only in a historical context. If that historical context has no more validity, as is the case with the romantic ironist, then her own subjectivity cannot positively appear. Therefore the ironist must not only poetically produce a world, she must poetically produce herself as well.

In order to maintain this hovering ironic detachment from the actuality of the historical world and from herself, the romantic ironist must "suspend what is constitutive in actuality, that which orders and sustains it: that is, morality and ethics" (CI,283). One way to suspend morality and ethics is to fail to be good to one's words, to be absent from them, not to own them and the responsibility that implies. This is what Kierkegaard means by saying that the romantic ironist lives completely hypothetically and subjunctively (CI,284). Such a mode of being, as manifest in this way of saying, is essentially noncommittal. This ironic mode of "speaking," in which first person present asseverations are suspended in favor of the abstract third person hypothetical and subjunctive absence of the speaker, fails to situate her in the historical world and her life "loses all continuity" (CI,284).

With this lack of continuity, the romantic ironist succumbs completely to mood. His life is nothing but moods (CI,284). But even his moods and feelings are poetized. "Thus the mood itself has no reality for the ironist, and he seldom vents his mood except in the form of contrast. . . . He hides his sorrow in the superior incognito of jesting; his happiness is muffled up in bemoaning" (CI,285). In the end, boredom is the only continuity left for the romantic ironist. "Boredom, this eternity devoid of content,

this salvation devoid of joy, this superficial profundity, this hungry glut"
(CI,285).

The ironic hovering of the romantic in which both self and world are
poetically produced is nowhere more clearly and tragically expressed than
in Goethe's *Faust*.

The Faustian Project

As Spengler has remarked in *The Decline of the West*, our modern age is
essentially Faustian. Others have said much the same thing: Thomas Mann
in *Doctor Faustus*;[2] Marshall Berman in *All That Is Solid Melts into Air*;[3] and
Harry Redne in *In the Beginning was the Deed*.[4] I do not take it as my task
to establish further what has been so well argued in these books. Rather,
what I want to do is to elaborate and clarify the thesis that our age is
essentially Faustian by setting it in the context of the Kierkegaardian claim
that Christianity introduced this possibility by first positing a world-picture
in which spirit and world are depicted as being related as idea and medium are related in a dynamic auditory phenomenon.

When I say that the Faustian project is the project of the modern age,
I choose the term 'project' deliberately. The modern age is, as Arendt has
told us, an age of the "vita activa"; that is, it is an age that finds its center
of gravity in activity. The paradigmatic human activity is what Arendt calls
action. For her, an action is first and foremost a historical, dynamic, political, and worldly pro-ject; it is an insertion of ourselves into the world
through the medium of the speech-act. This insertion of ourselves
plunges us into a temporally on-going, open-ended conversation with others concerning, among other things, the array of future contingent possibilities before us; and it presents us with the project of transforming some
of those possibilities, the ones that we jointly covenant and jointly declare,
into concrete historical actualities. To this extent, the modern age has carried on the dynamic *dabhar*-centered sensibility of the biblical narratives,
and to this extent, it is pneumatically qualified.

My claim, however, is that the modern age is demonic; that it is essentially musical. I am taking this to mean that in the modern age the dynamic spirit of *dabhar* has been twisted and deranged. This derangement
is subtle. Indeed, demonic activity is very much like the human speech-act,
the *dabhar*-centered project it parodies. Like the *dabhar*-centered act, demonic activity is also a dynamic project, a project that seems to aim at
"making a world appear." As Sartre—a Faustian of the first order—has
remarked: "To act is to modify the *shape* of the world."[5] Yet Sartre's elaboration of this modification of the world gives away both his reliance on
pneumatic categories and his subtle Faustian perversion of them. He says:
"The careless smoker who has through negligence caused the explosion
of a powder magazine has not *acted*. On the other hand the worker who

is charged with dynamiting a quarry and who obeys the given orders has acted when he has produced the expected explosion; he knew what he was doing or, if you prefer, he intentionally realized a conscious project" (BN,557). For all of this seeming affinity, even for all this real affinity, between Sartre's account of an act and the *dabhar*-centered act, one thing stands out: in the paradigm of an act that Sartre constructs, as that is embodied in his example of the worker at the quarry, a key element in action, namely, its aim of "modifying the shape of the world," is subtly twisted. The act here is in no way a calling forth of the world or some aspect of it into its determinate historical, lasting, and tangible actuality; rather, the act modifies the shape of the world by destroying or annihilating a part of it. Action in its demonic form is a transmutation of the positive power of the speech-act into a nihilistic power of destruction. In this subtle difference between the act as the instrument through which the world (and the self) appears in its full historical actuality, and act as the instrument through which the world is destroyed, lies the heart of our modern Faustian sensibility.

Human action came into its own and was fully authorized and legitimated for the first time with the advent of a pneumatically qualified world-picture. This world-picture vested human action, an already present but heretofore not-yet-fully-realized human possibility, with its rights, by vesting temporality and contingency with a heretofore not-yet-fully-realized reality. Yet the Christian vesting of the temporal order with its ontological rights was not intended simply as an affirmation of the flux *simpliciter*; Christianity did posit reality as dynamic, but not as *mere* flux. Indeed the Christian innovation is found in its understanding of time *as history*: historical time has within itself a structure of continuity absent in mere temporal momentariness. In positing time as history, Christianity also vested speech with its rights: speech is the historical medium par excellence. As essentially tensed, speech is able to express contingency, openness, transcendence; as semantic and reflexive in its formal structure, speech is also able to express continuity, tradition, permanence, and so forth. Such a historical understanding of reality was unimaginable in a psychically qualified cosmos.

When human action is understood as momentary, as mere activity, as coming from nowhere and as passing away into nothingness—that is, when human action is severed from the resources that provide it with stability, coherence, and continuity, namely, the resources of the speech-act—we have the emergence of the demonic. For the demonic individual, human actions are reduced to mere activities, to activities without continuity, to perpetual, frenetic movements without rest: this is the musicalization of human action. For the demonic individual, history is reduced to musical flux, full of sound and fury to be sure, but signifying nothing; words become fleeting notes disconnected from persons and from a worldly context; for the demonic individual, the world, as perpetually vanishing, loses all of its stability and continuity; in the demonic individual, words and deeds, self and world, are fatally severed. Such a demonic individual is nowhere more clearly found than in the demonic figure of Faust. Faust is pure frenzied activity, perpetual dissatisfaction, constant renewal; he is restless, frenetic, hyper, mad.

A key to Goethe's *Faust* is found in the scene in the scholar's study (Scene 3, Part I) in which Faust presents the first hint of his distrust of speech. The scene is preceded by hints of Faust's unbridled and infinite passion for perpetual spiritual renewal. His passion is realizable, Faust begins to think, not in words, not in books, but only in perpetual "pure activity"; that is, activity that keeps spirit alive by providing it a worldly space of appearance, but which also keeps it perpetually sundered from what Faust thinks are the confining and deadening "bonds" entailed by such an appearance *in the world*; bonds of commitment, responsibility, and reflexivity. This "insight" is behind his translation of 'word' into 'deed' in John's Prologue. My claim is that Faust's "insight"—his distrust of speech—coupled with his spiritual (pneumatically qualified) drive to appear in the world without getting trapped there, to be "free" without getting ensnared by responsibility, and so forth, produces a musicalization of both words and deeds, a musicalization of self and world. Although this musicalization is everywhere evident in Part I of the drama, in Faust's doubt, in his bargain with Mephistopheles, and in his seduction of Margaret, it comes to its apex in his reclamation project of Part II.

The story of Faust, as Goethe presents it, begins in Faust's despair. He is an intellectual, a renowned scholar; he has lived in and among books, in and among words; yet the breadth and depth of his knowledge has left him deeply and desperately dissatisfied with his life. His scholarly discipline has led him to a feeling of "being trapped" in his lonely, dingy, dreary hole-in-the-wall of a room. As the curtain opens on Scene I in Goethe's play, we find Faust cursing his "dungeon." In his despair he realizes that he has never, for all of his years, and for all of his putative success and worldly esteem, really lived.

What Faust found out is what every scholar who stops to reflect on his life of reflection discovers, namely, that the more one knows the more one is liable to doubt. Knowledge advances by questioning, by criticism, by discovery, and, as every freshman university student knows, these avenues of inquiry may well lead into an unsettling sea of uncertainty, into a storm of skepticism, and finally into a desert of despair. The more we know, the more possibilities are available, and the more we are acquainted with these possibilities, the more we recognize the parochial nature of our beliefs and life-metaphors, and so the more they, and along with them the stability of our world, are challenged. And with these challenges our childlike innocence is destroyed and we are liable to fall into a Faustian despair—a despair in which our world slips out from under our feet and all that is solid melts into air.

The point is that Faust has learned the great lesson that knowledge is an equivocal good. The enthusiasm and optimism of Wagner, replicating Faust's own younger intellectual passion, is based on a blindness to this fact. Wagner believes, as the young Faust did, that knowledge, infinite knowledge, will set him free. What the middle-aged Faust has discovered is that his pursuit of knowledge has led not to his freedom but to his present entrapment. Now Faust despairs, now he feels the acute pain of resentment: the resentment of having missed life, the resentment of having been robbed of his innocence, the resentment of having been exiled by his own excesses into his present prison. In his despair, Faust comes to realize that knowledge is gained only at a price, a high and painful price; "that knowledge is always an ambiguous good, concealing a *threat*; that catastrophe is associated with the loss of innocence."[6] In this respect, Faust is the modern version of the ancient western myths that teach us the same lesson. I mean the myths of Adam and Eve and Oedipus, both of which connect knowledge with an arrogance that leads to a fall and to exile.

Faust has lived in this arrogance and now he knows the pain of his exile from the world. He feels that he has lived as a god, high above the world. Now, however, he realizes that his life of the mind has isolated him from real life in the world. He desperately wants some connection to the life that has passed him by, to the world from which he has long been detached. Summoning up the Earth Spirit, he strains to find some way to plunge into life and into the world. But even this yearning to live— a yearning that now replaces Faust's scholarly yearning to know—is infinite, unbridled, absolute. He says: "You spirit of the earth, seem close to mine / I look and feel my powers growing, / As if I'd drunk new wine I'm glowing, / I feel a sudden courage, and should dare / To plunge into the world, to bear / All earthly grief, all earthly joy—compare / With gales my strength, face shipwreck without care" (462–467).

The Earth Spirit, however, recognizes that Faust's spirit and his own are alien, and vanishes, yet not before telling Faust that his ambition is the yearning of an *Übermensch*, a superman (490). As Marshall Berman has so aptly noted, perhaps the Earth Spirit is really saying to Faust that the two are alien for just this reason. Berman suggests that maybe the Earth Spirit is really saying to Faust that, instead of being a superman, he ought to "strive to become a *Mensch*—an authentic human being" (MB,42).

After the Earth Spirit vanishes, Wagner enters to converse on the intellectual joys of universal knowledge. Wagner is zealous in his quest to expand his knowledge. He says: "Though I know much, I should like to know all" (601). Faust is no longer interested in scholarly matters, for his pursuit has led him into his present despair, and he breaks off the conversation. And in a long soliloquy of thought he sees the folly of his life and resolves to commit suicide.

At this point he hears the church bells chime the dawning of Easter morning. It is not, however, Christianity, the resurrection of Christ, that saves Faust from suicide; it is rather his remembrance of his childhood, his lost innocence, and the possibility of resurrecting and renewing that youthful energy and carefree enthusiasm. He says: "And yet these chords, which I have known since infancy: / Call me now, too, back into life" (769–770). And further, "Sound on, oh hymns of heaven, sweet and mild! / My tears are flowing; earth, take back your child" (783–784).

Out of the darkness of his room, Faust enters into the world, now alive with the excitement of Easter morning, resurrection, and the delight of festival re-creation. Faust plunges into the crowd and is exhilarated by this renewed contact with the world he once knew but from which he had long been in retreat. Many in the crowd recognize Faust, remembering his early days as a medical doctor, a son of a physician. Faust has practiced medicine among these poor people of his old neighborhood. But his delight at renewing these acquaintances is short-lived, for Faust soon remembers why he left. As he and his father had practiced it, medicine was a hit or miss, crude and unrefined medieval craft. The people loved Faust and his father, but Faust was convinced that the two of them had killed more people than they had healed. In the wake of this guilt, Faust had retreated from this practical connection to the world and entered his detached intellectual quest, "the quest that has led both to knowledge and to intensified isolation, and that almost led him to his death" (MB,46).

Faust is now face to face with a dilemma: "Two souls alas are dwelling in my breast, / And one is striving to forsake its brother. / Unto the world in grossly loving zest, / With clinging tendrils, one adheres; / The other rises forcibly in quest / Of rarefied ancestral spheres" (1112–17). Faust knows that he cannot stay locked up in his intellectual isolation from the world, nor can he return to an existence in the world like the one he knew as a blundering physician—an existence he took to be mindless and confining. He must find a way to bridge the gap, a way to make a connection to the concrete world without getting mired down in it and deadened by its routines, by its banality; a way of making a connection to the world that will allow his spirit room to grow and develop.

At this point he returns to his study and rewrites the Prologue to John, replacing "In the beginning was the word" with "In the beginning was the deed." It is not in the word that all things are created, Faust comes to believe, but in the deed. In this is Faust's way of bridging the gap between his two souls: he can maintain the transcendence of spirit that he wants, the freedom of spirit that keeps it from suffocating in the world, and a connection to the world he needs to provide his life with meaning, substance, and content, only by being related to the world through (wordless) deeds of creation—what I will call musicalized deeds, deeds that pass away at the moment of their enactment, deeds that are perpetually self-annulling.

This connection to the world as its creator is, he imagines, just that connection that Yahweh, the God of the Hebrew scriptures, establishes to the world that he created out of nothing. He therefore decides to imitate God. Yet it is just at this point where the demonic perversion of spirit is disclosed; Mephistopheles appears. The God of the Hebrew story of creation is the God who speaks the world into existence, a God whose creative deeds are established in and through his faithful words. Faust does not imagine that words have any creative and sustaining power and so sees not only the word as lacking any essential connection to the deed, but the deed (pure activity) as standing on its own. In this ever so slight but ever so enormous twist, the full force of the demonic spirit of Faust is born; here the detachment of word from deed is a subtle transmutation of creative act into a brute force of destruction; here, when word and deed have parted company, as Arendt has remarked, words become empty and deeds become the brutal means to violate and to destroy and not the means to establish relations and create new realities (HC,179).

The twisted logic of Mephistopheles seduces Faust into thinking that he has indeed discovered the way to resolve the conflict between the two souls in his breast; the way, that is, to maintain a relation to the world that will not confine and deaden his soaring spirit. Mephistopheles presents an argument to Faust that has all of the dialectical flair of Kierkegaard's claim that Christianity brought sensuality into the world. As Mephistopheles has it, God, by his act of creation, paradoxically brought a demonic power of destruction into being at the same time.

As is the case in every effective deception there is some truth in Mephistopheles' reasoning. He is right to recognize a dialectical connection between creation and destruction in the biblical myth of creation. This connection is based, as I have argued, on the fact that the biblical world-picture is pneumatically qualified and as such presupposes, or more exactly posits the reality of, time and the temporality of reality. This means that what is brought into being in time also passes away in time. But the biblical pneumatic world-picture also provides a basis for stability and coherence, a kind of transhistorical absolute—indeed, precisely that basis that Faust and Mephistopheles have excluded, namely, God's providential and faithful *dabhar*. Without this stabilizing factor, all that is solid will melt into air, and everything created will be destined to vanish in the flux of time. When the world is pictured as having no basis of stability and coherence, when it is pictured musically as a series of sensuous moments that are perpetually vanishing, Mephistopheles appears as the spirit that negates all. This demonic spirit of negation stands in absolute opposition to the positive, creative spirit (God) of the biblical narratives who calls everything forth and bestows upon it its positive vocation, reality, and meaning. "I am the spirit that negates, / And rightly so, for all that comes to be / Deserves to perish wretchedly . . . " (1338–40).

Because Faust believes that deed ought to be separated from word, he readily agrees with Mephistopheles' characterization of the biblical dialectic as one in which creation issues in destruction. In this deception, Faust is set up for the next step in the seduction. If pure acts (of creation) issue in destruction, Mephistopheles reasons, then perhaps a pure act of destruction may issue in a positive creation. He says in answer to Faust's question as to his identity: [I am] "Part of that force which would / Do evil evermore, and yet creates the good" (1326–37). Mephistopheles knows that Faust has already concluded that he can resolve his inner conflict and find a way of being related to the world without being entrapped in it only if he can take up a relation to the world that is analogous to the relation God has to it as its creator. Now that he has been deceived by Mephistopheles into thinking that creation issues in destruction, he accepts the twisted proposal that the only path to creation open to him is the path of destruction. As Berman puts it, Mephistopheles convinces Faust that "he won't be able to create anything unless he's prepared to let everything go, to accept the fact that all that has been created up to now—and, indeed, all that he may create in the future—must be destroyed to pave the way for more creation" (MB,48).

With all of this, the stage is set for the famous bargain that Faust strikes with Mephistopheles. In Scene 4, in the study, Faust tells Mephistopheles of his restlessness, the weight of his existence, and his desire to die. Faust's quest for knowledge, infinite knowledge, resulted in a life of scholarly isolation which had caused him to miss life in the world. The only thing that had kept Faust from committing suicide was the chiming of the bells and the possibility of renewal they tolled. Mephistopheles tells Faust to stop feeling sorry for himself and offers to help him fulfill his longing for renewal. He tells him that he can rebuild the world he has missed, indeed, a better one: "More splendid / Rebuild it, you that are strong, / Build it within!" (1619–21). The price for Mephistopheles' help in this world is, of course, Faust's soul in the next. Faust tells Mephistopheles that if he (Mephistopheles) can quench his (Faust's) thirst for perpetual renewal, if he can make him satisfied and content, if ever he says *"Verweile doch! Du bist so schön!"* ("Abide, you are so fair!" [1700]), then his (Faust's) soul will be given up to Mephistopheles. The pact is signed with a drop of Faust's own blood.

What Faust wants is everything: perpetual youth, the excitement of the new, the sensuality of the worldly passion and beauty he has missed. But he wants to have it all without falling into the banality that he thinks inevitably accompanies life in the world. Worldly snares can be avoided and the spirit can freely soar, Faust thinks, only if spirit is perpetually disengaging itself from the sensuous and only if the sensuous is perpetually annulling itself. He says to Mephistopheles: "Show me fruit that, before we pluck them, rot, / And trees whose foliage every day makes new!" (1686–87). Faust declares that the essential thing is perpetual movement: "If ever I recline, calmed, on a bed of sloth / You may destroy me then and there" (1692–93). He wants to "Plunge into time's whirl that dazes my sense, / into the torrent of events! / . . . For restless activity proves a man" (1754–55; 1759).

Mephistopheles does not recoil from Faust's lusts ("Such a commission scares me not" [1688]), for, as he tries to seduce Faust into thinking, his power of negation is precisely a power to make all things "new." Faust is deceived by this logic and so fails to see that what is made "new" by this demonic power is momentary, fleeting, and so ultimately empty. In this deception, the pact is sealed and the quest for the satisfaction of Faust's lusts is begun. The first thing that Mephistopheles does for Faust is to make him young again. And feeling the passions of a young man, his first quest is focused on the seduction of the beautiful young girl, Margaret; Mephistopheles shows her to him in a mirror.

Margaret appeals to Faust because of her beauty, to be sure, but as Kierkegaard has remarked, what he desires most in her "is the pure, undisturbed, rich, immediate joy of a feminine soul, but he desires it not spiritually, but sensually" (E/O I,207). This immediate happiness of a feminine soul is the innocence and rest of the psychical world. Margaret lives in the world that Faust both misses and loathes. He thinks that her little world provides the traction needed for a fully human life, but he also knows that it has completely trapped and domiciled her within it. Faust's doubting soul desires the repose of this world, and what Faust desires in Margaret is not just the pleasure of the sensuous, but the immediacy of her psychical soul. As Kierkegaard says: "Faust seeks an immediate life whereby he will be rejuvenated and strengthened. And where can this better be found than in a young girl, and how can he more completely imbibe this than in the embrace of erotic love?" (E/O I,206).

Faust, being pneumatically qualified, cannot return to the psychical, but he can, as a stranger, return to it and there ironically feign an existence within it in order to succor its life's blood without suffering its confinement. But Margaret is not completely psychically qualified either, for she is restless in her little world, even though, owing to her lack of education and poor vocabulary, she is unable to express her unrest. She sees in Faust a way out of her confining little world; Faust sees an opportunity to create a new woman, the perfect lover, and in so doing fuels his lust for renewal.

Faust is a doubter; Margaret is an innocent woman of simple faith. But he does not seek to rob her of her faith—indeed, her childlike faith is precisely what he wants her to have. Faust exploits Margaret's simple faith; he seduces her with his knowledge and experience, becomes her mentor and teacher, her liberator; she transfers her faith to him. "But at the same time that he is building up her faith in this way, he is also undermining it, for he himself finally becomes the object of her faith, a god and not a human being" (E/O I,209). Faust overwhelms Margaret with his superiority, and in relation to him she becomes an absolute nothing: "Margaret completely disappears in Faust . . . he becomes everything to her. But just as from the beginning she is nothing, so she becomes, if I dare say so, less and less the more she is convinced of his almost divine superiority; she is nothing and at the same time she exists only through him" (E/O I,210).

Margaret's existence is a demonic inversion of faith. For Kierkegaard, faith is existence before God; the faithful individual is the one who is called into that existence before God and given by God's absolutely faithful and reliable word his vocation, his meaning, his purpose, his orienting center of gravity. Margaret, on the contrary, exists absolutely before Faust: "Not only has she loved Faust with her whole soul, but he was her life force; through him she came into existence" (E/O I,212). Faust, however, is the very opposite of the biblical God whose word is life and truth, for he is the *absolute deceiver*, the one who is absolutely unfaithful to his word. Existence before Faust is an existence destined for destruction.

Everything that Margaret is she owes to Faust, to what he has told her and she has wholeheartedly believed. Yet he was a deceiver. As Kierkegaard remarks, "His conduct, therefore, is not only a deception but an absolute deception, because her love was absolute. And in this way she will again be unable to find rest, because, since he has been everything to her, she will not even be able to sustain this thought except through him, but she cannot think it through him, because he was a deceiver" (E/O I,212).

In the end Faust is the demonic opposite of spirit; he is the absolute deceiver, demonic unfaithfulness. Margaret also turns out to be the demonic opposite of a faithful self, for her existence is before, in, and through deception and absolute unfaithfulness. For Kierkegaard, spirit is a positive reality; indeed, it is the ultimate and absolute source of all that is real; it is the positive transcendent ground of reality that Abraham knew as the absolutely faithful God who will provide, that Moses knew as the transhistorical *I Will Be, What I Will Be*, as the Psalmist knew as the Creator whose *dabhar* brings the world forth and sustains it. Faust is the opposite of spirit, for he is a liar; his words destroy and deceive.

Behind Faust's words there is nothing, for Faust himself is nothing. He is absent, or rather, perpetually absenting himself from what he says. He believes that he cannot speak with reflexive integrity for the tendrils of reflexively integral speech will bond him to the world and to others in commitment and responsibility; he fears that such a bonding to the world and to others will impede his freedom, deaden his spirit, keep it from soaring into the infinite, retard its constant growth, end its perpetual renewal. He thinks that he must hover above the world to maintain himself as free, as spirit. This hovering we have seen at the more sensuous level of passion and intoxication in the musical existence of Don Giovanni; now we encounter it as reproduced at the reflective level of Faustian deception. In Don Giovanni, speech has no place; in Faust speech is transformed into a musical sound and fury signifying nothing; in Faust speech becomes the twisted means for absolute deception, the absolute lie; in Faust, Don Giovanni's musical hovering is transformed into a reflective, sustained ironic detachment from the commitments entailed in reflexively integral speech.

Although words are for Faust, as they were for Johannes the Seducer, the means for violation and destruction, the irony in Faust looms much larger. Indeed, Faust is the absolute expression of romantic irony. The heart of this irony lies in the fact that Faust's words perversely imitate the reflexively integral words of the God of the biblical narratives: the words of the biblical creator, in whose image we were made, serve to call the world and us forth and to sustain it and us; as well, these words provide a fabric of stability insofar as they are spoken by one who is the paradigmatic faithful speaker; through his words covenantal bondings are established that produce historical constancy, continuity, and reliability in the midst of perpetual temporal change. The words of Faust lack the reflexive backing of an absolutely faithful self; in fact, because Faust is absolutely unfaithful, because he is not a self at all, because he does not stand behind his words in commitment and responsibility, because in the end he is nothing, they carry, and can only carry, the negative force of destruction and annihilation. In perverse imitation of creation, Faust's words become the means of destruction. Faust's words appear to have called Margaret forth, but, ironically, those words, lacking any legitimacy, authority, or ontological efficacy, end by destroying her. Faust's words are not the words of a faithful self, but the empty, effervescent, vanishing sounds of a perpetually vanishing ghost. Margaret's existence is therefore an existence before the nothingness of perpetual self/world negation. Again the irony, and the tragedy, of Faust's seduction of Margaret is that his apparent creation of her is, at a more profound level, her absolute annihilation.[7]

Much attention has been given to the episode of Faust's seduction of Margaret; so much so, indeed, that its prominence has virtually eclipsed interest in the second part of the tragedy. And in a certain sense, if one has grasped the Faust of Part I, then she knows the Faust of Part II. In fact it is safe to say that in Part II Faust does not take up something essentially new, an essentially new mode of being. However, what is true is that in Part II Faust's impulses are expanded, as Berman has noted, "from private to public life, from intimacy to activism, from communion to organization" (MB,61). In this stage, Berman goes on to say, Faust "pits all his powers against nature and society; he strives to change not only his own life but everyone else's as well. Now he finds a way to act effectively against the feudal and patriarchal world: to construct a radically new social environment that will empty the old world out or break it down" (MB,61). So while the spirit of negation is still the center of Faust's spirit, its demonic thrust has reached here its absolute realization. Because I want to claim, with Berman and others, that the modern age embodies the expanded and absolutized Faustian spirit of negation found in Part II of the tragedy, we must turn our attention, briefly, to it. My particular

slant on this, my Kierkegaardian interpretation of it, is my claim that in
Part II we find the absolute realization of the demonic spirit of the modern age insofar as we find there Faust's pneumatically qualified but demonic separation of word and deed—a separation that sunders self from
world, that reduces the deed to frantic activity, and the word to musical
sound—taken to its final and tragic consequences.

The real turn in Part II comes when Faust and Mephistopheles are on
a high mountain contemplating the fact that Mephistopheles' temptations
are running out and Faust's insatiable lusts are still unsatisfied. Just at this
moment Faust notices the sea—that ancient symbol of chaos and disorder—and is inspired with his greatest challenge to create (destroy). The
sea is so indifferent to man, ebbing and flowing according to the eternally
ordered psychical patterns, apparently outside and beyond the reach of
man's control. He tells Mephistopheles that it is time to assert his will
against this arrogant and fugitive force of nature, to subdue it, to harness
its meaningless surging to and fro, and bestow upon it a human purpose
and meaning: "This drives me near to desperate distress! / Such elemental
power unharnessed, purposeless! / There dares my spirit soar past all it
knew, / Here I would fight, this I would subdue" (10218–21, MB,62).

Faust expresses his desire to bring the sea, this force of is nature, into
the control of his creative will: he wants to create land out of the sea.
Mephistopheles tells Faust that his desire will easily be satisfied. The Em-
peror is in need of help and Mephistopheles hatches a plan to help him
in order to get rewarded with the stretch of sea coast that Faust wants to
develop. Faust is dizzy with the prospects; he outlines his reclamation program

> to harness the sea for human purposes: man-made harbors and canals that
> can move ships full of goods and men; dams for large-scale irrigation;
> green fields and forests, pastures and gardens, a vast and intensive agri-
> culture; water power to attract and support emerging industries; thriving
> settlements, new towns and cities to come—and all this to be created out
> of a barren wasteland where human beings have never dared to live.
> (MB,62)

Faust's energetic creative powers have now reached a new height, a
height that dazes and exhausts even Mephistopheles. No longer does Faust
dally in the folly of the isolated pursuit of knowledge and the self-devel-
opment and growth that pursuit had promised but failed to deliver; no
longer does he live in the fantasy of erotic romance, no longer is he animated by its project of creating, liberating, and developing his beloved,
for its promise of spiritual renewal had turned out to be empty; now his
energies are directed to a practical, material, worldly enterprise. As he
now recognizes, the given world *as it is*—nature and history—is not fit for
the human spirit. The reason for this, he assumed, is that the given actu-

ality binds, limits, restrains, retards, deadens, and traps spirit; therefore, we must create a whole new world! But we cannot let the new world stand fast, or it too will trap and confine spirit. The new world must quickly be destroyed to make room for the next. Faust's energizing motif is *development*; its guiding principle simply this: the given actuality must be perpetually destroyed, otherwise it will confine the human spirit. Modernity has come to call this process of perpetual destruction *progress*! Kierkegaard had long before called it a demonic perversion of the pneumatic qualification of the spirit/sensuous relation.

Faust finds the Archimedean point from high on a mountain peak—a standpoint essentially outside the world—and now he aims to move the whole world, to bring land out of the chaos of the swirling sea. And so delighted is he at this discovery that he does not grasp to any degree, as Don Giovanni in his sensuous intoxication did not, the dark side, the dreadful, the tragic dimension of his project of perpetual renewal. To the very end of the play, and literally at the end, he is blind to the tragedy of his program of world-development. He does not recognize to any fully responsible degree that he has used his own discovery of the Archimedean point against himself. Kafka, who saw more profoundly than most into the abyss of modern life, into the dark side of the tragedy of modern development, could very well have had Faust in mind when he said: "He found the Archimedean point, but he used it against himself; it seems that he was permitted to find it only under this condition" (HC,248).

Unlimited development is the driving force of the modern age. Indeed, so much so that in modernity the term 'modern' has come to be virtually identified with the term 'developed.'[8] However, the modern intoxication with this drive for renewal, for progress, for novelty, as I am interpreting it, is a perversion of the Christian emphasis on the future, on openness, on possibility, and so forth. In its intoxication with possibility, the modern age fails to see and to come to terms with the fact that in an open, radically contingent world, possibility is essentially equivocal. The idea that "anything can happen" is both exciting and dreadful. Modernity, like Faust, is virtually oblivious to this dark side of progress and development.

The dark side of Faust's project of reclamation is the dark side of the modern age. As such, the modern age is not free from the tragedies of development. This darkness of progress is measured in human cost, in human screams and spilled blood, in human suffering. We have already seen this in the story of Margaret. In Part II, Margaret's place is taken over by an old couple, Philemon and Baucis, whose little cottage, chapel with a little bell, and garden happen to be in the way of Faust's project.

Even the old couple, or at least the old lady, is caught up in the delirium of Faust's project. As she stands by the construction site, she thinks that there is something miraculous about the fact that things are changing so rapidly. She wakes up to a dam that the day before was not there. "Daily they would vainly storm, / Pick and shovel, stroke for stroke; / Where the flames would nightly swarm, / Was a dam when she awoke" (11123–26). The work is indeed so amazing that one wonders whether Mephistopheles is at work in this magical transformation of the landscape. But he seems not to be; in fact, in this section of the play Mephistopheles has virtually disappeared; or better, his role in the project has become peripheral to Faust's. Faust does not seem to need any help.

The key to Faust's discovery is the limitlessness of its vision. In this project spirit can soar to infinite heights without missing the joys of worldly life. The cost, however, of this infinity of spirit is the breaking down of all worldly bonds, all human boundaries. As Berman puts it: "The crucial point is to spare nothing and no one, to overleap all boundaries: not only the boundary between land and sea, not only traditional moral limits on the exploitation of labor, but even the primary human dualism of day and night. All natural and human barriers fall before the rush of production and construction" (MB,64).

Faust wants to eliminate what he takes to be the tragedy of human suffering—a tragedy he takes to be identical with either worldly confinement and its consequent limitation of spirit or spiritual isolation and its consequent emptiness. He tries to eliminate this suffering by creating what he takes to be a perfect world, a world that supplies all of the life blood needed to sustain spirit and give it its substance, and yet a world without bonds and limits that confine spirit. Ironically, however, his project to eliminate the tragedy of human suffering leads straight to it. This is the point of the Philemon and Baucis episode.

Philemon and Baucis are emblematic of the old world, perhaps the best of that world. They had come to be noted for their hospitality to strangers and to shipwrecked sailors in distress.[9] In addition to having all of the Christian virtues, selfless generosity, humility, and so forth, they also embody old world tradition and constancy. These virtues resist change and so stand in the way of progress and development. But this sense of tradition, constancy, and preservation are not virtues as far as Faust is concerned, and so these people who embody them, these people of the old world, must be seen as dispensable; they must, at whatever cost, be moved out of the way of progress.

Faust orders Mephistopheles to get the old people out of the way. He does not specify how, and he does not want to know the details of how. He wants to keep his hands clean but get the job done. The old couple's house is burned and they are killed. When informed of what has happened, Faust is outraged. He had not wanted anything to do with violence; indeed, he had wanted to remain aloof from the whole project, to stand on a hill at a distance and admire the work, to remain ignorant of what had to be done, of who had to be sacrificed to accomplish it. But herein lies the heart of the tragedy of development, the romantic irony of Faust and of the modern age: "the very process of development, even as it trans-

forms a wasteland into a thriving physical and social space, recreates the
wasteland inside the developer himself" (MB,67).

The supreme irony of the Faustian, the modern, project of development is that once all obstacles are removed there is then nothing to do.
What keeps spirit alive is the adventure of the destruction of obstacles, of
limits in the name of the creation of a better world. The Faustian wants
to create the world, he does not want to live there. As Dostoevsky has put
it: "How do you know, perhaps he [Faust, the modern developer, modern
man?] only likes that edifice from a distance and not at all at close range,
perhaps he only likes to build it, and does not want to live in it" (MB,6). But
when there is nothing left to build, nothing left to develop, when all obstacles have been removed, then there is no place for the developer either.
Now he must be ready to say that he is satisfied and is ready to die. The
bells in the little chapel were thus not only tolling for Philemon and Baucis, they were tolling for Faust as well. And as Berman says: "Goethe shows
us how the category of obsolete persons, so central to modernity, swallows
up the man who gave it life and power" (MB,70).

Faust and Modernity

What I have been leading up to is simply this: the modern age lives,
moves, and has its distinctive being within a world-picture that is fundamentally *demonic*. And I mean by 'demonic' what I think Kierkegaard
means, namely, that perversion and derangement of the pneumatically
qualified spirit/sensuous relation that is expressed first in Don Giovanni
and comes to its absolute expression in Faust. The irony of this perversion
of the spirit/sensuous relation is that it gets its traction as a possibility from
the positive spirit/sensuous relation as that is understood within the world-
picture that was first posited in the world by Christianity. In the demonic
world-picture that dominates the modern age, the self is essentially sundered from the world, and the medium that best expresses this mis-relation is music. This mis-relation of self and world was, however, made
possible by the prior positing of the Christian world-picture in which the
self is pictured as called into faith and into an absolute relation to God.
In such an existence before God, the self is dialectically sundered from its
psychical bonds to the sensuous, not, however, as an end in itself, but as
the means for establishing a new, personal, pneumatic bonding of self and
world. My claim is that the medium that best expresses this dialectical
relation, this double movement of faith, is the concrete, felicitous, reflexively integral speech-act; or more precisely, the speech-act insofar as it is
the act of owning and owning up to our words before some other.

In the Enlightenment, the breakdown of the medieval synthesis was virtually complete, and modern man found himself within a pneumatically

qualified, but demonically twisted, world. The medieval Church had managed to maintain the authority and efficacy of religious faith—to keep body and soul together; its breakdown entailed the collapse of the authority and efficacy of the biblical mythological framework of self-understanding. It is, however, just this framework that the speech-act requires to be fully vested with its rights. When the framework collapsed, modern man was left with a radically contingent world but without any absolutes, without any apparent resources for stability and coherence; for modern man, all that was solid had melted into air.

In the modern age the dominant metaphor for picturing the sensuous presence of the world has become the dynamic musical metaphor of perpetually self-annulling sensuous sounds. Here the world is imagined as forever fugitive in the flux of time, as forever slipping out from under our feet. And in this musical picture the self is pictured as a vanishing ghost, a spirit perpetually emancipating itself from the sensuous; forever hovering above the world; forever dis-placed, without any place to stand, without any place to enact its freedom; forever alienated from the world and its own sentient and motile body; forever alienated from the full realization of the self it is intended to be.

It was to this radically destabilized situation that Descartes, the father of modern philosophy, was responding. For Descartes, all former opinions, all traditions, the old world that Faust loved and hated, all that was solid, had, under the energizing power of the emerging science of his day, melted into air.[10] Descartes felt the dizziness of his own doubt, of the instability it had generated, and set out on a quest for certainty, a quest that ended in his discovery of that famous rock of indubitability, "I think, therefore I am."

Descartes then, we might say, is Faust in his first stage, Faust as scholar, as intellectual. For both Descartes and Faust, though in different ways to be sure, the full impact of the Christian picture of the world as radically contingent was dawning. But both were also Enlightenment skeptics for whom the authority of Christian faith had given way to "reason." This combination was deadly: because of the impact of Christianity, both Descartes and Faust pictured the world as radically contingent, the sensuous as perpetually annulling itself, as perpetually in flux; but because of their skepticism, the same skepticism that had eroded the authority of the Christian framework in which speech was given its legitimation and ontological efficacy, they were left with no resource for establishing constancy, coherency, and stability. Descartes was left with the task of trying to establish certainty in a world that was at best particles in motion, a vast empty space with no center, a world essentially alien to spirit. Descartes concluded that the space of the sensuous world is not real, or at least not bedrock, for its reality must be derived from the reality of the Cogito. Meanwhile what is bedrock, the thinking self, he concluded, can be immune to the flux of radical contingency only if it is conceived as radically sundered from historical time and place. He formulated, accordingly, a picture of the self as essentially severed from its own body, from its own orienting bodily senses and motility; a picture of the self (spirit) as wholly disengaged from the sensuous.

What is ironic in the case of Descartes' quest for certainty is his attempt to rehabilitate psychical, visual, categories. It is to these atemporal truths of reason (*logos*) that Descartes appeals as the pillars that will eventually support a rebuilt certainty, that will support a newly created world that is immune to the threats of historical contingency and temporal change. Although he does have a place for god in this rebuilding process, this god is a highly abstract one—a god of the philosophers, as Pascal called it— and not the historically implicated God of the biblical narratives. Seduced by the Enlightenment into an arrogant rational skepticism, liberated from the bonds of religious faith, from the shackles of the Church's authority, the possibility of appealing to a *dabhar*-centered, transhistorical absolute was ruled out. It was, however, only an absolute that could stabilize this pneumatic chaos. In this predicament, Descartes's only alternative was to return to a kind of *logos*-centered, Platonic—that is, visualist—framework. But, of course, it was not possible for him to return to the psychical garden in his post Christian situation; therefore his attempt to rehabilitate psychical, atemporal absolutes, the absolutes of reason and mathematics, took an ironic pneumatic twist, a twist at the heart of the modern demonic world-picture.

Let me digress for a brief moment to rehearse what I mean by the term *logos*-centered world-picture, especially as that is formulated in the greatest metaphysician of the psychically qualified world, Plato. Despite the fact that he is called a "rationalist," and has a prima facie disdain for the senses, Plato employs visual metaphors as the primary terms in which he conceives of the work of reflection. For Plato, the mind and not the physical senses serves as the primary organ that gives us access to the real; but this mind is pictured by him as an inner *eye*.

For Plato, of course, the "seeing" that is accomplished by the mind's eye is a reduction of our ordinary seeing to an introspective, passive, inner spectation. The Greek predilection to reduce all knowing to a kind of vision now, under Plato's influence, is superseded by an inclination to reduce vision itself from an embodied, concrete, and sensuous experience in the world to a private intuition of ideas. This reduced "inner sight" is identical to what we might call psychically qualified reflective immediacy.

The discovery of this psychically qualified reflective immediacy was accompanied by the development of a certain kind of metaphysics—a *logos*-centered metaphysics. Plato tells us that the object and lure of thought is *being*, what truly *is*. On his view, what truly is, is eternal, immutable, indestructible, static, at rest, harmonic, and peaceful and apprehendable only through a passive abstract contemplation which is an intuition of the mind's eye. If we abstract from the actual, concrete, embodied, and temporal phenomenon of the visual perception of something in the world, we can readily understand how the resulting abstract structure of vision is neatly correlated with an abstract ontology of eternal forms. In its abstract essence, vision apprehends objects that are determinately there before the (mind's) eye, all at once, with no temporal successiveness. That is, the objects in this visual field consist of gestalten all of whose parts are simultaneously co-present in a kind of eternity. The visual reduction of embodied seeing to the visually modeled reflective immediacy of a disembodied eye has therefore the consequence of reducing the full-bodied sensuous and temporal objects of ordinary embodied seeing to the metaphysical and eternal objects of abstract theoretical vision. The visualistic reduction is now complete: the first reduction was a reduction of all the senses *to vision* and the second reduction was a reduction *of vision* to an imaginative theoretical attitude which reduces reality to abstract metaphysical objects, spatial, eternal, and mute.

This visualistic double reduction is strikingly evident in Descartes. In one place, Descartes says: "But, since I assign determinate figures, magnitudes, and motions to insensate particles of bodies, *as if I had seen them,* whereas I admit that they do not fall under the senses, someone will perhaps demand how I have come by knowledge of them."[11] His answer to this demand is that what we know *as if seen* by the external eyes is actually known in an inner imaginative theoretical perception where the objects of the understanding are "seen" clearly and distinctly. Commenting on Descartes' visualism, Don Ihde describes his reduced objects of "in-sight" as follows: "the now geometrically reduced object even at this insensible level retains certain 'abstract' visual properties. However, the 'real' object is now thought to be a bare and reduced object distinctly different from the rich thing found in experience" (LV,11).

The visual reductionism of Descartes, however, is very different from that found in Plato. Descartes was situated within a context that was deeply influenced by Christianity. His image of the human "knower" was shaped by Christian ideas—ideas that emerged with all of their infinitizing energy in the wake of the modern "emancipation" from the authority of the religious faith in which those ideas were originally posited. We can put the difference between Plato's visualism and Descartes' as follows: what is "present" to the eyes of the mind for Plato was present in a static psychically qualified reflective immediacy; in Descartes, ideas passed before the "eyes" of the mind in pneumatically qualified, dynamic reflective immediacy. In Descartes, the "thinker," "seer," is virtually transposed into a "hearer"—one who listens, as it were, to the ideas of the mind, to voices that are perpetually passing away.

Descartes' pneumatically qualified reflective immediacy rules empiricism no less than it does rationalism. John Locke, for example, speaks of ideas that we know from "experience," though it turns out that for him the realm of "experience" is the realm of reflection, not the concrete experience of the embodied senses. For Locke, ideas consist of either subjective abstract secondary qualities such as yellow, white, heat, cold, soft, hard, bitter, sweet, and so on, or objective abstract primary qualities, the "real objects" of "sense" (thought). These "real objects" (ideas) seem to be visual and spatial, at least in the reduced senses of these terms; that is, the "real objects" of "sense" turn out to be mental "sense" objects and seem to be very similar to the mental objects of Plato's visualistically modeled intelligible world. On closer analysis, however, what seems true is not. Secondary qualities have no stability in Locke's framework—they exist only in the moment of their presentation. That is, secondary qualities seem more like sounds that are perpetually passing away than stable visual objects. Primary qualities have a similar fate: though these qualities would seem to have a more stable existence, to be more like visual objects, they too are fleeting, ever changing; they too seem more like sounds than visual objects; indeed, what these "real objects"—solidity, extension, figure, motion, rest, and number—qualify are particles whose most distinctive feature is *motion.*

From the beginning, the modern attempt to restabilize reality by attempting to return to the visualistic categories of the *logos*-centered psychical world-picture was doomed to failure. The psychical framework, I have argued, was irreversibly overturned with the Christian positing of spirit in the world: Christianity effected a triumph of pneumatic contingency. As a consequence, the modern search for certainty, for stability, is a search inextricably bound to that pneumatic framework; yet in modernity that framework of radical contingency has been uprooted from its stabilizing grounding in God's absolutely faithful *dabhar.* Because the substratum of the modern age is a pneumatically qualified world-picture, its attempt at finding stability and coherence in psychical categories cannot be successful.

Because modern thought is dynamic, it cannot find expression in a static medium; having ruled speech out, it seems to be left with the only other dynamic medium, music. However, modern thought cannot find its model in music simpliciter; modern thought is, after all, *thought,* and thought requires a reflective medium for its expression; music is not a medium of reflection. What then are the modern models of reflection? I suggest two answers: *mathematics-as-music* and *speech-as-music.* The former is the medium of modern science, the latter is the medium of modern humanistic studies. In the next two sections of this chapter, I will consider each of these modern pictures of reflection.

The modern world-picture is Faustian; it is a musical picture of the spirit/sensuous relation; it is demonic. It is a picture that forms the basis for almost all modern accounts of virtually all of our practices, religious, scientific, political. We encounter it in the gnosticism that has almost completely taken over popular Christianity; we see it in the irony of the scientist's account of his own scientific enterprise, an account that reduces

the scientist to a mindless, mechanical entity; we encounter it in the bru-
tality of a Third Reich that would clean up the world and make it a better
place at whatever the human cost. The demonic world-picture is ubiquitous as the basis of our modern accounts of our existence; and in all of
its multiple manifestations, however subtle, it undercuts the power of the
speech-act by transforming words into musical sounds that point from nowhere to nothing; in this musical reduction, words—what is left of them—
serve either to carry the spirit (as disembodied thought) aloft into wild,
demonic passion, or aloft into passionless, cold, demonic calculation.

The triumph of the demonic world-picture in modernity is no more nor
less present in the sciences than in the humanities. In fact, that very di-
chotomy between the sciences and the humanities is a product of the dominance of the musical model of the spirit/sensuous relation. In the
remainder of this chapter, I will restrict myself to dealing with the salient
features of modern scientific and humanistic reflection. In the discussion
of science, I will focus on features of scientific reflection that indicate how
it undermines speech (and so spirit) by attempting to replace speech with
mathematics; and on features that indicate the irony of this replacement,
that is, the irony that the scientific understanding of mathematics is pneumatically qualified—that mathematics for science is ultimately mathematics-as-music. In the discussion of the humanities, which I will carry
forward into the next chapter, I will focus on features that indicate the
deep suspicion of speech within the humanities, a suspicion that is based
on the conviction that language is too restrictive to express the fully disengaged spirit, a suspicion that ultimately leads to the attempt to transform speech into a medium that can express this absolute disengagement,
namely, music. This transformation of speech into speech-as-music within
the humanities is deeply ironic, for words are at the center of the humanistic enterprise.

Modern Science and Mathematics-as-Music

Modern science began in skepticism. One of the things discredited in
this skepticism was the authority of religious faith, and consequently, the
authority of biblical myths, metaphors, and models. Modern science would
soon call the basic biblical doctrine of creation into radical question. The
effect of this skepticism was the discreditation of *dabhar*; this discreditation
entailed a discreditation of the human speech-act, to the extent that it was
modeled on *dabhar*. The demise of the authority, legitimacy, and efficacy
of the speech-act (as *dabhar*) meant the loss of the last and only medium
with the semantic and reflexive resources necessary for establishing a integral relation of a disengaged spirit within a radically contingent world.

Scientific skepticism, however, did not question the pneumatic picture
of the self as radically transcendent, or the picture of the sensuous as
radically contingent. Science accepted, in other words, the pneumatic

spirit/sensuous relation as one of opposition and exclusion. Yet this acceptance was combined with its rejection of, its discreditation of, the speech-act. Accordingly, modern science was left with a picture of spirit as free floating; and it was left with a picture of the world as perpetually self-annulling and as completely devoid of spirit. In the scientific picture, self and world unalterably parted company; but more importantly, its discreditation of the speech-act left it with no resources for integration.

While Don Giovanni finds a deracinate sensual hovering in mid-air to be intoxicating and feels only the slightest hint of the darkness and dread of such a hovering, such an aesthetic existence, as Faust knows, leads inevitably to despair. The self (spirit) is condemned to despair, and ultimately to madness, if it cannot find its feet. To avoid this, a new grounding for the self must be found. My claim is that the task of finding this new grounding, the task of finding a solid footing, translated in the modern age into a project of *constructing* a new world. This task of world-construction bred of world-alienation is the project of modern science; it is a Faustian project.

The immediate stage of the rise of modern science, its euphoric liberation from the sensuous world, came to its full expression with the invention of the telescope and the Copernican Revolution. The telescope allowed Galileo, the chief exponent and hero of his dawning scientific age, not only to confirm the Copernican theory but to call radically and irreversibly into question the evidence of the unaided, embodied senses (HC,259–260).

Despite its ironic rhetoric to the contrary, then, modern science began with an explicit renunciation of the evidence of the senses and a preference for artificially constructed instruments of "perception." (As Don Giovanni knows so well, the embodied senses are fleeting.) These instruments, most notably the telescope, were thought to provide the best window on the world as it really is, as it is beyond the flux of sensuous appearance, as it is from a so-called objective standpoint outside the world. With the aid of these instruments, the Copernican theory was confirmed beyond doubt: for the first time, it was clear that the sun did not move across the sky as it had appeared to, that the earth was not the center of the universe as it appeared to be, and indeed that nothing was as it appeared to be. For science everything that had appeared to the senses to be solid was actually quite different: things that appeared to be dense actually consisted of swirling atoms; things that appeared to be hot or cold, red or green, actually consisted of bare particles in motion that were in themselves neither hot nor cold, red nor green. From this new perspective, all that appeared to the senses to be solid had melted into the flux of motion and change.

After the exhilaration of being liberated from the shackles of an earthbound perspective, modern science turned to its Faustian task. Unable to abandon its newfound liberation from the senses, its euphoria in being delivered from the confinement of an earthbound perspective, yet unable to do without some source of stability, coherence, and certainty, the Faustian task of modern science was clearly defined. In response to the uncertainty, instability, skepticism, and world-alienation that the Copernican Revolution, the discovery of the telescope, and the general renunciation of the senses produced, science resolved, in a Faustian, god-like, supererogation of will, to create its own world, its own basis of stability and certainty. This new ground was not the given historical actuality, but a *construction* of the intellect—an intellect now completely liberated from any limits, from any confinement within the given; that is, this new world was the construction of a pneumatically qualified disembodied intellect.

Again, I remind you that this construction process is at the very heart of what Kierkegaard refers to as romantic irony. Recall that, for Kierkegaard, the romantic ironist assumes the task of providing actuality. He assumes this task precisely because he has come to think that the given actuality has eroded into nothingness. As Kierkegaard has remarked, romantic irony assumes the power to do everything: "If it allowed something to remain established, it knew that it had the power to destroy it . . . It knew that in general it possessed the absolute power to bind and to unbind" (CI,275–276).

The medium that modern science uses for its reconstruction of actuality is mathematics. As Galileo put it in "The Assayer," the universe is written in the language of mathematics.[12] Mathematical certainty, he thought, the certainty of two plus two equals four, is the very paradigm of stability and reliability. It was this paradigm that was operative in Descartes' Cogito and this paradigm that has subsequently served as the basis of certainty for the modern age in general. The re-constructed real world for modern science then came to be identified with the totality of entities that are mathematically quantifiable, with what Galileo called *primary qualities*. Such a world was not the world of appearances, it was not the actuality given to embodied perception. This world of mathematically quantifiable primary qualities was, in the end, a theoretical construction, and it existed only within the scientist's own disembodied consciousness.

The world that science composes for itself is altogether too familiar. It is the world as the great machine that Floyd Maston speaks of in *The Broken Image*,[13] the cold hard world that E. A. Burtt describes in chilling detail in *The Metaphysical Foundations of Modern Science*,[14] the world of the primary qualities of extension and motion that Galileo describes in "The Assayer." Indeed the scientific picture of the world has been described so widely and is so familiar that I will assume it is in no further need of description. My interest is in the fact that this brave new world is a world that is the product of scientific construction, that indeed *world-construction* is at the center of the scientific enterprise. But beyond this, I am interested in the medium of construction, namely, mathematics. If we focus on these issues, I think that it will become clear once again that the modern age is dominated by a pneumatic, albeit demonically twisted, world-picture.

The challenge the scientific community undertook was to construct a new world that would replace the old world that had suffered the ravages of a radically secularized pneumatic world-picture. That challenge, I want to claim, was the same challenge with which Faust was confronted. The issue was how a new world of stability can be constructed without having that world entrap the newly liberated self. Attempting to meet both sides of this challenge has produced some uniquely modern ironies.

In an effort to find stability, a world that was reliable and dependable, science constructed a new world—a world as a great machine, causally determined in its every aspect. Unable to abandon its new found freedom, however, the scientist had to construct a world with absolutely no trace of spirit *within* it. This resulted in a staggering irony: the world that was constructed to provide stability and coherence for the topsy-turvy existence of a pneumatically disengaged spirituality turned out to be a world essentially alien to spirit. The world that science constructed was a world in which the self was reduced to a mechanical object. Again, the aim of the reconstruction of the world was to find a way to provide the self with a ground; the problem was that the ground that was constructed was no place for the self. As Floyd Maston has put it, in modern science, man "disappeared from the world as *subject* in order to reappear as *object*. Mind itself was dissolved into particles in motion by the neutralizing solvent of the new physics" (BI,13).

This Newtonian-Galilean picture of the world as a causally determined machine did offer stability, dependability, and predictability. In fact, this newly reconstructed world was almost a return to the psychical world; but not quite. The new world was as determined as the psychical world, although the forces of determination were no longer the anthropomorphized fates, but the natural, impersonal forces of cause and effect; and in some ways the new world was a return to the psychical model of stability and coherence wherein the real is depicted as consisting of abstracted visible, static objects in space, even though these objects no longer included moral or aesthetic objects, value, or intentional structures, as was the case in the psychical world-picture. As well, the new scientific world, like the psychical world, was not a world in which spirit could appear; not, however, because it lacked an appropriate transcendence as was the case in the psychical world, but because it lacked the resources for reestablishing any bonds within the world from which it had been sundered.

Most importantly, however, the fact is that even in its attempt to recover a kind of psychical stability, the dynamics of the pneumatic world-picture carried the day in the modern search for stability and coherence. This is nowhere more apparent than in the fact that the Newtonian world-picture, even though it still has its adherents, was short-lived. In a pneumatically qualified world, the self could not long stand for its reduction to causal mechanisms. The reassertion of the self came when the full impact of the nature of the world-machine was recognized as a *mathematical construction*. This realization came when Newtonian mechanics was challenged by other systems, Einstein's theory of relativity and quantum mechanics, and when Euclidean geometry was challenged by new forms of geometry, for example Riemann's geometry of curved and boundless space. In this latter case, what was realized, as Spengler has put the matter, was that Euclidean geometry was nothing but a *hypothesis* (DW,88). And by analogy, what was realized was that the actuality of the world machine was simply a useful hypothesis, a mere mathematical hypothesis with practical applications but without ontological import.

The stage for this realization, however, had long since been set by Descartes. Descartes had already put into motion a wholesale reduction of the common world of sense perception to the contents of consciousness and so put that world, as Arendt has remarked, "on the same level with a merely remembered or entirely imaginary thing" (HC,282). Arendt has also pointed out that for Descartes, man is thought to carry whatever certainty he can achieve only *within himself* and that therefore that certainty is essentially a mathematical construction, a construction without reference to anything outside of itself (HC,283).

When the Newtonian world began to break up, the full impact of the Cartesian reduction of the common world of sense to subjective mental processes was felt. Modern science now accepted the Cartesian premise that stability and certainty must rest only with what man can, with the aid of mathematics, produce wholly within his own consciousness. In a topsyturvy world, where all that is solid is perpetually vanishing, the sensuously given world is finally replaced by a framework of mathematical formulas that are *produced by the thinking mind*. "It is this replacement," Arendt comments, "which permits modern science to fulfill its 'task of *producing*' the phenomena and objects that it wishes to observe. And the assumption is that neither God nor an evil spirit can change the fact that two and two equal four" (HC,284).

The dividend of this reduction of the sensuously given common world to subjective processes was a second "liberation" of the self. This time the self was "liberated" not from the bonds of psychical immanence, but from the bonds of a different sort of deterministic world, the deadly bonds of mechanical causality. When the great world machine was exposed as one possible world-model, as a mere theory, what scientists realized was that we *can* think of the self as a causal mechanism if this is useful, or we *can* construct other models if they prove more fruitful, if their utility value is higher. We are free to do this for there is no given actuality, there is no world over against us, nothing with which we must reckon. Now actuality has been transformed completely into possibility. The pneumatic world-picture shattered the stability of the Newtonian world of absolute space and time just as it had shattered the stability of its ancient and kindred psychical world.

At last science had arrived at a way of meeting its Faustian dual demands. It had found a way of making a world that would serve the purpose of providing a source of order and coherence in an otherwise shifting chaos of appearances, without compromising the freedom and transcendence of the self. As world-constructor, the scientist could remain radically free in relation to the constructed world without being trapped in it. So long as the world that was constructed had no trace of spirit in it, the self could remain free from that world. In this freedom the self was able to take up a relation to this de-spirited world: that relation was as its absolute lord and master. The self can be connected to the world as its creator, but it cannot live in that world since that new world is constructed without a trace of spirit in it.

The development of this self/world relation was tied to a pneumatic transformation of mathematics. The transition from a closed cosmos to an infinite universe opened the way for the development of an understanding of mathematics that would transmute that old understanding of it as a system of finite geo-metric form into the mathematics of the infinite, a mathematics of abstract point, number, and symbol. As Spengler has noted, this new mathematics was not the geo-centric, finite, spatial form of geometry, but the nonspatial form of analytic geometry or algebra: "The liberation of geometry from the visual, and of algebra from the notion of magnitude, and the union of both, beyond all elementary limitations of drawing and counting, in the great structure of function-theory—this was the grand course of Western number thought" (DW,86–87).

The old mathematics of geometry, the earth-centered math of finite line and magnitude, was being replaced with a new math of function and variable, the mathematical systems of algebra and analytic geometry, systems that had no essential connections to anything outside themselves. This liberation of the new mathematics from any essential connection to the finite world opened up an infinite potential for theoretical construction: it enabled modern science to construct a world that was completely without a trace of spirit; a world over which the scientist could exercise absolute control.

The modern scientific renunciation of the senses and its affirmation of an Archimedean perspective on the world from outside it, was not, however, a return to Platonism. As I have argued, Plato's preference for the intelligible over the sensible was a preference from within the confines of the psychical world-picture. The intelligible forms that the "eyes of the mind" behold, for Plato, find their best analogy in the mathematics of *geo*-metrical form; and geometry, "as the name indicates, depends on terrestrial measures and measurements" (HC,265). Moreover, these intelligible forms, for Plato, were not *produced* by the intellect, but rather were *given* to the eyes of the mind as the sensuous world is given to the eyes of bodily vision. The "eyes of the mind," then, on Plato's reckoning, are still *eyes*, and as such, still within the bounds of spatiality, even if that spatiality is abstracted into geometrical form.

Once every relic of visual space and magnitude has been removed from mathematical points, once they have been reduced to number groups and number groups reduced to equations of variables, then the new mathematics has, as Arendt has pointed out, "succeeded in freeing itself from the shackles of spatiality" (HC,264–265). At this point we can begin to grasp the pneumatic character of the new mathematics; it begins to be clear that the new mathematics of modern science finds its closest analogy no longer in geometric spatial form, but in the acoustical, abstract infinity of *music* (DW,85).

It is commonplace to remark on the similarities between music and mathematics. I do not intend to add to this, but only to set the comparison within the context of our present concerns. In this light, I simply call your attention to the following important elements in the comparison between music and mathematics. For one thing, musical tones in a musical composition, like mathematical variables in a proof or theorem, or mathematical expression of a theory, have no resources for making reflexive or semantical connections; or what amounts to the same point, musical compositions are like mathematical proofs insofar as both are self-contained systems of expression with no personal, demonstrative, or possessive pronouns, and hence without the resources necessary for reflexive and semantic reference; both are self-contained systems, the meaning of which is not essentially related to the composer of the mathematical proof or musical score. In addition, musical notes are analogous to mathematical points insofar as neither have any essential bearing on the world—in any concrete, embodied sense of the term; indeed, both point beyond themselves to worldless ideas; as well, neither musical notes nor mathematical points are in time in any concrete, essential, that is, historical, sense; there are no tenses in either mathematics or music.

Of course there are obvious disanalogies. For one thing, mathematics does not take place in time in either an essential or unessential sense; there is no tempo in mathematics as there is in music. Even though mathematics is like music in having no tenses, but unlike it in having no tempo, modern mathematics is essentially connected to *motion*. Given that nature is thought by modern science to be particles in motion, and that mathematics is the language of nature, then mathematics—as the perfect medium for expressing nature-as-particles-in-motion—is thought to be the perfect medium for expressing this perpetual motion. This connection between modern mathematics and motion makes it closer to music than may be first imagined.

It is also true that mathematics, unlike music, is not an auditory phenomenon. Yet, and this is the most important point of analogy between the two, mathematics, like music, *annuls the sensuous*. That it, the numerals, symbols, and so forth, in mathematics, *point beyond themselves to ideas that lack any trace of the sensuous*. Mathematics is the perfect medium for expressing ideas that have been completely disengaged from the sensuous. Modern mathematics, unlike its classical counterpart, is not about the world; indeed, its points, its rays, its lines, its curves, have no concrete spatial dimensions; modern mathematics is about nothing. Like music, the mathematics of modern science is perfectly suited to expressing worldlessness, to expressing ideas that are completely *sundered* from the sensuous; completely *sundered* from the concrete world; completely *sundered* from the mathematician himself.

What I am trying to get at by drawing attention to this comparison between music and mathematics is that modern science's attempt to reconstruct the world mathematically shows the extent to which modern science reflects what I have been calling the demonic world-picture. That picture, recall, is a perverted pneumatic world-picture in which the self is understood as essentially sundered from the world and the world is understood as perpetually vanishing; or, as we might summarily put it, the demonic spirit is the spirit of worldlessness, spirit as it is without any bonding resources, spirit as perpetual hovering.

Although modern science tries to recover the stability of a common world, its attempt is profoundly ironic. The "world" that modern science constructs out of mathematics is a world in which there is no trace of spirit and so a "world" that cannot provide the traction spirit requires for its life blood, a traction essential for providing it with the stability necessary for making it a common human world. Or to put this more pointedly, modern science is so thoroughly informed by the dynamics of the pneumatic world-picture that its attempt to reconstruct a stable, predictable, and coherent common ground for human beings—a ground that had melted into air in the aftermath of the ravages of the destabilizing pneumatic sundering of self and world—ends, ironically, in a radical retreat from such a common world.

This retreat from common sense and from the common world entails that for modern science "world" is no longer understood as *one common* world, but *many* worlds or many world-models, or world-possibilities. Such world-models are composed in the way that musical scores are, namely, out of the imagination of the composer. These world-models are not attempts to understand the world as it is in its given actuality; indeed, the assumption is that that world is perpetually vanishing, that as such there is no stable and reliable given actuality. All actuality has melted into possibility; the world has collapsed into the subject; relativism has become the only constant. Within this climate of relativism and subjectivism, the modern scientist is careful when he poses his world-models to avoid any ontological commitment; this, however, seems a small price to pay since such an ontological neutrality opens him to the exhilaration of an infinite and limitless horizon of possible worlds. The modern scientist would be lost, perhaps beyond retrieval, in his god-like fantasies were it not for the fact that his theories remain subject to the adjudication of utility. Yet even this limit of practical application is radically relativized in the modern scientific world-picture: what is of practical value is constantly changing, forever shifting, in the chaos of a musicalized flux of need and desire.

If this all sounds a bit like madness, I am duly making my point. This is the modern age; it is an age in which the given actuality has collapsed into a chaotic flux of disembodied mental music; it is an age in which ideas come into and pass out of existence in a perpetual vanishing; it is an age that is demonically possessed.

The madness of the modern scientific enterprise of world-construction reaches its full demonic, its full Faustian proportions, when the exhilaration of the infinite possibilities of world construction give way to the nightmare of the infinite possibilities of world-*destruction*. The scenarios of wonder and terror here are all too familiar: the wonders of the creation of life itself and the terror of it as the life created is transmuted into a monster and turns back on the scientist who created it to destroy him and perhaps even the whole world; the wonder of nuclear power, and the terror that it will be the very means of our utter annihilation; the wonders of technological advancement and the terror of dehumanization and the annihilation of the very earth, the air we breathe, the water we drink, the very conditions of earthly life. In these scenarios of wonder and terror we begin to grasp the full force of the demonic transmutation of its disembodied and limitless powers of world-construction into the nihilistic powers of world-destruction.

Alas, however, the modern age has tended to ignore the terror in all of this and to lose itself in the wonder. Perhaps we can see this when we put the matter in terms of *progress and nihilism*. The Faustian age is smitten with the lure, and with the intoxication, of scientific and technological "progress." As one advertiser has put it, progress is our most important product. In such a dizziness of possibility and progress the other side of the Faustian project, its inherent nihilism, is often eclipsed. Many appear to recognize this. For example, Harry Redner in his book on Faust, *In the Beginning Was the Deed*, says: "We know now that Progress and Nihilism belong together, and that the latter is no mere unfortunate side effect of the former which might somehow be avoided" (BD,xi). But in curious remarks before and after this claim, Redner indicates that nihilism, with a little redefining, is not all that bad a price to pay for progress. Nihilism needs to be redefined and reapplied and when this is done then it "is no longer to be recoiled from with aversion and horror and contrasted with Progress . . . On the contrary, [Redner's book] attempts to show that some of the most daring achievements of mankind in the modern age are part and parcel of its Nihilism" (BD,xi). What Redner demonstrates is the amazing capability of the modern demonic world-picture to neutralize any criticism of itself: it simply takes up within itself its own liabilities and transmutes them into virtues.

Similar demonic transmutations have taken place within the philosophy of science. One such example is the account of science that is given by Karl Popper. On his reckoning, the proper method of scientific inquiry is falsification. To follow this method, a scientist must not only propose world-hypotheses, he must immediately attempt to *destroy* them. He puts his method as follows: the scientist puts forth bold conjectures with no commitment to their truth and then tries to overturn them, to refute them, to falsify them. As he says: "Using all the weapons of our logical, mathematical, and technical armory we try to prove that our anticipations were false—in order to put forward, in their stead, new unjustified and unjustifiable anticipations, new 'rash and premature prejudices,' as Bacon decisively called them."[15]

In Popper, the Faustian demonic world-picture has reached its perfect expression and its deepest irony: the absolutely sundered, absolutely disembodied intellect establishes its freedom and its only essential connection to the world through an ironic posture toward the world, a posture from which it constantly overturns that world, from which it constantly destroys the very thing that it has created.

While the actual practice of scientific inquiry is tied to the world and to the scientists who inquire, the predominant modern account that is given of the enterprise is one in which "world" and, on some accounts, even the scientist himself, become synonymous with what can be expressed mathematically. Because mathematics as a medium, like music, lacks tenses, personal pronouns, and so forth, the "world" that it expresses is free floating; and the scientist who composes that world is a disembodied intellect in no way implicated in responsibility for the world he has created out of nothing. Modern scientists picture themselves as liberated from any bonds to the given actuality, for they think there is no such thing. In this situation, or rather, outside of any given situation, the scientist imagines that he is absolutely free to compose an infinity of *possible* situations. These possible worlds, in their possibility, lack the stability, the solidity, and the traction, of a historical actuality. Such a historical actuality places us within a context that is given, a context that requires something of us. The given historical actuality bumps up against our unbridled will; sometimes it has its own way. The possible worlds of the scientific imagination provide us with no such solid ground.

This is the ultimate triumph of the musical world-picture: in this picture "world" has been reduced to a dynamic process of perpetually vanishing world-models; these world-models are, like the sounds of music, perpetually coming into and going out of existence. In this pneumatically qualified but demonically perverted world-picture, the sensuous is depicted as perpetually vanishing and spirit is depicted as hovering above it in what is taken to be an absolute freedom and autonomy. The dilemma here is that spirit needs some kind of grounding for the full realization of its freedom and autonomy; at the same time, it is thought that any grounding of spirit will limit, confine, entrap it. Therefore demonic spirituality, in its search for coherence, must satisfy its need for actuality by creating its own actuality, its own world; at the same time, it must satisfy its contempt for the actuality it creates—a contempt that is based on the assumption that actuality kills spirit, and on the assumption that this bonding inevitably limits possibility—by perpetually breaking out of it. It is in this attempt of demonic spirituality to safeguard and maintain its unfettered freedom and autonomy that the terror of the demonic power of perpetual annihilation, of negation and destruction, has its all-too-real existential expression.

The next chapter will say a bit more about the ironies of the modern scientific perversion of the pneumatic world-picture in preparation for an extended discussion of a similar demonic perversion of this picture as manifested in the humanistic perspective of the modern age, a manifestation that has culminated in a "movement" called "post-modernism," and ultimately in the destruction of the humanities. In preparation, the final section of this chapter presents a brief introduction to my thesis that the humanities are no less negatively impacted by the perversions of the demonic world-picture than are the sciences.

The Humanities and Speech-as-Music

Modern science, being under the suasion of the modern musical world-picture, does not think that "the real" can find its adequate expression in speech. At the most superficial level, the modern scientist treats speech as a flawed medium because she is after a univocal certainty that speech, because of its rich open texture of metaphorical intentionalities and ambiguities, cannot provide. On the deepest level, however, the modern scientist rejects speech as a medium for the expression of the real because of the fact that speech—as an essentially semantic and reflexive medium—entails an inherent bonding of the speaker to the historical actuality.

The reason that the modern scientist rejects speech and its inherent semantic and reflexive bonding of speaker to others and to the world, is that he thinks—as a good Faustian—that such an entrance into the given historical actuality fails to reckon with the modern discovery of the perpetual flux of things, a flux in which all that was previously thought to be stable, solid, and continuous, has melted into the air of a perpetual temporal vanishing. Moreover, the modern scientist is convinced that the bonding effects of speech among speaker, other, and world serve only to entrap spirit, to limit its possibilities, to compromise its freedom and autonomy.

In place of speech, the modern scientist accepts mathematics—in its modern musicalized form—as the perfect medium for expressing "reality," or better, "reality possibilities." Because of its formal properties as a medium, mathematics allows the scientist to entertain reality in all of its dynamic but ahistorical contingency. As a medium, mathematics, like music, is a semantic system of expression without tenses, without pronouns, without reflexive resources. Because of the fact that mathematics is essentially tenseless, it is a perfectly suited medium for the expression of the myriad ahistorical relations that can obtain in a de-spirited world that is at base a swirl of atoms in motion, and ultimately, only energy. And because mathematics is without reflexive resources, it allows the scientist a way of constructing possible worlds while remaining completely commitment-neutral in relation to these "worlds." In this timeless dynamic, detached process, the scientist happily overturns old mathematical models for new ones while professing no moral or ontological commitment to any. Like Don Giovanni, he hurries on his way from one world hypothesis to the next, energized by this perpetual movement; like Faust, he maintains his absolute power, freedom, and autonomy vis-à-vis the present historical actuality by constantly destroying it in a relentless quest for something new and better.

We might think that while modern science distrusts and ultimately rejects speech as the appropriate medium for the full expression of the real, the opposite would be true of the humanities. The modern humanistic world-picture, however, agrees with the modern scientific world-picture in its distrust and ultimate rejection of speech as the most appropriate medium for expressing the real. This distrust and rejection of speech in the humanities is staggeringly ironic, however, because it is precisely in the field of the humanities, if anywhere, that words seems to have their inalienable place. After all, it is in the humanities where we find history, poetry, drama, and narrative. Without words, of course, the humanities would be reduced to painting, sculpture, wordless music, dance, and so forth, and therefore robbed of its capacity to *say* anything in any assertive mode.

In the humanities this distrust and rejection of speech does not manifest itself, as in modern science, in the substitution of another medium (mathematics) for speech. The humanities abandon speech in a much more subtle way, that is, without abandoning it. Modern humanists continue to retain words as their primary medium, but they also radically transform them. While continuing to live in words, the modern humanistic perspective robs speech of its semantic/reflexive potency. The humanities take seriously the dynamic and transcendent dimension of speech but not the reflexive power of words to bond speaker to others and to the world. They do this by reducing speech to an aesthetic system of emotive and subjectivistic expression. In this aesthetic reduction, words are emptied of their power to connect the speaker to the world and the world to the speaker. The aesthetic model in the reduction is music. From this perspective, words become virtually indistinguishable from the notes of a musical performance.

Within the humanities, the place of speech is reduced to a vehicle for communicating our inner private thoughts and ceases to be the inhabited instrument of shared thinking and acting. As such, speech becomes the means for making private thoughts and feelings public rather than the embodied instrument for generating and establishing a common world, a common space of appearance. In the aesthetic reduction of speech to speech-as-music, words have no essential role to play in the constitution or appearance of the self; here the self is imagined as constituted alone in thought and not before some other and from within some given tradition and world.

Modern humanistic studies imagine that the self is private and essentially inaccessible to others while inerrantly accessible to its own immediate introspection. Along these lines, the poet might claim that no one can really understand his thoughts and feelings because to do so the other would have to feel those very feelings and think those very thoughts, which is perforce impossible; for then the other would cease to be the other. Such a subjectivist might remark: "I know how and what I think and feel, and you can know how and what you think and feel, but I can't be you and you can't be me, and so we can never really know what is inside each other; we are finally hopelessly isolated from each other." Indeed, this remark is the logical conclusion of the subjectivistic premise that the self is constituted alone and outside the realm of public discourse.

The suspicion that modern humanistic studies exhibit toward speech is, again, distinguishable from the suspicion exhibited by the scientist. As I have said, the scientist distrusts speech because it consists of metaphors, subjective connotations, and the like, making it too vague and imprecise to be useful and effective in the task of describing and explaining the real world. A better language for this purpose, the scientist reasons, is the language of quantification, that is, mathematics, statistics, and graphs. The scientist prefers the language of mathematics because of its univocal exactness. Moreover, the scientist particularly distrusts first person discourse and prefers, when he is forced to enter public discourse, for example, in scientific journals, to speak hypothetically and subjunctively with detachment and noncommitment. To put it another way, the scientist does not communicate himself, he does not speak in his own voice, he does not own or own up to his words, but contrives to disguise his own presence in his words so as to make room for the pure exchange of the information in his head to some other head or heads. Here speech has been reduced to communication and communication to data exchange. In this context, the language of quantification is much more efficient than ordinary speech.

When communication is thus perceived as information exchange, a process more suited to a system of quantification than to a system of words, what becomes of words? One answer is that they become empty of their power. Words now are not only perceived to be untrustworthy because of their equivocal nature and their tie to the subjective intention of the speaker but empty of their power to establish a space in which human beings can appear to one another and form a community and tradition. What then are words good for? One staggering reply is that words are useful tools to advance self-interest, if used cleverly and effectively. On this view, words are not the means of mutual appearance, but the very opposite: they become masks behind which the pursuit of self-interest is discreetly hidden.

The humanities simply present a counterpart to this scenario. In the humanities, speech is not trusted any more than in science, but for different reasons. Why don't humanists trust words? Not because they are too subjective, too ambiguous, as the scientist would put it, but because they are not subjective enough. Words are too clear, too precise, and too shallow to capture and reflect the depth of feelings and emotion inside the soul; speech is essentially public, the self essentially private. Here we might hear the humanist saying that his feelings just can't be adequately captured in words; indeed, he may even feel that words get in the way of their expression. As a recently popular song has it, "I tried to say 'I love you,' but the words got in the way."

It is common to hear the modern humanist say such things as "I know what I feel, I just can't put it into words." We may imagine that the force of the 'can't' here is the 'can't' of "I can't find *the right words*," but I think that the actual force of the 'can't' is the stronger claim that the speaker believes that *no words* can adequately express his feelings and intentions. In taking this position the humanist brings words under a very dark shadow of suspicion.

In this shadow, we are likely to hear humanists vent their frustrations in such standard code phrases as, "Words, words, words . . . what do I need with more words?" The point here is that this humanist thinks words are empty, impotent of expressive power. A hug, a look, a touch, a smile, he would suggest, can *say* so much more than *mere* words. No doubt such a person would identify with the commercial that tells us we should "say it with flowers."

Modern humanists are often inclined to nature; inclined to appreciate its immediacy uncluttered by words. For such humanists, public discourse is pictured as useless verbiage and insignificant in relation to the wordless sounds of nature. The babbling brook, the singing bird, the whistling trees, all create a symphony of musical expression beyond the reach of words.

In the final analysis, the modern humanist favors music over speech. Just as mathematics offers a more precise alternative to speech for the scientist, so for the humanist speech as lyricism, speech as poetry, and ultimately speech-as-music offer an alternative to what he takes to be the shallowness and emptiness of speech. Music moves us, it lifts us out of the world and into our inner selves.

I can think of no better image of such a humanist than someone who is completely engrossed in a piece of music to which she is listening through a set of headphones attached to a Walkman. Here the whole outside world is eclipsed and the self is lost inside of her own self. While there is nothing wrong with listening to music in this way, there is a problem when the listener comes to believe, however tacitly, that this emotional flux inside her own private self is the primary reality and the world of public discourse is inferior and secondary in comparison.

As I have argued, music does not have within itself the resources for making any claims; musical pieces are neither true nor false. In other words, self-reference and reference to the world and others is impossible in music alone and therefore as a medium it is not able to provide the resources for establishing relations among persons and relations between persons and the world. In music it is not possible for a person to speak in his own voice; indeed, in music, one cannot speak at all. Music lacks pronominal, demonstrative, declarative, and other semantic and reflexive resources apart from which nothing can be said that has any power to establish truth and the bonds of moral responsibility and commitment. This bonding power is absolutely essential for the establishment of community and tradition; and community and tradition form the worldly context that is absolutely required for the self to realize its telos, to respond to its vocation and to come to itself.

When music is prized for its expressive power and held to be superior to words and yet where words cannot be eliminated, the only alternative is to turn words into music, or what is the same thing, to turn our relationship to words into a relationship appropriate to the one a singer bears to the words in a song he sings. As Alasdair MacIntyre has put it, "the relationship of our beliefs to sentences that we *only* or *primarily* sing, let alone to the music which accompanies those sentences, is not at all the same as the relationship of our beliefs to the sentences that we primarily say or say in an assertive mode."[16] What is missing in music is any connection between its elements, that is, its notes, and the world and any reflexive connection between the music and the musician. It is this lack of semantic and reflexive resources that renders music impotent to speak, to bind together and to establish a space of mutual human appearance. Insofar as words are turned into music, words are emptied of their unique power of bonding human beings to the world and to each other.

When speech has become impotent as the means of moral action, as the medium of human appearance within the world before others, words are liable to be demonically transmuted into weapons of assault, force, and violence. When this happens, words no longer create a condition in which freedom is allowed positively to appear, rather, just the opposite. Now words are the instruments of tyranny and are used to invade and threaten the freedom of the other. Here words form only a ghost of authentic human discourse masking behind them the darkness of the inhuman.[17]

The reduction of words to music and the consequent evacuation of their power to establish a moral world is linguistic nihilism. Nowhere does this nihilism come more into prominence than in the latest intellectual movement within the humanities known variously as "deconstructionism," "post-structuralism," or "post-modernism." Here it is declared, with a funny kind of evangelical enthusiasm, that the old ideas—for example, that words bear a relation to the world, and to the truth, and that they have within them the power of disclosing personal presence—are ideas that have to be "deconstructed." In place of the view that words have a semantic and reflexive dimension, the deconstructionist turns words into signs that have a "reference" only to meanings that are forever fugitive and illusive, forever changing and undecidable; that is, he turns words into musical notes that are, as such, always outrunning themselves, always disconnecting themselves from the concrete context of their enactment.

For the post-modernist, it is not only that words cannot get to the truth, rather it is that the idea of truth itself is called into question. Truth is, on this view, a lingering relic of a bygone metaphysics of presence. The post-modernist is correct that truth can appear only within a context established by speech; he realizes all too well that truth is connected to speech, that speech alone with its semantic and reflexive resources is able to establish a tie between the knower and the known. In perfect deadly consistency, the post-modernists—in redefining speech so as to excise from it its reflexive dimension and in so turning it into a system of dynamic signs/notes—"declares" the end of truth, the end of a metaphysics of presence and embraces the dawning of the "post-modern" era of absence, a/theology, and nihilism.

Such an open and enthusiastic embracing of nihilism is, to my mind, incredibly puzzling. I must admit I am inclined to wonder, along with Joseph Prabhu in a recent symposium on post-modern a/theology, whether the deconstructionist who celebrates the demise of truth, God, and value has perhaps not curiously retrieved the bath water in order to bless it after having thrown out the baby.[18]

In the next chapter, I will take up a more extended discussion of the position of post-modernism insofar as it constitutes the clearest example, not, as it would have it, of a *post*-modern world-picture, but, as I would say, of the modern world-picture carried to its final and fatally demonic conclusion. As such, the post-modernist world-picture will serve as a foil in terms of which I will try to present my concluding meditations on the Kierkegaardian alternative to the modern world-picture.

V

POST-MODERNISM AND THE TRIUMPH OF THE DEMONIC

> . . . the [romantic] ironist frequently becomes nothing, because what is not true for God is true for man—out of nothing comes nothing.
>
> (S. K.)

The most staggering irony plaguing the modern age is the fact that our basic understanding of ourselves is radically discrepant with the way we live our lives, with our existence. This ironic existential-conceptual contradiction is clearly manifest when we realize that the accounts we stand ready to give of our existence—that is, the ways we represent ourselves to ourselves and to others when called upon to respond to the philosophical question, "Who are we?"—are governed in modernity by a fundamental assumption, namely, that we, in our essential selfhood, are outside of the world. We regard ourselves as essentially *sundered* from the world, as essentially hovering in an aesthetic musical flux above the given historical actuality of the world and above our own embodiment in it, because we have come to think (due primarily to a demonic twist of the pneumatic impact of Christianity on the human imagination) that it is the only way to insure that we, as essentially god-like "spiritual" beings, will remain absolutely free. We assume that to remain as such we must remain absolutely unbounded, absolutely sundered from what we take to be the confining snares of a worldly existence. And we assume that the key to remaining aloof from the world is found in withholding our commitment from our words, in the avoidance of speaking in our own voice, in refusing to own our words before some other; for we know too well that, owing to the semantic and reflexive properties of the speech-act, speaking with reflexive integrity will situate us within the worldly bonds of responsibility that, so we think, can only compromise our unbounded freedom and deaden our spirits. At the same time, in our existence, and in stark ironic contradiction to this self-understanding, we find ourselves, at least from time to time, and perhaps inescapably, speaking in our own voice to some other, and in doing so assuming the authority, legitimacy, and efficacy of our words and thus taking up a stand before that other from *within* the world.

At Kierkegaard's suggestion, I have been posing the basic contrasts between the Christian and the pagan self-understanding and the Christian and the regnant modern self-understanding in terms of the contrast between the aesthetic and the existential, between *art* and *act*, *art* and *life*. I have contrasted paganism and Christianity/modernity in terms of the differences between a world-picture that consists of visual and thus static metaphors and models—the plastic arts (paganism)—and a world-picture informed by auditory and thus dynamic metaphors and models—speech and music (Christianity/modernity). The contrast between Christianity and modernity has focused on the differences between speech and music. (Again, the predominant modern self-understanding is taken here to be a demonic perversion of the Christian self-understanding, a perversion ironically made possible by the Christian introduction of the pneumatic world-picture.) The modern self-understanding, in which the self and world are radically sundered, finds its perfect medium of expression in the aesthetic medium of music; the Christian self-understanding, in which the self is radically sundered from and bonded to the world, finds its perfect medium of expression in the concrete existential speech-act.

It is possible for a thematized self-understanding to undermine the authority, legitimacy, and efficacy of our existence. Indeed, that is exactly our modern predicament. However, it is important, first, to circumvent a possible misunderstanding of the relation I am trying to establish between our existence and our thematizations of existence. A thematized self-understanding, even if it radically contradicts our existence, cannot provide a sufficient basis on which completely to obliterate the authority, legitimacy, and efficacy of that existence and the practices that define it. To be more specific, it is possible that the authority, legitimacy, and efficacy of our speech-acts can continue in spite of the fact that they are (mis)placed within a self-understanding that works to undermine that authority, legitimacy, and efficacy. Or what is even more ironic, it is possible that the authority, legitimacy, and efficacy of the speech-act is presupposed as the condition of the possibility of the formation of the self/world thematization in which speech has no authority, legitimacy, or efficacy: here the thematized self-understanding nihilistically aims at its own destruction. Let us consider a strikingly ironic contradiction implied in the modern scientific/mathematical self-understanding.

In the last chapter, I argued that the modern scientist prizes the medium of mathematics over the medium of speech. The modern scientist, however, transmutes the psychically qualified geocentric system of finite measurement (classical geometry)—a system that requires an embodied (visual) point of view—into a multiplicity of pneumatically qualified, universal, and self-contained systems of abstract point and analytic geometry;

or as we might say, the modern scientist transmutes mathematics into music. Such abstract mathematico/musical systems enable the mathematician/scientist to assume an Archimedean, universal perspective—a "standpoint" outside of the world—and so fail, necessarily, to provide a place for her to stand or to take up a stand from *within* the world-hypotheses that these systems create. Moreover, this sundered relation that the self has to the (selfless) worlds described or created in these mathematical systems generates an intoxicated celebration over this liberation of the self. Here the self celebrates its complete detachment from the world, for now the world, understood as a mere mathematical hypothesis, one among many possibilities, can no longer bind us. Rather we are in control, we are the world's absolute lords and masters, for the world is subject to our god-like omnipotence, a power that can, at will, overturn one world in favor of another.

The mathematician/scientist, as one species of Kierkegaard's romantic ironist, attempts to undermine the legitimacy, authority, and efficacy of the given actuality of the concrete, historical, embodied speech-act; and yet this same mathematician/scientist goes on speaking and, at least when she is not thinking about it, taking what she and others say with a seriousness that is at ironic odds with her explicit denigration of speech as a medium for expressing the real. The impact of the explicit denigration of speech then does not entail, indeed could not entail, a complete disengagement of the mathematician/scientist from her words and from the given historical actuality. What I mean here is that even under the most intense and explicit attempt to deny authority, legitimacy, and efficacy to the speech-act it will nevertheless, and inescapably, have such an indispensable role in our actual concrete existence.

But there is a more staggering irony here: despite the scientist's intense and explicit effort to denigrate the authority, legitimacy, and efficacy of speech, the very enterprise of science depends on realities that cannot be expressed mathematically (or musically), but only linguistically. The scientific enterprise involves in its essential structure far more than empirical data gathering and computation (mechanically conceived). As Michael Polanyi has demonstrated, moral, normative, rational, affective, conative, intentional, and semantic dimensions play an indispensable role in the actual practice of science. Mathematics has no resources for expressing these existential dimensions of human knowing and being. Indeed, it is ironically just for these reasons that mathematics is thought by science to be pure and the appropriate medium for expressing a reality with every trace of the human (spirit) excised from it. Only in speech can the moral, the normative, the reflexive, etc., be posited in their full existential reality and power. The extent to which the scientific enterprise depends on these human factors is the extent to which the medium of the human—speech —is indispensable to its success.

I make no claims to originality in noticing this irony in the scientific enterprise. It has become commonplace to notice that the scientific pretension of offering us the most rational picture of the world ends up offering instead a theory of reality in which all rationality has been reduced to mechanical causality. Commonplace or not, there is certainly a devastating irony in the claim that all events are either rigidly determined by the laws of physics and chemistry, mechanically construed, or else random chance occurrences; such a view provides no place in the mechanical (or perhaps musical) play of particles in motion for freedom, action, value, and intentional structures, and hence no place for the scientist or the scientific enterprise. Polanyi has claimed that this contradiction "stems from a misguided passion—a passion for achieving absolutely impersonal knowledge which, being unable to recognize any persons, presents us with a picture of the universe in which we ourselves are absent. In such a universe there is no one capable of creating and upholding scientific values; hence there is no science."[1]

This illustration is drawn from modern science, but it has a wider application. While our modern self-understanding, in any of its manifestations, either in the sciences or in the humanities, is radically discrepant with and intensely and explicitly works against the authority, legitimacy, and efficacy of the given actuality of our bedrock existential speech-acts, at the same time the speech act exhibits what seems to be an invincible resistance to attack; whatever our self-understanding happens to be, we continue to speak to one another; indeed, not only can no self-understanding utterly obliterate the authority, legitimacy, and efficacy of the speech-act, it is ironically the case that every thematization of our self/world relation depends ultimately on the integrity of the speech-act, even if that self-understanding seeks to destroy or to displace speech.

But this is not to say that our speech-acts do not suffer, are not weakened and battered, when placed in a self-understanding in which they have no essential place and in which they cannot acquire the traction they need to be fully authorized and ratified. It seems obvious that speech has indeed felt the impact of its denigration in modernity. It is scarcely a matter of controversy any longer to dispute the claim—the claim that George Steiner, for one, has so eloquently argued in his *Language and Silence*[2]—that speech in the modern age has become radically impoverished. The vocabulary of our ordinary conversations, in comparison even to our recent past, is relatively monosyllabic. Moreover, the standard rules of grammar are routinely disregarded. The subjunctive mood, for example, is disappearing. But if only that "was" the extent of it! In matters more substantial, words have suffered demonic perversions in the modern age. For one thing, they have been transmuted from instruments of revelation into instruments of deception; for another, they have been transmuted from instruments that bind human beings into political networks of freedom and equality into brutal weapons of tyranny, assault, and even death; as such, words divide us and destroy human community. Using words cleverly to deceive or to manipulate is called marketing, and the better we are at this, the more we are rewarded. And we assume that the harsh reality of the world of politics requires brutal force, for in the end, politics is ultimately about nothing more noble than manipulation and domination.

Under the influence of a new movement, one that ironically originates from within the humanities and is sometimes called post-modernism, sometimes deconstructionism, the prospect that this situation will improve seems remote. The new movement began in the field of literary criticism. It was spawned by various French literary critics and philosophers, but most often is associated with the name of Jacques Derrida. The project that Derrida calls deconstruction, I take to be a project that is designed to invade, attack and destroy the legitimacy, efficacy, and authority of the speech-act.[3] It is not a project that seeks to displace words with another medium in the way that, for example, science seeks to displace words with mathematical symbols; rather, deconstruction seeks to undermine the legitimacy, authority, and efficacy of the speech-act by radically reinterpreting it. In brief, it seeks to show that speech ultimately derives from writing, a derivation that it is possible to understand only when the so-called modern distinction between speech and writing is deconstructed, after which, a new picture of all language as writing emerges. This new picture is supposed to be a "post-modern" one. I will, however, take this deconstruction of the speech-act into writing to be a thoroughly modern picture of language, a picture that does not move beyond the modern but simply takes the assumptions of the modern age to their final demonic conclusions.

What I will argue in the next section is that the "post-modernist's" deconstruction of the speech-act and his attempt to establish the priority of writing over speech, or better, to establish speech as a species of writing, not only fails to move beyond the modern demonic self-understanding, but shows the depth of the hold that it has over even our most explicit and concerted efforts to move beyond it. I will point out that the characterizations of writing that the deconstructionists provide—despite the obvious fact that an emphasis on writing seems to entail a nostalgia for the visual and the psychical—are, ironically, characterizations that perfectly fit the pneumatic medium of music. I will show that in the deconstructionist's reduction of the speech-act to writing, he fails to notice that he has also reduced writing (and speech) to music. In the end, therefore, the deconstructionist's critique of the speech-act does not move him beyond the modern; on the contrary, it reveals his project to be an ironic illustration of the final triumph of the modern, a final triumph of the musical and the demonic.

In the final section of this chapter, I examine the post-modernist attempt to assimilate Kierkegaard into its camp. This attempt, I will claim, trades on a common misreading of Kierkegaard on word and spirit, a misreading that denigrates speech and that transmutes spirit into a demonic hovering above the world.

Speaking as Reading, Speaking as Writing, and Writing as Music

Derrida's post-modernist program of deconstruction maintains that *all* language is essentially *writing*. This assertion that language is essentially and primordially writing does not dismiss the speech-act, but encompasses it as a form of writing. As he says: "In all senses of the word, writing thus *comprehends* language."[4] This reduction of all language, including the speech-act, to writing requires a deconstruction of the commonly accepted understanding of writing and speaking, an understanding upon which the commonly accepted distinction between them rests.[5]

I shall not attempt to trace Derrida's complex argument for the reduction of all language to writing. However, I am interested in exploring his claim (whether it is in the end Derrida's own claim or not—and if Derrida is correct, its being his own claim or not is irrelevant to its interpretation) that all language is essentially writing. I intend my comments—even though for Derrida what I intend is irrelevant to the meaning of what I am now writing—as a commentary and critique of a claim that seems, if not to have originated with him, and if not to be still held, in some form, by him, then at least to be associated with him—though from Derrida's point of view, these connections of the claim to the claimer are also irrelevant to interpretation. What I will do, then, is to submit this (Derrida's?) naked assertion that all language is writing to a Kierkegaardian analysis and critique.

It should be obvious what is at stake here. Kierkegaard's remark that language is the perfect medium for expressing man's essential idea, namely, spirit, can be comprehended only when language is understood as an essentially dynamic, auditory medium, that is, as *speech-act*. For Kierkegaard, the speech-act does not get fully vested with its rights as the dynamic medium that it essentially is, until, with the advent of Christianity, spirit is posited in historical time. Because speech (*dabhar*) is essentially a dynamic medium, it becomes the perfect medium for expressing the dynamic movement of spirit in its dynamic disengagement from the sensuous. This dynamic and auditory property of speech makes it more analogous to music than to any visual medium. At the same time, it should also be obvious that writing, at least "on the surface," seems to be essentially visual.

On a purely historical level, it is universally accepted that speaking is prior to writing. Historically, writing is understood as an alternative mode of expressing, through a system of visual marks or signs, the same thing that is expressed in the sounds of speech. Writing as an alternative mode of speaking, however, had to wait for the invention of a system of signs.

One such system, among others, of course, is the alphabet. The invention of these systems of signs as an alternative mode of speaking was obviously historically later than the emergence of speech, just as the appearance of speech was obviously a later phenomenon than the gesticulatory and exclamatory antecedents from which it emerged. Because of the historical priority of speech in relation to writing, the tendency has been to interpret writing as an actual or hypothetical speech-act that has been transcribed; on this view, speaking is the primary phenomenon and writing is derived from it and remains essentially parasitic on it.

Derrida thinks that the speech/writing opposition is a function of a logocentric metaphysics of presence that the modern age inherited from Plato. For Derrida, logocentrism is the same as 'phonocentricism' (OG,7–8). Derrida identifies *logos* with speech (*parole*), voice, sound, etc. Or to put it in terms of this study, Derrida identifies a logocentric world-picture with what we have been calling a *dabhar-centered* world-picture. But here we meet with a deep confusion. When Derrida characterizes the logocentric world-picture as based on an ideal of *presence*, he abandons his emphasis on the dynamics of sound and speech (*dabhar*) and takes up metaphors and models that are essentially static and visual. For Derrida, a logocentric metaphysics of presence seems to be identical with what I have characterized as the presence within a psychical world-picture—a picture in which *logos* is the central token of an eternally and statically present reality. Derrida would be right if he had said that *this* is Plato's heritage to us; for indeed, this is logocentrism and it is this visualism that informs every modern lapse into a nostalgia for Hellas. But this logocentrism of (visual) presence has nothing to do with the dynamics of presence (and absence) in sound and speech. Logocentrism is not *phonocentric*, it is *photocentric*.

For Derrida, logocentrism generates a whole nexus of oppositions: truth/fiction, male/female, literal/metaphorical, etc. He claims that in all of these cases, the first term inevitably gains ascendency and ontological and axiological priority at the expense of the second term. Consequently, the second term always suffers from repression and dominance. The task of deconstruction is not simply to give the second terms their due, but to reverse the terms of the logocentric dialectics, to liberate the second terms from their repression and domination. This provides an opening into a new way of understanding things that is *beyond* the old repressive logocentric oppositions. Derrida's claim is that when the classical dialectics are reversed, the oppositions they embody are superseded by more comprehensive concepts.[6]

The speech/writing opposition, Derrida argues, has been generated by the logocentric metaphysics of presence. As in all of these oppositions, the left hand term dominates and defines the right. In line with this, Derrida thinks that speech has dominated and repressed writing since Plato. He sets out, then, on the task of reversing this standard, or as Derrida calls it, this "classical" interpretation of writing as derived from and parasitic on speaking. His aim is to find a broader "conception" of language that will encompass and transform both speech and writing in their classical senses. Strangely enough, however, the word 'writing' or at least the neologism 'grapheme' is retained as the name of this "new concept."[7]

I am puzzled by Derrida's claim that speaking has dominated writing in the Platonic logocentric tradition—the tradition that he thinks still dominates modernity. I have already indicated that for Plato it is the *visual* (photocentrism), not the *auditory* (phonocentrism), that serves as the primary resource for his metaphors and models of the real and for his self-understanding. Indeed, we can certainly find in the modern philosophic tradition strains of thought that are animated by a kind of hellenistic nostalgia, a nostalgia that is a longing for precisely that (visual, logocentric) *presence* that Derrida is trying to undermine. This nostalgia is a longing for a total presence of reality comprehended all-at-once before the mind's eye, before the spectator who passively beholds, in a static moment, a slice of visual space. But again, such a hellenistic nostalgia is photocentric, not, as Derrida claims, phonocentric. But more importantly, this search for a logocentric presence is not the primary animating force in the modern age. Indeed, for the most part, modernity has taken such an attempt to stop time to be its primary enemy.

This aside, there is something even stranger in Derrida's claim that speaking has repressed and dominated writing in the modern age. Contra Derrida, we in modernity have tended toward the opinion that writing is more stable, somehow more reliable, than speech. This really, if anything, is our modern logocentrism! The predominant tendency in modernity is to think of the spoken word as we think of music, namely, as being effervescent, temporary, even unreal. By contrast, we think that when something is written down, when it is visually and spatially present, then it must be important, if not true. A signed document or a published writing, we think, is charged with a seriousness, stability, reliability, and reality that is missing from the mere speaking of words, missing from their dynamic coming into and going out of the temporal now.

What would lead us to think that the agreements we enter into with the pen are more serious, more binding, more real, than the bonds we establish in the act of giving our word to one another in the oral/aural reciprocity? And what would lead Derrida to think, to the contrary, that speaking has dominated writing since Plato? Let me deal with the second question first.

Speaking, as opposed to writing, is more evidently tied to the intentions of the speaker, to the co-presence of speaker and hearer and to the temporal and singular context of the production the speech-act. Derrida's contention is that when writing is defined in terms of speaking, the focus is on the intentions and presence of the writer (and reader) and the context of its origination. For Derrida, making this tie prevents us from recognizing the extent to which the meaning of what is written does not depend on the intentions or presence of the writer or the reader or on the context of original production. Our failure then to appreciate writing on its own terms is a function of our persistence in thinking of writing as a kind of hypothetical speaking.

In contrast to Derrida's contention that speech has dominated writing, there are good reasons to think that since Plato, and especially since the invention of the printing press,[8] the tendency has been to bestow an ontological and axiological primacy to writing over speaking. This modern tendency, ironically, is a function of recognizing just that feature of writing that Derrida thinks has been ignored in favor of speaking, namely, the fact that writing has a durability, tangibility, and permanence that enables the expression to endure across time and to persist even in the absence or death of its author or reader. By contrast, the speech-act is a once-and-for-all act that depends on the presence of the speaker and hearer and is tied to the context of its enactment. Writing has just that kind of solidity and durability—indeed, a kind of eternity—that speech seems to lack; and this suggests that writing is an appropriate medium for expressing a permanence we think essential to the real. Derrida seems to want to remind us of this; however, we already know it all too well. While Derrida thinks that the dominance of speaking over writing is evidence of our lingering logocentrism, I want to suggest that wherever such a lingering logocentrism is found it is always connected to our modern tendency to favor writing over speaking.

We might think that the permanence of writing in contrast to the transitoriness of speaking is simply a contrast between the stasis of the visual and the dynamics of the auditory, or between what we have earlier called the psychical and the pneumatic. We might think that language naturally would be understood as writing in a psychical world-picture just as in a pneumatic world-picture language would be understood as speaking. This is only partially true.

What is written is visual. As such, writing is present all at once before the eyes of the beholder and so seems to have the qualities of the real as that is defined within the premises of a psychical world-picture; as such, contra Derrida, writing and not the dynamic, phonocentric act of speaking, seems to be essentially a logocentric phenomenon. (Just as clearly, I might add, speaking has its home within the premises of a pneumatic world-picture). But something is wrong here, something at the very heart of this whole discussion. Something is left out when language is represented as either speaking *or* writing. That crucial dimension of language that is left out of this speaking/writing opposition is *reading*.

The written word is to be *read*. Writing itself, however—the process of producing something to be read—is, therefore, not quite as unequivocally visual as the process of reading something, especially something that never has been written, that is, something that has never come into existence as written, but has always existed ahistorically as a kind of eternal *logos*. This distinction between reading and writing and, in turn, the distinction between both and speaking needs to be elaborated. In this elaboration, I want to work toward the following conclusions. First, in the psychical world, in Plato's *logos*-centered, visually conceived world, what Derrida rightly calls logocentrism, reading, and not writing or speaking, is the operative paradigm of language. In this world-picture, speaking and writing are defined in terms of reading. Second, the post-modernists' rejection of Plato's logocentric metaphysics of presence leads them to a similar but different sort of redefinition of language. For the post-modernists, all language is redefined in terms of writing. The similarity and the difference between Plato and the post-modernist critique of Plato is found in the similarity and difference between reading and writing. Third, when the post-modern understanding of writing is analyzed, it begins to be apparent that its operative model is *music*. Indeed no other model could be more suited to the redefinition of writing as a dynamic play of signs.

In summary, then, post-modernism is in fact a rejection of logocentrism, of Plato, of the psychical, of what I have called a *logos centered, psychical world-picture*, and so forth; but it is not a rejection of phonocentrism, and it is not a rejection of the pneumatic. At the same time, post-modernism is a rejection of speech, or better a redefinition of it in terms of writing, and a redefinition of writing in terms of music. I will try to establish that the key metaphor for logocentrism is reading, and that the post modernist emphasis on writing does constitute an alternative to it. Further, I want to contend that the post modernists' alternative to *logos* = *reading* is not *dabhar* = *speaking*, but *writing* = *music*. If this analysis is correct, then it is clear that the philosophic movement of post-modernism is hardly *post-modern*; on the contrary, it seems to be but the latest manifestation of the hold that the demonic, musical self-understanding has on the modern imagination.

As I have argued, in Plato's world the real is pictured in terms of visual metaphors and so as static, timelessly eternal, and essentially *present* to the eyes of the mind. This is the world that post-modernists associate with Plato in the way that original sin is associated with Adam. The post-modernists claim that the original sin of the modern age is the sin of a logocentric metaphysics of presence. The claim is that this metaphysical predisposition to seek static presence is ubiquitous in modernity and manifest in its nostalgia for a system of thought, a system of truth, in which everything at last will be seen face to face as it really is. This longing for certainty, for clarity, for truth and for meaning is, the post-modernists argue, a mortal wound in the modern spirit that will not heal; it is a wound that will ultimately bring the modern age to an end.

For Plato, there is no better model for the real than an eternal and immutable book. By saying that it is eternal and immutable, I mean to indicate that it has no author, and its text did not come into being by being written down by someone at some (beginning) time. Like it or not, all humans and even the gods are subject to and determined by the order and the course of events defined and set in this eternal and immutable text. For Plato, reality is exhaustively embodied in this text. The task of the knower of the real is the task of reading what is there to be read, of passively beholding the Truth.

In a completed book, all of the elements are present all-at-once. We can skip over to the last page, or go back and reread previously read pages. In this picture all that will be already is and all that has been can and will be again in the course of an eternal return. The reader has no significant role in the constitution of this text, no role in the constitution of the real, as a passive spectator has no role in the constitution of a piece of sculpture, or architecture, or painting. In fact, we might say that reality, as modeled on the visual metaphor of a book, is essentially *complete* and so in the *past*. The task of the knower of the real, as Plato says, is *recollection*. When the real is complete and in need of being recovered in a backward and passive beholding, there is no place in reality for time, for novelty, for freedom, for contingency, no place for an agent whose acts have ontological efficacy, and ultimately no place for the person. This means that even speech becomes a kind of reading, or a reading-off, and a person's life is understood as the role of a character in that book. As we live, as we read further, we find out what our character is fated to "do." If we could only have flipped over a few pages we could have seen what "will be for us" because what "will be" already is; it has always been there, from all eternity, set and fixed. On this self-understanding, it is impossible for me to speak with reflexive integrity, to own my words before you, for the words that I "say," I actually read off from the eternal text of reality. These words are not, and indeed they cannot be, my own, for rather than being initiated by me, they are determined for me, externally imposed by the text of the book.

Plato's enemy was the flux. Although his notion of becoming seems to be a concession to the reality of time, in the end, time is subsumed under eternity. He was aware that in our ordinary existence we inescapably have a sense of time, of possibility, of contingency, of our own self-determining power. For Plato, however, this ends up being a function of our ignorance. Because we are ignorant of what "will happen" in the next pages of the text of our lives it is natural to get excited, or worried about what may or may not take place; we speculate about what will happen; but, more to the point, we act as if we can have some influence on the shape of the future. However, like Heraclitus, Plato cannot grant to time, to contingency, any place as real. For Heraclitus and for Plato, behind the veil of the flux is the stasis of the eternal text, the eternal and immutable *logos*. It is this that keeps the flux in check, that puts it to *rest* and ultimately robs time of its reality. As Kierkegaard has put it: "Greek culture did not understand the moment" and "did not define it with a forward direction but with a backward direction" (CA,88).

Here we meet with what the post-modernist objects to in the metaphysics of presence. The post-modernist thinks of presence as static, as a kind of eternal all-at-once *now*. Accordingly any philosophy, perhaps all philosophy since Plato, that aims at stilling the flux, at subverting becoming by Being, time by eternity, is included in the camp of logocentrism. Logocentric presence is anti-movement, it is rest and repose; its perfect model is the stasis of visual presence. As one commentator put it, "The philosopher is no friend of movement, and the Platonic account of motion is in fact a theory of anti-movement" (RH,13). The basic impulse of the metaphysics of presence, of logocentrism, is to find a way to think itself out of time, change, and movement.

For these reasons, reading becomes the perfect model of knowing and an immutable and eternal text the corresponding perfect model of the real in a logocentric metaphysics of presence. While things appear to "happen" in the course of reading a book, what will be is already *present*, already determined, already fixed. Except for the contingent fact that the reader has not gotten to the end of the book, it is nevertheless essentially over, the book is already finished. Time within the book is but a moving image of eternity, and the movement of the book is but an aesthetic illusion.

There is, of course, a major difference between the reading of a book and the writing of one. For one thing, the process of writing a book implies a context of possibility and contingency. As well, the writer is not a passive ingredient in the process, but stands at the very center of it. What will be on the next page is not already there, but will be what the writer, subject to the context already established by what has gone before, determines it to be. This process then is a dynamic one, and an essentially temporal one. In other words, writing does not seem to be a process in which becoming is supplanted by Being, time by eternity. Rather, writing presupposes an ontological context other than that provided by the logocentric metaphysics of presence. If writing is to be vested with its rights, it must be placed within a context which provides the conceptual resources in which temporality, contingency, possibility, freedom, action, and so forth, make sense and are accorded reality. As I have been arguing, the pneumatic world-picture provides just this necessary context.

Derrida is correct that writing is not a logocentric enterprise. However, against what he says, speaking is not either, for speaking requires a context in which temporality is not put to rest, in which it is accorded reality; as much so as writing. As I have just suggested, writing, as a model for all language, is in fact an alternative not to the model of speaking but to the model of reading. As such, writing as a model for all language does in fact constitute a real alternative to logocentrism. What Derrida does not see, however, as I shall pursue presently, is that speaking *and* writing—as models for all language—are both alternatives to logocentrism; both require a pneumatic world-picture in order to be vested with their respective rights as media.

What then is the *difference*, and why does Derrida want to define all language in terms of writing? What is the hidden agenda here? One thing that Derrida wants to avoid is the idea that language is the communication of, or transmission of, intentions.[9] The reason that he wants to avoid this is connected again to the idea of presence. If the intentions of the communicator determine the meaning of the communication, then, so he reasons, not just the presence of the communicator, but his *pure presence* is required. I do not know what justifies this move, and I cannot find in his writing such a justification. Nevertheless, Derrida does make the jump from the requirement of presence to the requirement of *pure* presence. At work in this jump is the pivotal "concept" of *iterability*. For Derrida, iterability is the bedrock structure of all language, precisely what makes all language writing, or graphematic. This comes out most clearly in Derrida's dispute with John Searle and J. L. Austin. In a key passage of *Limited Inc*, he says:

> What is limited by iterability is not intentionality in general, but its character of being conscious or present to itself (actualized, fulfilled, and adequate), the simplicity of its features is *undividedness*. To cite once again: "In such a typology, *the category of intentionality will not disappear*; it will have its place, but from that place it will no longer be able to govern the entire scene and system of utterance [*l'enonciation*]. . . . given that structure of iteration, the intention animating the utterance will never be through and through present to itself and to its content. (LI,105)

What is *pure* presence? And why does the structure of iterability make such a *pure* presence impossible? I can only speculate that a pure presence is a *total* presence; in other words, a complete, and thus an immutable and eternal presence, a kind of *frozen* and thus atemporal presence. This concept of presence is indeed logocentric; its basic model is visual: the all-at-once, through and through, presence of a static, spatial phenomenon.

On a Derridean analysis, the structure of language includes iterability at its most basic level. This means that the bedrock character of all language is its essential and primordial *detachability* from the original context of production and from the original intentions and presences that animated it. Iterability is just that property of all language that makes it citable and repeatable, that allows the "same" words to be grafted into another context different from the one of original production, original intention, and original presence of speaker/hearer, writer/reader. This implies, Derrida thinks, a necessary relativizing of meaning, and makes the dream of a pure, total (that is, visual, logocentric) presence impossible. Derrida thinks that because writing is essentially iterable, that is, separable from the context of its production, that the meaning of writing is fundamentally indeterminate. While Derrida might agree that it is the context, the particular circumstances of a communication, including the intentions and uptake of the interlocutors, that fixes meaning, his point is that iterability implies a radical relativity of contexts, a constantly shifting ground, in which meaning is dynamically and perpetually outrunning itself.

The key element in the structure of iterability is what Derrida characterizes as *the break*.[10] As I understand it, the break has to do with the relation of idea to medium. As I have argued, there are three possible such relations. The first is psychical and the second two, the Christian and the demonic, are essentially pneumatic. In the psychical world-picture, idea is wholly confined within the spatial presence of the sensuous. Here there is no essential break of idea and medium; idea and medium are bonded in harmony and accord. This bonding however has the effect of supplanting the temporal and encompassing it within an immutable and an eternal stasis of rest and repose. It was Christianity that introduced the break between idea and medium, between spirit and the sensuous, for Christianity understood the relation between idea and medium in auditory and hence essentially temporal categories. Within these categories, spirit, idea, meaning, like the present moment in a temporal succession, was pictured as perpetually fugitive, as perpetually breaking out of its sensuous medium of expression. This is the pneumatic self/world relation, a relation presupposed in both Christianity and in its demonic perversions. In Christianity, spirit breaks out of the world, relativizes it, teleologically suspends it, in order that the world may be given back every inch; in the demonic, spirit perpetually erases the world leaving no trace of itself behind.

It is iterability, for Derrida, that makes language an essentially dynamic medium. Because of iterability, meaning is always changing, always undecidable, always breaking out of its original context of production and always breaking away from the original intentions of the speaker/writer. This breaking force in language, this separation, this disengagement of signs from both signified and from signifier, never stops to allow us to get a fix on "pure" meaning. For Derrida, such a fixed "pure" meaning would be immutable and eternal; it would require a total presence of consciousness, of intention. Iterability teaches us that such a logocentric dream for "pure" meaning would require that we arrest the dynamic play of signs, and deny the primordial *break* that iterability implies, a break that is built into the very structure of all language. Because of iterability, because of the essential break that this implies, meaning is never purely present but constantly breaking out of one context and hurrying on to another. It is not that meaning doesn't require a context: for Derrida, it certainly does. But contexts themselves are constantly shifting, radically set into dynamic motion, radically destabilized, radically relativized.

In this respect, I think that meaning, for Derrida, is very much like spirit; writing, for him, is a pneumatically qualified medium. Writing, for Derrida, is constantly in motion, constantly shifting, never at rest. However, I also want to suggest that the spirit of writing for Derrida is a *demonic perversion of spirit*. The spirit of writing is, by definition for Derrida, a perpetual breaking, a perpetual *sundering*, a perpetual hovering, a perpetual play of signs. The spirit of writing is essentially disembodied, essentially a break with the world; it is just the spirit that Don Giovanni and Faust express. Writing, for Derrida, is essentially *music*.

Music, of course, is an aesthetic medium, a form of art. In order to interpret, that is, comprehend, appreciate, and understand a work of art, it is not *necessary* for one to know anything about *who* produced it, that is, the intentions of the artist; nor do we need to know anything about the historical circumstances of the context of its original production. The fact that a work of art can be *anonymous* and still meaningful shows the essential irrelevancy of the artist's intentions and the essential irrelevancy of a knowledge of the original context of production. A work of art has a life of its own, and although it expresses an *intrinsic intentional structure*, the presence of this structure should not be confused with the *intentions* of the artist. As soon as the artist finishes her work there is a *break*—the artist's presence, her intentions, the context of production, and so forth are no longer components in the work.

I want to contend that both logocentrism and post-modernism are essentially aesthetic, but also as different within the aesthetic world as are music and the visual media. For logocentrism, the text-to-be-read, the *logos* of reality, is analogous to a work of art—an anonymous poem, for example—insofar as it does not depend on knowing the intentions of the one who wrote the text, for, in this case, and unlike human poetry, no one ever did write it: *logos* is eternal (static) and impersonal and the only place for the self in such a world-picture is as the passive and distanced reader of that text. Logocentrism is *psychically aesthetic*.

For Derrida, and for post-modernism, writing is also like a work of art, also essentially aesthetic, but with important differences: for Derrida, writing is not an eternal text of reality for us to read, but a *project* for us to undertake. As a consequence, the self (spirit) is at the very center of Derrida's conception of writing, although ironically so. For Derrida, writing, unlike reading, requires a context of contingency in which something can be *originated*, that is, produced *by someone*. This means that post-modernism is *pneumatically aesthetic*. However, in a manner reminiscent of the demonic irony of Faust's creation/destruction of the world, for Derrida, the self is not only centrally *present* in the pneumatically qualified creation process of writing, it is also and essentially *absent*. The process of writing denies and presupposes the self: immediately after its "execution," the writing crosses out and breaks away from the self that originated it and from the historical context of its production; the now detached self turns back upon the writing to deconstruct it.

Poetry, painting, sculpture, architecture, and so forth (either as completed or as in process) fall into the category of what Hannah Arendt calls *work*.[11] Arendt radically distinguishes *work* from *action*. This distinction corresponds to a basic distinction in Kierkegaard, namely, the distinction between the *aesthetic* and the *existential*, or between (a work of) art and life. The distinctively human act, as Arendt understands it, and as I think Kierkegaard understands it also, is the speech-act. The speech-act, in contrast to an aesthetic work, is essentially an *existential* phenomenon. This is so precisely because of the unique *semantic/reflexive* properties of the speech-act, properties that tie the speaker and hearer to one another, and both of them to the context of origination, and to the world. Although I have been presupposing this distinction between the aesthetic and the existential throughout these meditations, I must pause again to bring it into focus for further elaboration.

All art is characterized by what Michael Polanyi calls a framing effect.[12] The frame in a painting, the stage in a theater, serve to isolate and separate the art work from our concrete historical existence. We are well aware of this aesthetic suppression of the historical/existential when, at the theater, we witness a "murder" on stage. The artificial frame separates what "happens" there from actual historical actions, for what is going on is after all a "play" and the "actions" issue not from the intentions of the persons, *as themselves*, but from the text of the play. Art work may, and usually does, arise out of history/existence. Stories involving these events and actions have an existential and historical content, but the framing effect transforms the story into a work of art and thus separates it from actual existence and history. Indeed, the frame serves to carry us away from our ordinary lives and provides a "time," or a kind of suspension of time, in which we can rest from existence.

The frame in art, the aesthetic suppression of history/existence such a frame implies, makes all art *abstract*. That is, all art is abstract in relation to the concrete realm of historical time and action. This does not destroy the traditional distinction between abstract and representational art; rather, it simply relativizes it. This means that representative art is more closely related to historical time and human action than abstract art. As I have already argued, it is for this reason that sculpture as medium is more concrete than architecture. Yet even the relatively concrete medium of sculpture is abstract relative to the more concrete and dynamic medium of poetry; and yet poetry is more abstract than the first person speech-act in concreto.

At this point, we need to recall and to define more precisely Kierkegaard's distinction between the aesthetic and the existential. I find no clearer such definition of the distinction than in an article by Stephen Crites, "Pseudonymous Authorship as Art and as Act." In this essay, Crites describes the aesthetic as follows: "The ideality bodied forth in a work of art is always an abstraction from experience. It arises out of the temporality of experience, but it achieves a purified form as a self-contained possibility, free of temporality. That is why both artist and audience are able to come to rest in it" (AA,210). Crites contends that Kierkegaard uses the term 'aesthetic' to signify a certain modality of existence: "The aesthetic way of life is a strategy for giving life a coherence of a sort. It is a strategy modeled on the work of art, extending that model so far as possible to one's experience as a whole. Here Kierkegaard has in mind the romantic ideal of making life into a work of art" (AA,211).

The aesthetic is contrasted, Crites says, to the existential, or what we could call the historical, field of human action in concreto. Both the aesthetic and the existential modes of life are achievements of coherence, "but *unlike* the aesthetic, the existential integration occurs through a projection into temporality through action" (AA,214). Further, Crites maintains, "The aesthetic strategy, however, proceeds by negating that temporality, the existential movement by intensifying it through passion giving it a form that is itself temporalized" (AA,214).

The framing effect in art, then, transforms the existential into the aesthetic by isolating or separating a certain aspect of existence and abstracting it into an ideal form. This abstract quality of the work of art due to its frame also separates the work of art from the artist. The work of art is cut off not only from the concrete field of human action, but also from the one who produced it. As Polanyi has put it: "From the vantage of this analysis, we can see that poems and also paintings, sculptures, and plays are so many closed packages of clues, portable and lasting" (MP,87). And, referring specifically to poetry, but implying a general characteristic of all works of art, Polanyi says: "strictly speaking, it is the *poem* that speaks to us, not the poet . . . the poem is not the voice of the poet and its meaning is not conveyed by its prose content" (MP,86).

I do not want to denigrate poetry or the aesthetic in general. Poetry surely has its place, especially in the enterprise of indirect communication. In fact, Kierkegaard himself took up the strategy of the aesthete in his pseudonymous writings. As Louis Mackey has put it: "As the poet is silent in his poem, so Kierkegaard is silent in his books: 'I always stand,' he [Kierkegaard] wrote, 'in an altogether poetic relationship to my works, and I am, therefore, a pseudonym' " (KP,250). Of course, this claim of Kierkegaard, found in one of his works, is not poetry and he is not absent from it. As well, against Mackey, I think that there is more of Kierkegaard in his writings than there is of the poet in his poetry; or to put it differently, Kierkegaard's himself is not absent, but present indirectly (as absent) in his pseudonymous writings; he is present as the one who aims to establish and to assert the truth of the religious modality of existence. But what Mackey says about poetry seems to me to be correct not only about it but about all art, about the aesthetic modality of existence: namely, that in a work of art, the artist disappears, and in an aesthetic life, the aesthete vanishes.

Again the aesthetic mode of existence stands in radical contrast to the existential, especially to the fully actualized existential modality as that is found in religiousness B. The perfect medium of the existential, for the religious, from the Christian point of view, is the faithful word as that is embodied in the paradigmatic Speaker, Yahweh/Christ. When I speak in good faith, that is, seriously, in my own voice, in the first person, present tense, indicative mood, active voice, and so forth, I take up and enter into semantic and reflexive bonds of commitment and responsibility in relation to the world, to others, and establish my own identity as a self. In the context of such a reflexive integrity, I am also necessarily self-transcendent, for it is after all I who must take up and own my words before some other. In the dialectical movement of reflexive integrity, in the dialectical sundered/bonded self/world relation that it expresses, I am established as the concrete I that I both already am and am called to be. "In acting and speaking," Arendt has pointed out, "men show who they are, reveal actively their unique personal identification and thus make their appearance in the human world" (HC,159). This reflexively integral use of the word in the concrete speech-act is the realm of existential appearance, the realm of dynamic existential presence, not the realm of aesthetic anonymity, the realm of aesthetic absence, either of the static or of the dynamic sort. There is here no ultimate break with the historical existence; indeed, quite the contrary.

Derrida thinks that writing is more fundamental to language than speaking precisely because of what he takes to be the more obvious iterability of writing as compared to speaking. Clearly a writer, the writer's intentions, and the particular circumstances of the writing can disappear and change; indeed, the writer himself can leave, or die, just as soon as he is finished writing, and yet the writing can endure, can be repeated, cited, and grafted onto an unlimited array of contexts. In writing—at least, in writing as a kind of poetry—as opposed to speaking, we are not obliged to ask, "Well, what did he *mean* by that?" This is an essentially aesthetic understanding of writing, as opposed to an essentially existential understanding of it. On the latter view, writing can be construed as a hypothetical speech-act and so necessarily tied to the existential context, to the speaker, and so forth. As aesthetically construed, writing implies an essential suppression of historical context—a break with the world and with the writer.

Certainly the process of producing a work of art is in some sense a worldly activity and it takes place in time, though again, I must qualify and say "in some sense." The process of writing something, poetry, a play, a novel, a letter, a will, etc., is a dynamic activity that takes time, but no more nor less so than the creative processes of painting something, or sculpting something. But the aesthetic process of creating a work of art not only takes time, it also takes place within a context of contingency and possibility. The artist, after all, creates something, brings something new into the world. This creation implies a break with the past, an augmentation of reality. In this respect, writing (as a process) is unlike reading (as a process), for reading, though it takes time, does not bring anything into existence, does not produce or originate anything. As such, reading is a better model of logocentric, visual, presence than the *processes* of sculpting or painting; reading is more analogous to viewing a completed painting, a cathedral, or piece of sculpture. As *completed* products, sculpture, architecture, painting, and a text-to-be-read, are equally atemporal, for all of these products are essentially closed to novelty and contingency. Even if there is the appearance of historical time, as for example, in a novel, movie, or play, once complete, nothing new occurs; all that will be for the reader, or viewer, already is.

We can say then that all aesthetic media involve a suppression of historical existence, a suppression of spirit. Spirit, therefore, cannot find its full existential expression in any aesthetic medium. But we must again distinguish between two forms this suppression of spirit can take: the suppression of spirit when it is engulfed within the sensuous (the psychical) and the suppression of spirit when it has been completely cut off from the sensuous world, from its own body (the demonic). This difference is one between the pneumatically qualified aesthetic medium of music and the psychically qualified visual media. Writing, for Derrida, I contend, is an aesthetic medium of the first sort.

In the final analysis, Derrida leads us to imagine that speaking, like writing, is a process in which the meaning (the idea) is constantly disengaging itself from both the speaker (writer) and from the words that are spoken (written). Even the reader, the interpreter of the writing, cannot get a fix on the meaning because of its dynamic and perpetual disengagement from its sensuous medium. The medium of writing/speaking, for Derrida, is one in which the relation between idea and medium is perfectly analogous to the relation between spirit and the sensuous in the medium of music. In music, recall, idea (spirit) is perpetually disengaging itself from the sensuous (the world, the historical actuality). The musical break with historical actuality is no psychical arresting of time by a static eternity; rather, musical transcendence breaks with the historical actuality not by encompassing time within space, or by arresting time, but precisely by destroying history with a demonically perverted temporality that perpetually transcends the world in a musical hovering.

To use Kierkegaard's idiom, we can say that Derrida's musicalization of language presents us with a musical picture of human existence—a picture that amalgamates *both* Don Giovanni and Faust, and that is, as such, radically demonic. On the one hand, the writer, for Derrida, is perpetually disengaging himself from his words just as Don Giovanni is forever hurrying along, forever hovering above the world. Just as clearly, however, writing expresses the spirit of Faust, for writing is a *reflective* project of creation/destruction.

For Derrida, to write is to repeat, and to repeat is to make, indeed, to make anew, and so to write is to create. Faust's task—given that the stable old (logocentric) world had slipped out from under his feet—was to create (to write) a new, better world. This world, however, had to be, for him, a product of his own consciousness, and subject to his own will—it had to be a "world" over which he could exercise absolute control. For the Faustian there is much *work* to be done; the world must be renewed at every moment. For Faust, however, we must not let any world stand, for if we are not careful, the world that we create will turn on us and confine us and ultimately destroy us. Progress demands that the world as it *is* be perpetually destroyed; actuality is always imagined to be inferior to possibility. Just under the surface of this omnipotent, disembodied, Faustian creative/destructive will lies a deep and intense hatred of the given actuality, a fundamental world-alienation.

The right side of the creation/destruction opposition in Faust's spirit seems to dominate in Derrida and is reflected in the very name of his enterprise: deconstruction. We find Derrida saying that we must not let any interpretation stand, we must not allow ourselves to come to rest, we must not allow meaning to be captured in any determinate way. For Derrida, meaning is always disengaging itself from its context of production, from its author, its time and place, and so forth. Because it is so fugitive, so thoroughly caught up in the dynamic flux, we cannot be content with any fixation of meaning, and we must destroy every pretension otherwise.

There is also something in Derrida that seems deeply akin to Don Giovanni. Faust is serious, Don Giovanni is not; Faust feels the burden of much work to do; Don Giovanni, by contrast, is giddy with the excitement of another conquest always just ahead. In terms of these contrasts, Derrida seems to be much more like Don Giovanni than Faust. As Caputo has paradoxically put it: "The *work* of deconstruction is not *work* but *play*. . . . We must understand that any talk of solicitation and anxiety in Derrida is subordinated to a Dionysian laughter and exuberance. He is no captive of the spirit of seriousness" (RH,147, italics added).

The parallels between the spirit of writing in Derrida and the spirit of Kierkegaard's Don Giovanni and Faust are too uncanny to go unnoticed. For Derrida, writing is a project that combines the destructive reflective immediacy of Faust with the sensuous immediacy of Don Giovanni's playfulness. For Derrida, undecidability, iterability, *difference* leaves us "with no footing, on constantly shifting, slipping grounds. It keeps us off balance in the *ebranler*, the trembling" (RH,188).

The next section will take up the post-modernist attempt to appropriate Kierkegaard as one of its own. In rejecting this move, I also want to present again what I take to be Kierkegaard's subtle alternative to both logocentrism and the post-modernist "rejection" of logocentrism.

Coping with the Flux

It has become popular of late to include Kierkegaard as a forerunner of the post-modernist movement. Indeed, a university press has even es-

tablished a series devoted to the topic, Kierkegaard and Post-Modernism.[13]
To my mind, the best of these recent attempts to appropriate Kierkegaard
as a post-modernist is that of John D. Caputo, the already-cited *Radical
Hermeneutics: Repetition, Deconstruction, and the Hermeneutic Project*. What is
so striking about its argument is not that it is correct, but rather that in
it Caputo manages to locate the central thrust of the post-modernist critique of philosophy (i.e., logocentrism, the metaphysics of presence) more
pointedly and more clearly than his post-modernist allies. The import of
this is that it allows us to assess more accurately Kierkegaard's contribution
to and his differences from the post-modernist movement.

It is certainly understandable why some post-modernists think not only
that they have found a kindred spirit in Søren Kierkegaard, but that, indeed unbeknownst even to Kierkegaard himself, he was the "first" and
perhaps the father of the movement. I think, however, that this is a mistake—but an instructive mistake. It is instructive because it can lead to a
deeper than usual understanding of Kierkegaard's project.

Why is it that post-modernists are attracted to Kierkegaard? There are
no doubt many reasons, including Kierkegaard's supposed fideism, his
supposed irrationalism, his critique of reason, his emphasis on will and
decision, and his practice of pseudonymous authorship. It is arguable that
these "affinities" would go away on other, and indeed quite plausible, interpretations of Kierkegaard. On my view, however, there is an affinity
between the project of Kierkegaard and the project of the deconstructionist that is more substantial: both Kierkegaard and post-modernism launch
similar attacks on what the latter sometimes calls *logocentrism*, sometimes
the metaphysics of presence.

Caputo has given us a characterization of logocentrism that penetrates
to the very heart of the matter. As I have already noted, for Caputo,
logocentrism is a sustained attempt to deny temporality, change, and
movement: logocentrism aims to still, put to sleep, or otherwise take the
sting out of what he calls "the flux." Caputo thinks that Kierkegaard
ought to be placed within the post-modernist camp precisely because he
recognizes that the logocentric search for rest and repose is antithetical to
Kierkegaard's project. He thinks that Kierkegaard and post-modernism
share a common project of affirming the flux and, in Caputo's terms, of
restoring "life to its original difficulty." On this point, Caputo seems to me
to be absolutely correct. As he puts it: "Kierkegaard . . . thinks that philosophy [i.e., logocentrism, the metaphysics of presence, etc.] makes things
too easy for itself. It is ready to sneak out the back door of existence as
soon as life begins" (RH,12). Against logocentrism, so Caputo argues,
Kierkegaard proposed that Being is essentially becoming, that existence is
essentially repetition, and that repetition is simply "an existential version
of *kinesis*, the Aristotelian counterpoint to Eleaticism, a movement which
occurs in the existing individual" (RH,11). More generally, he notes:

> Kierkegaardian repetition is the first "post-modern" attempt to come to
> grips with the flux, the first try not at denying it or "reconciling" it, in the
> manner of metaphysics, but of staying with it, of having the "courage" for
> the flux. Kierkegaard wants resolutely to avoid turning the world into a
> frozen *eidos*, stilling its movement, arresting its play, and thereby allaying
> our fears. He wants to stay open to the *ébranler*, the wavering and fluctu-
> ating, and to keep ready for the fear and trembling, the anxiety by which
> the existing individual is shaken. (RH,12)

The issue between the post-modernist view and logocentrism is the
same as, in Kierkegaard, the issue between Christianity and paganism, or
more precisely, between Christianity and paganism's perfect expression in
Greek culture and thought. That issue has to do with temporality, movement, change, contingency, the flux. And the issue is this: how do we cope
with the flux? The logocentric response, that is, Plato's response, the response echoed by all those who are but footnotes to him, is *denial* or *subversion*. "What we get from the philosophers is either the outright denial
of motion, as in the Eleatics, or some spurious theory which takes the
teeth out of motion, even as it professes to be on its side. In philosophy,
becoming is always getting subverted by being" (RH,13). Both Kierkegaard and the post-modernists want to deny this logocentric denial of motion and to subvert the logocentric subversion of becoming. For
Kierkegaard, the realm of becoming, the realm of time and history, is
precisely where spirit is allowed its rights, its freedom, as spirit. The logocentric attempt to still the flux is for Kierkegaard the same as paganism's
containment of spirit; the same as what the Bible calls idolatry. Both Kierkegaard and post-modernism are essentially iconoclastic.

The impulse of logocentrism—that is, the impulse to still the flux—is,
for Kierkegaard, the most prominent characteristic of Greek culture. For
him that impulse was radically thwarted with the advent of Christianity.
This is not to say that the advent of Christianity put an end to every
remnant of a hellenistic nostalgia; it certainly did not. However, a radical
and momentous shift was effected with the Christian positing of spirit as
spirit. Once spirit was released from its bonds within psychical immediacy,
once it drank of the champagne of temporal transcendence, once it was
thrust into radical contingency, novelty, and change, it could not look
back. The positing of spirit as spirit was absolutely irreversible: the flux
is no longer the problem as it was for Plato; now the problem is located
in those who would presume to still it, in those who would presume to
capture spirit, to restrict freedom, to deny or subvert time and change.

For the post-modernist, it is as if nothing has changed between the time
of Plato and our own; it is as though the post-modernist were just discov-
ering what happened nearly two thousand years ago. While it is true
enough to say that the Greeks were dominated by a world-picture in

which change and time were problematic, and that their impulse was to flee from the terror of the flux and to find rest and repose in an immutable, eternal order, certainly the post-modernist cannot expect us to believe that modernity is essentially a culture in which time and change are denied and subverted. Again, it cannot be gainsaid that there are elements in the modern age that could rightly be called logocentric (perhaps the most notable example of this hellenistic nostalgia has been among professional philosophers). The overwhelming impulse of modernity, however, seems to be anti-logocentric. If anything characterizes the modern age it is certainly the fact of its affirmation of the flux and its celebration of the liberation and disengagement of spirit, and, I might add, its suspicion and even its hatred of all attempts to deny or subvert the flux. As such, then, the clarion call of post-modernism and its attack of logocentrism is, ironically, identical to the clarion call of the modern age and far from what it pretends to be, namely, the announcement of a "post-modern" era.

I agree with Caputo that even among the Greeks there was an anticipation of the "post-modern" affirmation of the flux, of time, and of change; but I do not find that anticipation as clearly evident, as he does, in Heraclitus and in Aristotle. Caputo's argument is that Heraclitus, in his notion of the flux, and Aristotle, in his his notion of *kinesis*, are forerunners of the "post-modern" celebration of time and change and so are exempt from the general Greek logocentric tendencies. I think that this argument fails. It is arguable against Caputo that the Heraclitean flux was always understood against the background of a static and eternal *logos*, and that even though Aristotle did find a place for "change"—for the dynamic interplay of potency and act—his view that the actual is *prior* to the potential reduces, in the final analysis, *kinesis* to a backward "movement" and so makes it more akin to Platonic recollection and logocentric presence, than Caputo and even Kierkegaard have noticed.[14]

My agreement with Caputo on the fact that we can find an anticipation of the modern celebration of time and change among the Greeks has another rationale. As I have argued, the given actuality of our human existence is essentially and inescapably dynamic. This means that even if one has a world-picture that is essentially alien to time and change, it will never be able completely to still the flux. Given that the flux is ever present in our pre-thematized, concrete existence, it would indeed be surprising for it not to be at play in every thematized self-understanding, even if only negatively; as well, it ought not to be surprising to find that the flux is, on occasion, positively appraised and even celebrated. I think that this is exactly the case with both Aristotle and with Heraclitus and that this is why Kierkegaard admires Aristotelian *kinesis*. I simply want to add that the world-picture that was the substratum of their inquiries prevented their flirtations with time and change from being anything more than simply flirtations: a kind of playing with the possibility of possibility. The logocentric world-picture they both inhabited—perhaps inextricably—

kept them from letting time, history, and radical contingency awaken in their full existential energy and power.

My argument throughout this book has been based on Kierkegaard's contrast between the *psychical* and the *pneumatic*, a distinction that allows us to understand that the Greeks had no place for spirit in their world-picture. At best, spirit was present in the Greek world as psyche, as soul, and existed therefore in a wholly immanent relation of harmony and accord with the sensuous. This relation between psyche and sensuous is perfectly paralleled, for Kierkegaard, in the relation between idea and medium in the visual arts, painting, architecture, and sculpture—the arts that were dominant in Greek culture. The reason that spirit did not— could not—break into the Greek cosmos, that is, break forth in all of its existential power and energy as spirit, was that spirit, as spirit, is essentially temporal, essentially on the move in time, in history, and so essentially in a relation of opposition and strife with the sensuous. In the Greek world-picture, reality is essentially static, eternal, timeless.

What Christianity posited, according to Kierkegaard, is spirit in its radical temporal transcendence—a transcendence that radically disrupted spirit from its rest and repose within the sensuous and set it into motion and into radical opposition to the sensuous. This Christian spirit is spirit in its full pneumatic qualification as spirit. So qualified, spirit is in strife with and excludes the sensuous. Spirit cannot find its absolute medium of expression in the plastic arts of Greek culture, where idea is in harmony and accord with its medium; rather, it requires a dynamic auditory medium from which the idea is constantly disengaging itself.

When we focus on Kierkegaard's distinction between the pneumatic and the psychical, we are able to articulate rather succinctly and clearly just that point at which Kierkegaard is a friend to the post-modernist. For Kierkegaard, Christianity supplanted the psychical with the pneumatic; as I understand it, the post-modernist critique of logocentrism is simply a reassertion of this triumph of the pneumatic over the psychical. Insofar as Kierkegaard and the post-modernists join hands in this pneumatic critique of the psychical, it seems quite proper to say that Kierkegaard was the first to take up the post-modernist project. But this partnership quickly disintegrates.

Kierkegaard diverges from the post-modernist in the way he understands the pneumatic self/world relation. While both agree that spirit is radically transcendent, that spirit, as spirit, is perpetually disengaging itself from the sensuous, and that as such we ought to avoid any attempt to still that flux in which spirit lives and moves and has its life, they do not agree as to what is required of spirit in order for it to sustain its existence within the "thunderstorm" of the flux. The post-modernist is always on guard against a recurrence of the logocentric impulse, however subtle it might be, to find a way to deny or to subvert the flux, and so again to reconfine spirit and restrict its freedom. Spirit can survive, the post-modernist reasons, only if it is perpetually breaking out of every "presence." Kierkegaard, however, thinks that in modernity this is no longer the main threat to spirit: in modernity, that is, after the impact of Christianity was fully felt, spirit can no longer be swept under the rug, not for long anyway. In the modern age, Kierkegaard reasons, spirit is not as subject to logocentric or *psychical subversion* as it is to a *pneumatic perversion*.

To avoid the quest for a pure presence, to avoid logocentrism, and to allow spirit its free reign in its pneumatic disengagement from the sensuous, the post-modernist proposes, like Kierkegaard, that we understand the spirit/sensuous relation, the self/world relation, analogically in terms of a dynamic relation between an idea and a medium of its expression. The media of the plastic arts are obviously altogether too psychical, too logocentric, too static to serve the post-modernist, or Kierkegaard, as the paradigm of the pneumatic spirit/sensuous relation. A more dynamic medium is required. Among the choices here are speech and music. And it is precisely in this choice that Kierkegaard and the post-modernist part company: for Kierkegaard, spirit finds its perfect medium in speech; post-modernism will have nothing to do with the so-called logocentrism of the speech-act; in its place, it suggests *writing* as the paradigm of the expression of meaning; the post-modernist definition of writing, however, ends by transmuting it into music.

The post-modernist prescription for coping with the flux is simply to let it have its play. But this is not as passive as it may seem. Indeed, we must actively and militantly preserve and defend the flux at all costs against the tyranny of logocentric presence; we must defeat presence whenever it raises its head. For the post-modernist, the most productive way to do this is to redefine language, for it is in language that the metaphysics of presence continues to hold sway over our imaginations, leading us astray into the illusion of a stability of meaning and truth.

Why is presence seemingly so inexpungible from language? The post-modernist reply is that presence seems to be inexpungible from language only because we have misunderstood language by thinking of all language is essentially a kind of speaking—by subsuming writing under speaking. On one point, at least, the post-modernist seems to be correct: in the speech-act the presence of the speaker and hearer, the singular context of the act, the intentions involved, and so forth are essential elements in the determination of meaning. In other words, the post-modernist rightly recognizes that speech is essentially a *semantic/reflexive medium* that ties the speaker to the world, to the other, and to the singular historical context of production. Ironically then, the post-modernist understands perfectly well that the speech-act has a meaning only insofar as it is reflexively *bonded* to some particular actual speaker, and only insofar as it is situated within a concrete historical world; for the post-modernist, it is precisely the inexpungible semantic/reflexive dimension of the speech-act that leads to the metaphysics of presence.

At this point, it is well to remember that Kierkegaard distinguished between two manifestations of spirit: one, spirit as such, the other, a demonic perversion of spirit. The first finds its perfect medium in speech, the other in music. Spirit as such, spirit in its pneumatic qualification as spirit, is constituted in a dialectical sundered/bonded relation to the world; the demonic perversion of spirit is constituted in a pneumatic mis-relation of spirit to the sensuous, that is, spirit as either de-spirited sensuality (Don Giovanni) or deracinate thought (Faust)—spirit sundered from its true place, its world, others, and its own body. We must also recall that while speech and music are both auditory and pneumatically qualified media, speech has resources in it that are lacking in music. They are, to name a few, demonstrative and personal pronouns, a system of tenses and moods, and a system of syntax and grammar, and they provide speech with its *semantic/reflexive dimension*, its power to refer to the world and reflexively to bond the speaker to the world. If it were not for its bonding resources, what is to be heard in the speech-act, like what is to be heard in music, would be perpetually *sundered* from its sensuous particulars. It is precisely because of these resources unique to speech that a speaker is able to refer to the world and reflexively to own and own up to his claims before some other. Music, as an essentially semantic/non-reflexive medium, is, as such, the perfect medium for expressing the demonic mis-relation of spirit to the sensuous, the demonic sundering of self and world. Speech, like music, is also a dynamic (semantic) medium, but, unlike music, it is a medium with a reflexive dimension. Because of its semantic/reflexive resources, the meaning of the speech-act not only outruns its sensuous particulars, it is constantly recalled back into the world, and tied to some actual speaker in some concrete time and place. It is these semantic/reflexive resources that make speech the perfect medium for expressing the dialectical sundered/bonded relation of spirit to the sensuous.

For some strange reason, the post-modernist thinks that it is the bonding resources of speech—and all language modeled on the speech-act—that leads to the metaphysics of presence. As an alternative, the post-modernist suggests the subsumption of all language under a redefined conception of writing. According to this new definition, writing is constantly in motion, constantly shifting, never at rest. In this respect, the meaning of writing is like spirit, and writing is transformed from a psychical to a pneumatic medium.

For Derrida, the structure of iterability makes writing—in this new sense of the term—essentially different from speech. Writing lacks any essential reflexive ties between the writing and the writer, the reader and the writer, the writer and reader, and the context of the writing/reading. Because of its iterability, its essentially non-reflexive character, the mean-

ing of writing is, for the post-modernist, always undecidable, always indeterminate, always breaking away (disengaging itself from the sensuous)
from its historical context and from its authorial connections. In other
words, for the post-modernists, the meaning (the idea) of writing is pictured as a dynamic quality analogous to spirit, and the medium itself analogous to music. And yet writing, as this is defined by the post-modernist,
turns out not to be spirit in its positive reality and power, but a *demonic
perversion of spirit*.

The spirit/meaning of writing is a demonic perversion of spirit since it
is, by the post-modernist's own definition, a perpetual breaking, a perpetual *sundering*, a perpetual hovering, a perpetual play of signs. The
spirit/meaning of writing is essentially disembodied for it is a perpetual
breaking with the world; again, this is just the spirit that Don Giovanni
and Faust express.

What it amounts to, then, is that writing is not, as it might first appear,
a visual phenomenon in its essential structure; rather writing for the post-
modernist has all the properties of a sonic medium. When we recognize,
however, that writing, for the post-modernist, has the dynamic qualities
of a sonic medium but lacks an essential reflexive dimension, then we
begin to realize that this redefinition of writing transforms it into something like *music*. As Kierkegaard understands it, music is a pneumatically
qualified medium, but at the same time a medium that is without any
resources for the bonding of spirit to the world. Music is just such a system
of meaning. As medium, music hurries along in a perpetual vanishing
from the world just like the ideas it expresses—the ideas of restlessness,
tumult, and infinity. As I think Kierkegaard might look at it, for the post-
modernist, graphematic marks are ultimately vanishing tones and meaning is a fugitive spirit constantly disengaging itself from the sensuous,
from the here and now of historical existence.

The mistake that the post-modernist makes is her assumption that presence is always and ultimately static, eternal, and atemporal. If this is what
presence is, that is, if we let Plato and logocentrism define what presence
is, then of course the post-modernist is right that pure presence is a
dream, an illusion. Having made this assumption about presence, the post-
modernist attempts to liberate meaning from its confinement within the
logocentric illusion. Is there another sense of presence? a pneumatic and
dynamic sense of presence?

It is certainly arguable that presence can be defined pneumatically, that
there is a viable sense of presence that is essentially dynamic, essentially
temporal and historical. What the post-modernist cannot bring herself to
acknowledge is the possibility of *constancy, stability, or reliability* in the *midst
of the flux*. Such a constancy, however, does not necessarily entail logocentric presence. The constancy I am talking about here is the constancy of
faithful speech, the presence of a speaker in her words before some other.
That presence cannot be said, but forms the background and the context

of what is said. This background of personal presence is a critical element in the determination of the meaning of a speech-act. It has nothing to do with the static logocentric presence; it is a dynamic transhistorical presence.

As speakers we are quite aware, when we are attentive, of whether we are present in, or absent from, the words that we are speaking or whether those who address us are present or absent. Indeed, there is nothing more offensive than to be in the physical presence of someone who is actually somewhere else; nothing more insulting than to be with one who speaks words of promise, words of love, words of commitment, and yet is absent, or rather, perpetually absenting herself. To speak in good faith is just to offer ourselves as reliable and to offer to the other the restful confidence and assurance that we will deliver on the word that we have given. Though we can certainly be deceived, we can also find that our faith has been well placed.

The constancy of faithful speech finds its paradigm in the spirit of the biblical God whose word, unlike the grass that withers and the flower that fades, endures forever. God's presence in his words is not an atemporal presence, it is *transhistorical*: "I will be who I will be." This is not logocentric presence, it is pneumatic. And although the constancy of God does bring rest within the flux, it does not deny it. With this as a model of constancy, I am enabled to live in faith, to own and own up to my words before some other. This faith stabilizes and takes the sting out of anxiety, but from within it; in the way that a promise provides the courage to move forward into a radically open and radically contingent future. This is not logocentrism; it might be called *dabhar-centrism*.

In the language of Kierkegaard's stages, what I am suggesting is the intelligibility of an *ethical*, as opposed to an *aesthetic*, presence.[15] Whenever I speak with reflexive integrity, I give my word to some other, that is, make a promise and enter into a covenant with the other. In reflexively integral speech then, I freely bond myself to the world, to others, and take my stand within the world and before the other. The commitments and responsibilities implied in my speech-acts are essential for establishing not only my identity in the world, but also that web of relationships that is *my world, my place*. In owning my words before some other I freely take up myself as the speaker already present—I actualize the given actuality of my concrete, given existence; I become a self by coming to myself. In my responsible speech-acts, I take a *stand* in the world, a stand before others. To take this stand is to stop hovering over the abyss and to live an ethical existence.

Without some sense of constancy and stability, we are mad. Ethics works against insanity. The qualities of an ethical existence—constancy, continuity, and steadfastness—are qualities of presence, an existential, dynamic presence, a presence that does not deny the flux but lives within it and presupposes it. The continuity of ethical, existential presence is the conti-

nuity of historical consciousness; it is the continuity of a promise, a covenant, that establishes a stability in time and across time and in the midst
of contingency. For Kierkegaard a paradigm of this, in contrast to the
aestheticism of Don Giovanni and Faust, is the marriage of Judge Wilhelm.[16] In the marriage vows, the radical contingency and the radical uncertainty of historical existence are at once acknowledged as real and as
stabilized. We acknowledge that we do not know what may befall us, sickness or health, riches or poverty, etc., yet before these witnesses, including
God, we declare that we will stand fast in our commitments to each other.
The visible and invisible covenantal bond that is established is as real and
as palpable as anything can be.

It is the reliability and stability of an ethical existential presence that is
missing from the post-modernist prescription for avoiding logocentrism.
Lacking this *dabhar-centered* alternative to logocentric presence, the post-
modernist ends by simply affirming the flux itself and abandoning all
hope of stability, constancy, and continuity.

To address this issue, let us return to Caputo's version of post-modernism, what he calls radical hermeneutics. Caputo recognizes that it looks as
though radical hermeneutics, as an alternative to logocentrism, ends by
throwing us to the wolves (RH,209). Has it?

No doubt this is the central question in a pneumatically qualified world-
picture. In such a world-picture it is easy to see why it would seem that
every attempt at finding a stabilizing truth and a determinant meaning
would be itself caught up in a relativizing temporal slippage and so fail.
Once the historical subject is recognized as being at the center of the
real—that equivocal Christian contribution to world historical consciousness—then it is a short step to thinking that everything is "subjective," that
every thought is a radically idiosyncratic construction, a social, linguistic,
historical, contingent construction that, as such, is subject to being deconstructed. But, as I have argued, to make this move would pervert the
pneumatic innovation. In the wake of this perversion, all that is solid will
melt into air; and all that will remain will be the Faustian dialectic of con-
struction/destruction. In this world, or rather, in this worldlessness, what
can we know and what are we to do? How is science possible? How is
ethics possible?

Caputo says that science, in its pretension to discover the true nature
of things, constitutes the hard case against keeping the flux in play. While
relativism and subjectivism may reign supreme within the humanities, so
we have come to think, in the hard sciences, we find out what is true
across culture, across time and space, what is objectively and universally
true independent of an embodied observer, independent of a historically
situated subject; in the hard sciences we find the *logos* of nature that lies
behind the appearance of the flux. If we conceive of science in this logocentric way, then it is indeed difficult to see how the flux can have any

more of an essential role to play within science than it had within the psychically qualified ancient world. But this would be to conceive of the modern scientific revolution as merely a continuation of the logocentric ancient world. There is, no doubt, something to this.

As I have argued earlier, it is certainly true that a strong impetus in the rise of modern science has been its tendency to want to recover the stability of a well-ordered, psychical cosmos, to retreat into a visually oriented, logocentric world-picture. It is this side of science, its reductionistic, positivistic, deterministic side, in which it is most difficult to keep the flux in play. But as I have also argued, this side of the modern scientific enterprise has virtually collapsed (except perhaps in the social sciences) under the pneumatic critique. The pneumatic critique has forced science to recognize the flux, to recognize the historical context of its enterprise, and the central role the scientist plays in determining scientific theory and truth. It is this new understanding of science that Caputo wants to highlight and to celebrate; it is an understanding of science that enables it to make its claims without having to deny the flux; it is an understanding of science that has been made available to us through the works of Kuhn, Popper, Feyerabend, Lakatos, and Polanyi.

In this list of innovators in the philosophy of science, it is unfortunate that Caputo concentrates on Thomas Kuhn instead of Michael Polanyi. Although Polanyi and Kuhn are often thought of as doing the same thing, there are important and subtle differences. Arguably, Kuhn's analysis of the structure of scientific revolutions could be construed as a relativistic account of science. If it were so construed, Caputo's question becomes more pointed: how then is science possible? On a strict relativistic account of science, there would be no stilling of the flux, but by the same token, the idea that a scientific theory can provide us with a true account of some natural phenomenon would collapse. What is missing from Kuhnian paradigms is reflexivity. That is, Kuhn's paradigms are self-contained systems, free floating, shifting, moving in the flux; paradigms, in short, are like musical compositions, free floating aesthetic packages of intrinsic meaning without reflexive resources for establishing referential bonds between scientific theory and the world, and reflexive bonds between the scientific theory and the scientist who holds and sustains it with his commitment.

Polanyi would be a much better example of how it is possible to take the flux seriously without falling into relativism. The key in the whole matter is, again, the semantic/reflexive aspect of a scientific theory, its contact with something outside itself and its dependence on a subjective ground of belief, choice, and commitment. Perhaps it is best to let Polanyi speak for himself: "[The scientist's] gropings are weighty decisions . . . The choices are made by the scientist; they are his acts, but what he pursues is not of his making" (TD,76–77). And further: "By trying to say something that is true about a reality believed to be existing independently of our knowing it, all assertions of fact necessarily carry a *universal intent*" (PK,311).

It is remarkable that Polanyi's descriptions of the scientific enterprise bear striking similarities to Kierkegaard's religious epistemology. Central to the latter 's the claim that truth is subjectivity. Yet neither Kierkegaard nor Polanyi are subjectivists. Neither thinks that truth is constituted by the subject, by a decision. To think that the subject decides what is true would leave no room for distinguishing between truth and fantasy; this would entail the collapse of rationality itself. Decisions, for both Polanyi and Kierkegaard, are crucial in the process of discovery, but they do not determine what is true. For both Kierkegaard and Polanyi, a subject must be at the very center of the process of arriving at the truth; indeed, both would agree that there is no truth in science, in ethics, or in religion, unless that truth is owned and owned up to by an actual, historically situated "I": there is no truth that is not the truth *for someone*.

By grounding truth reflexively in the historically existing subject who speaks in his own voice with universal intent, Polanyi is able to find a way to understand the scientific enterprise in which the flux is taken seriously and in which we are not thrown to the wolves of relativism, subjectivism, and ultimately nihilism. Is there a similar prospect for ethics? As Caputo says: "The [post-modernist] critique of metaphysics included within its sweep every metaphysical ethics. And that poses the question of the possibility of an ethics *after* metaphysics, of a postmetaphysical ethics" (RH,236).

If we do not try to still the flux, to contain it and arrest its play, then where are we to look for ethical guidelines? Are we not thrown to the wolves of a relativism that says there are no such guidelines? Perhaps, says the post-modernist, but there is still much work for the ethicist to do. What work? The work of deconstructing every ethical scheme, of every binary opposition that leads to power, control and objectification, oppositions such as ruler/ruled, cause/effect, master/slave, rich/poor, male/female, privileged/underprivileged. Such would be an ethics of *dissemination*: "Proceeding from a salutary deconstructionist mistrust of all such binary schemes, [an ethics of] dissemination is directed at constellations of power, centers of control and manipulation, which systematically dominate, regulate, exclude. Its model is the Socratic work of showing up the contingency of every scheme" (RH,260).

For Caputo, the task of the ethicist of dissemination is to keep things difficult, not to let us fall into easy solutions to ethical dilemmas, to keep things *fair*. In order to do this, we must keep the conversation moving, always preserving the right of dissent and always allowing the idiosyncratic its rights. Caputo's own questions, however, are right to the point: how are we to insure that public debate is fair? How shall we adjudicate between competing viewpoints? What will guide ethical deliberations?

How will we be able to make a decision so as to *act?* To press these questions, Caputo seems to think, is to fall into a foundationalist compulsion, a Cartesian anxiety. All we must do is to keep the free assembly of diverse points of view open and fair and above all restricted to pragmatic and local strategies for local action. As Caputo puts it: "[The ethics of dissemination] does not speak in the name of a master plan; it speaks only of a series of contingent, ad hoc, local plans devised here and now to offset the exclusionary character of the prevailing system. Its role is to break up clusters of power, constellations of ruling interests, to put them on the run, to keep them in play. It bears no name beyond its disclaimer not to know the master name" (RH,263–264).

As I see it, a post-modern ethics of dissemination has to face the questions that any ethical relativism must face. If the flux is all there is, then whence any sense of "fairness"? Doesn't the idea of fairness itself bespeak of constancy, of stability, of basic human rights, of ethical principles that cut across time and sociology? If all idiosyncratic rights are granted, then are we going to say that racism and bigotry, slavery and domination should be allowed to have their day? Isn't it the case that behind the postmodernist attempt to keep things open, there lies the assumption that openness is a good for all people regardless of historical situation? As well, isn't liberation a universal good for the post-modernist? And are the dominators not always condemned by the ethics of dissemination? So what is wrong with such ethical principles? Apart from being able to rely on such principles we are indeed thrown to the wolves; apart from our reliance on them we cannot have any sense of coherence and consistency, and we remain without standards for judgment, guidelines for action, a sense of continuity; in short, apart from such resources for stability we are mad.

Perhaps our need for stability and constancy, for something to rely on in order to steer our way through the flux, does bespeak a deep-seated anxiety in us. Why, however, must we be forced to think that this is just a Cartesian anxiety in search of foundations? Isn't it possible that the anxiety at stake here is a universal human anxiety, a human terror of a flux without order and coherence? Isn't this the universal human anxiety of groundlessness, the anxiety that finds its demonic intensification in Don Giovanni hovering over the abyss, and in the frenetic anxiety of Faust's perpetual renewal? Isn't this the anxiety we all feel when we come face to face with madness? with the demonic? As far as I can see the ethics of dissemination does not provide us with the resources for establishing a stability and coherence that will allow us to endure these anxieties and to find a place to stand, a ground from which to act. Caputo's worry seems justified: ethics, even an ethics of dissemination finally collapses into relativism. Unless ethical claims can be vested with a semantic/reflexive dimension and with a universal intent then they become merely musical expressions of emotion and preference. The vesting of ethics with a semantic/reflexive dimension however seems impossible for the post-modernist, since for him ethical systems are social constructions perpetually shifting in the flux. Central to any ethics, as Kierkegaard has told us, is world-bonding steadfastness, commitment, constancy, and continuity; but, as the post-modernist insists, every such bond to the world threatens to still the flux and to fall prey to a metaphysics of presence. For some reason it does not occur to the post-modernist that it is at least possible for ethics to attempt to find its way in the flux without denying it. Indeed, the reality of the flux may be just the reason why ethics arises: if we are not to be engulfed in the terror of the flux, we must find at least a measure of stability and coherence, continuity and reliability. Against the post-modernists, however, it certainly seems possible to find this stability *within the flux*. The stability of a promise, for example, provides me with an anchor of reliability not by denying the radical contingency of the future but precisely by presupposing it, by declaring from within the radical contingency of the flux: "this much you can rely on." Ethical stability thus does not, as the post-modernists claim, still the flux as much as it presupposes it.

Caputo gives us an equivocal answer to the question of whether, in a post-modernist critique of metaphysics, ethics is possible. On the one hand, we are advised to keep the flux in play, to acknowledge the groundlessness of our life within the flux, our life over the abyss. On the other hand, Caputo says that we are not thrown to the wolves, and that the ethics of dissemination does not leave us in the bankruptcy of aestheticism, in a hovering worldlessness. Caputo seems to know that a thoroughgoing aesthetic hovering over the abyss is nothing less than madness. He knows with Kierkegaard that the ethical individual is one who has learned to "hold fast in time, both by finding constancy in the midst of the flux, and by finding novelty in the midst of the customary and everyday" (RH,29). He knows, again with Kierkegaard, that "ethical repetition means the steadiness of the unbroken vow, the enduring bond of the lasting marriage, the capacity to find ever new depths in the familiar and selfsame" (RH,30), and that in the ethical life we are provided with just that worldly context we need in order to come to ourselves. But he also knows, again with Kierkegaard, that the ethical must eventually come to grief: "Ethics suffers from the illusion that repetition lies within its power" (RH,31). And finally, Caputo acknowledges that, at least for Kierkegaard, the only way to make it through the flux is in faith. It is at this point, however, where we meet with the deepest level of Caputo's equivocation.

According to Caputo, the man of religious faith "takes his stand in the abyss" for "in the abyss of the God-relationship the individual is able to move ahead" (RH,32). But how it is possible to take one's *stand* in the abyss? Certainly, for Kierkegaard, the God-relationship does not place us in the abyss but rescues us from it; moreover, insofar as we picture ourselves as hovering above an abyss it makes no sense to speak of "moving ahead"; indeed, it is thanks only to faith that we are provided with the traction we need to move through the flux, for faith provides us with an absolutely reliable ground within the flux, a source of constancy, stability, and coherence. That ground is found in a *presence* to be sure, but a pneumatic, not a psychical presence. *Such a presence is both historical and absolute, dynamic and steadfast.*

A pneumatically qualified presence is essentially personal, for in the pneumatic world-picture, presence is paradigmatically defined as the personal presence of an absolutely faithful speaker, a speaker whose word is life and spirit; this dynamic personal presence provides us with our human space of appearance, our world, our place to stand, our ground, our context for ethical action. That space of our mutual appearance is perhaps what Pascal meant by "our true place," the place from which we in the modern age have fallen. As I have tried to argue, that place, our place in the world is paradigmatically a place *before God* and derivatively a place *before some other self within the world.* This space of appearance is established in its full existential reality only within a world-picture in which words are fully vested with their rights. Only within the premises of such a world-picture is it possible to speak with reflexive integrity *before some other.* Such an owning and owing up to my words in reflexively integral speech involves a double relation to the world, what I have called a dialectical sundered/bonded self/world relation. In this dialectic, I am at once liberated from a psychical bondage to the world into a pneumatic transcendence, a transcendence that opens the possibility of establishing a bonding to the world and others that is of my own choosing. In this personal bonding, I not only choose to be the self that I am called to be and already am, that is, I not only choose to be *myself,* I also establish the world as *my* world, and the other as *my* neighbor.

The impression one gets from Caputo is that such a Kierkegaardian faith might be just one more way of "bailing out of the flux." Or at least it seems to him that faith may become just another way for trying to sneak out of time.[17] But this is hardly a Kierkegaardian understanding of faith. It is the knight of infinite resignation that sneaks out of time and out of the world. In the double movement of faith, the knight of faith receives the fullness of the temporal back again from the hands of the Eternal. But because of Caputo's anxiety over the possibility that faith may end up becoming just another strategy for stilling the flux, because of what we might call his anxiety over the good, he ends up advocating, paradoxically, an "ethics" of aesthetic hovering, an ethics without a ground, an ethics in mid-air. But this is the ethics of a perverted pneumaticism, an ethics whose demonic aim is the destruction of ethics, the collapse of ethics into aesthetics. I do not know how it is possible for a post-modern ethics of dissemination, lacking as it does a center and a ground, to avoid ending up in this demonic madness.

Is there a way to make sense of ethics, to provide ethical decisions and actions with grounds and with as much universal intent as any scientific claim and at the same time allow these claims to be made from within the flux and to presuppose it? The argument of these meditations implies that there is. Kierkegaard has provided us with the clues for seeing that an alternative to an ethics of dissemination would be something like an ethics of covenant, an ethics of promise, an ethics of reflexive integrity.

I certainly am prepared to grant the essential frailty of an ethics of reflexive integrity. But this frailty need not force us into nihilism. We can admit of course that human beings are not always reliable, that there is a darkness deep in the human heart; we can admit that we can never know what the full consequences of our ethical actions, our commitments, our covenants, our promises will be; this is the price we pay for our freedom. But we are not therefore forced to abandon our reliance on others. Indeed, it is all we have in a pneumatically qualified world. It will not be enough if our dream is to secure the future in all directions; that would entail that we forfeit our freedom and it would render every ethic self-defeating. This is the dream of a metaphysics of presence, a metaphysics that would arrest the flux. On the other hand, an ethics of reflexive integrity will be too much if we will have nothing to do with any isolated islands of predictability and guideposts of reliability, if we are simply engulfed by the flux. This, it seems to me, just is the demonic nihilism of post-modernism, the nightmare of abandoning ourselves to the play of the flux. The ethics of promise, the ethics of covenant, the ethics of the reflexively integral speech-act, steers a course through the flux, a course that does not put temporality to rest but, quite to the contrary, presupposes the radical contingency of the world. Without the presupposition of radical uncertainty, promising makes no sense, but without the power of promising, radical uncertainty is madness (HC,213).

Promising is serious business. When this seriousness is combined with the darkness of the human heart we may well end up in profound disappointment and eventually in despair. The aesthete knows full well the dangers of entering into the ethical life and so he avoids it. He wants the joys of freedom and transcendence but without their liabilities. But to avoid the latter, he must not permit himself the seriousness of commitment, the seriousness of reflexively integral speech. The aesthete is convinced that to own his words and to own up to them before some other would establish bonds that would confine and deaden his spirit. And so he retreats into a detachment from the world, a demonic hovering over the abyss. As I have tried to argue, this is precisely the move of post-modernism. If my analysis is correct, however, it is hardly a "post-modern" move at all; indeed, it seems to be modernity brought to its final demonic conclusion.

But there is something to the post-modernist worry about the seriousness of an ethics of reflexive integrity. Kierkegaard is aware that the ethical life may smother spirit. He offers a response to this problem that is different from that of the post-modernist. In place of a sustained aesthetic, demonic retreat from the world into the free play of the flux, Kierkegaard offers an alternative way of coping with the dangers of the ethical life. The name Kierkegaard gives to this alternative response to these dangers is *mastered irony*. In the concluding Epilogue, I will try to show how an ethics of reflexive integrity is incomplete apart from being tempered by the spirit of mastered irony.

EPILOGUE

MASTERED IRONY AND THE RECOVERY OF SPIRIT

> Anyone who does not understand irony
> at all, who has no ear for its whispering,
> lacks *eo ipso* what could be called the
> absolute beginning of personal life.
>
> (S. K.)

In these concluding remarks, I will present one last expression of what I take to be Kierkegaard's alternative to the modern (and "post-modern") demonic world-picture. This alternative, for brevity's sake, is Christianity. Beyond the naming of this alternative, however, I want to continue Kierkegaard's project of radicalizing our understanding of the Christian world-picture. For Kierkegaard, to be a Christian in the most radical sense of the term is to exist in the world in an ethico-religious modality—religiousness B. Religiousness B is ethico-religious insofar as it is constituted within a double relation: it is religious insofar as it requires that we exist before God, that we are absolutely bonded to him as the center of our lives; it is ethical insofar as it also requires that we exist in a sundered/bonded relation to the world, the center of which is our neighbor. For Kierkegaard, to exist in this mode is to be fully human, to exist as a person, as oneself; it is to be willing to be the self that we are called to be; it is to actualize actuality.

The difficulty of faith is not so much found in the God-relation as it is in the world-relation; or more precisely, the difficulty of the God-relation is that it entails a certain kind of world-relation, a relation that I have characterized as *sundered/bonded*. I don't mean to suggest that it is easy to be absolutely bonded to God, but if this bonding entails only the first movement of faith, the movement of infinite resignation from the world, one's faith is at least simplified. The difficulty of the life of faith in its fullest sense is to make the double movement. The knight of faith must learn how to be absolutely committed to God, and yet to affirm the world. It is not an easy matter to embrace the world, every inch, without falling into idolatry; and the constant temptation of faith is to sneak out of time, prematurely "to join what God has put asunder."

The world that faith requires us to affirm is the concrete space of our human appearance. It includes a whole matrix of bonds, many of which are determined by the given actuality of our natural and historical embodiment in a particular time and place. Most importantly, however, the world includes the presence of others. Indeed, as a knight of faith, I am required to *choose* the world, to *choose* the other, for my task is to affirm the world as *my* world, and the other as *my* neighbor. When the world becomes mine, when I become my brother's keeper, I enter into covenantal bonds of ethical and moral responsibility and commitment, bonds of continuity and steadfastness, bonds that require something of me, bonds that will surely entail my own suffering.

And yet, the knight of faith must tread lightly in the world. He has a worry not shared by the knight of infinite resignation; he must guard against the self-deception that subtly transforms the relative into the absolute. How does the knight of faith avoid this slippage? How does he live within the paradoxical sundered/bonded self/world relation?

I have claimed that the perfect medium for the expression of the sundered/bonded self/world relation is found in the reflexively integral speech-act. It may be easier, however, to see how reflexively integral speech provides the proper medium for constituting and embracing the worldly bonds of ethical action and its attendant commitments and responsibilities than how it is, at the very same time, the perfect medium for enabling us to avoid absolutizing the relative. To be sure, the reflexively integral speech-act has an intrinsic moral seriousness, a kind of ethical heaviness that brings us down to earth, that plants our feet firmly on the ground, firmly in the world. It could not be otherwise when we existentially own and own up to our words, when we are present in them, when we say what we mean and mean what we say. Given its intrinsic ethical heaviness, how can reflexively integral speech provide us also with the resource for treading lightly in the world?

As I have claimed, to speak with reflexive integrity is also to *act*. That is, when I engage in reflexively integral speech, I am actively involved in doing much more than simply producing word-sounds: as Austin has put it, I am doing something with my words; I am engaging in an act that is essentially linguistic, that is, an act that is possible only in, through, and by virtue of words. But there is also an essential moral dimension in this act. As I have claimed, every felicitous speech-act is a giving of one's word, essentially a *promise*. But this *giving* (of my word) also implies another activity—a *taking*, or more properly, a *taking up*. In reflexively integral speech, I not only actively take up as my own what I say to some other, but ultimately take up the incipient personal presence implied in the words I say as my own. In doing this, in being actively present in my words before some other, I show not only that I have chosen the words I speak, that they are my words, I also show that I have chosen myself. In the same act, I am both revealed and constituted as the self that I am called to be. As Poteat has put it: "My actually existent speaking mind-body, though subject to the principles of causality, is always something that I, *as existing*, am engaged in taking up as my own. . . . [A]s a tonic mindbodily being in the world, a necessary condition of my existing *at all* is that I not merely 'consent' to exist, but that I positively 'intend' to do so" (PM,95).

To put this differently, we can say that the speech-act is essentially and intrinsically *free*. Freedom, however, is essentially and intrinsically connected to transcendence, or, what is the same thing, spirit. I can only own and own up to the words that I speak to the extent that I *transcend them*, that I am *free in relation to them*.

The upshot here is that in reflexively integral speech I constitute and reveal both my freedom and my inextricable bonds to the world. Speaking with reflexive integrity constitutes and reveals, as nothing else can, my transcendence, my spirit, and my worldly embodiment, my sundered/bonded self/world relation. The difficulty here is to grasp and to live this dialectic concretely. To be sure, insofar as I own and own up to my words before some other, I enter into a web of moral interconnections, commitments and responsibilities that go far beyond what I can, at the moment I speak, possibly know. My word, as we say, is my *bond*. So far so good. The trick, however, is to realize not only that my word-as-*bond* does not translate into my word-as-*bondage*; indeed, just the opposite: the word as *my* bond is the decisive sign of my most radical freedom.

This distinction between the word-as-bond and the word-as-bondage can bear some clarification. The term 'bondage,' it seems to me, is necessarily associated with *unfreedom*, the condition of slavery. Granted the term 'bond' *can* be so associated, but it also seems to have other linguistic connections. Certainly my promise to someone is a bond, and certainly I am bound by it, but insofar as I freely enter this promise, I show by my act that I am free, that I am no slave. A covenant that is not freely entered is paradoxically not as binding as one that is freely entered. As Judge Wilhelm might say, the bond that unites two people in a marriage, at least ideally, is no bondage. The marriage relationship, again ideally, is no master/slave relation, no domination/submission relation, it is a relation of mutuality, a relation in which the freedom and individuality of each partner is expanded in and through the bond that holds them together.

Consider the ordinary human activity of holding hands. I don't mean by the term 'holding hands' the phenomenon in which one person is simply grasping another's hand, perhaps even against the other's will. Rather, I mean the phenomenon which we could felicitously describe as "holding hands." We would certainly distinguish between the case of a parent and child holding hands and the case of a parent keeping a rambunctious child in hand. Even though there is a rich variety of contexts that determine the nature and meaning of the act of holding hands, a common thread in these cases is the fact that in this phenomenon we have a bond that is formed between two or more individuals on the basis of their mutual intent and consent. What is important in this bond, and what makes it different from a bondage, is the fact that it is freely formed and sustained by the individuals involved. An ever-present *positive* reminder that this bond is not a bondage is found in the awareness—however tacit—that it originated in the mutual will of those involved, in their mutually exchanged consent and intent. Beyond this, however, an ever present *negative* reminder of the sovereignty that each has in relation to this bond is found in the fact that each is aware that the bond can be broken, that the two have it within their own power, mutually or individually, to let go, to withdraw.

This power of withdrawal is essential for the positive determination of spirit, for it is precisely this power that keeps our worldly bonds from being transformed into our bondage. This negative spiritual power, this power of withdrawal, is an essential corrective to the ethical life; it continues to whisper in our ears the subtle danger of the ethical life of reflexive integrity, the ever-present danger of turning bonds into bondage, of absolutizing the relative. The negative power of withdrawal knows that the moral heaviness of reflexively integral speech can easily cause us to forget our transcendence; it knows that the speech-act, the very medium in which our transcendence finds its most decisive realization, where spirit is posited in its full existential reality and power, can easily become the very means for stifling and ultimately suffocating spirit in unfreedom; it knows how easily our word can be transformed into our bondage. This negative spiritual power of withdrawal is *irony*.

Kierkegaard tells us that irony provides us with an antidote for the bankruptcy of the psychical/aesthetic life. But the irony that has a positive role to play in the positive determination of spirit is not of this Socratic type; it is not the irony that is the healthy antidote to the psychical confinement of spirit in the unfreedom of innocence and ignorance. But neither is it the romantic, demonic irony that traps spirit in the insidious unfreedom of worldlessness and inflicts the modern age with a cultural sickness unto death. The irony that keeps the ethico-religious modality of existence from collapsing into the purely ethical mode, that keeps ethical bonds and commitments from collapsing into bondage, the irony that ever reminds us from *within the bonds* of our transcendence and freedom, is, as Kierkegaard puts it, *irony as mastered moment*.

The master of irony disowns his words before some other in order to provide himself with a *temporary* way out of the ethical demands of commitment and responsibility implied in reflexively integral speech; the master of irony practices a "teleological suspension of the ethical." The double irony in this is that the telos of this suspension of the ethical is the ethical. It is in this respect that mastered irony is unlike the unhealthy modern species of ironic detachment, that is, romantic irony, which seeks a *sustained* avoidance of the commitment and responsibility entailed by reflexively integral speech, an avoidance that amounts in the end to a permanent aesthetic retreat from the ethical.

Even though all irony is a negative determination of subjectivity, such a negative determination can and, Kierkegaard insists, *must* have an essential dialectical role to play in the positive determination of spirit. He says: "Just as scientists maintain that there is no true science without doubt, so it may be maintained with the same right that no genuinely human life is possible without irony" (CI,326). The irony that Kierkegaard thinks is essential for an authentic life, again, is *mastered irony*. This healthy form of irony has an indispensable role to play in the positive determination of spirit precisely because its *sundering* effect is always in the service of bringing us down to earth. Mastered irony reminds us of our transcendence by reminding us that our worldly bonds are *our own*. As such, mastered irony is an absolutely essential element in the dialectic of a pneumatic sundered/bonded self/world relation—and an absolutely essential element in the life of spirit. Kierkegaard explains:

> Anyone who does not understand irony at all, who has no ear for its whispering, lacks *eo ipso* what could be called the absolute beginning of personal life; he lacks what momentarily is indispensable for personal life; he lacks the bath of rejuvenation, irony's baptism of purification that rescues the soul from having its life in finitude even though it is living energetically and robustly in it. He does not know the refreshment and strengthening that come with undressing when the air gets too hot and heavy and diving into the sea of irony, not in order to stay there, of course, but in order to come out healthy, happy, and buoyant and to dress again. (CI,326–327)

How does mastered irony serve to keep our worldly ethical bonds from collapsing into a bondage of unfreedom? As irony, that is, as a negative determination of subjectivity, mastered irony plunges us into a detachment from our words. When I speak ironically, when I say the opposite of what I mean, and do not mean what I say, when I am not present in my words, "my" words cease to be my own. This mis-relationship to "my" words is the very opposite of the relation I bear to my words in reflexively integral speech. In irony, I *dis-own my words before some other*. This ironic disowning of my words becomes mastered irony when it serves as a sign of my radical freedom to own them. In other words, what makes mastered irony healthy is that it bears (negative) witness to a higher positive determination of subjectivity, namely, subjectivity as spirit, as self. When we become aware that the words we are hearing are empty, that no one is present in them, it brings concretely into focus the radical relation of freedom that a speaker bears to the words he speaks. Apart from this radical freedom, it would be impossible for the speaker to own and own up to them, that is, to speak with reflexive integrity. The master of irony withdraws from his words in order to be all the more present in them.

To put this differently and paradoxically, mastered irony reminds us of the fact that our relation to our words, in reflexively integral speech, is radically *contingent* as well as radically *necessary*. That is, being absent from our words testifies negatively and indirectly to the *necessity* of presence as an essential factor in the determination of meaning; at the same time it testifies to the *contingency* of that presence. A speech-act is tied to its speaker necessarily insofar as the personal backing of the speaker is pivotal in the determination of what is said; a speech-act that is not connected to someone who speaks before some other in some singular context of enactment is essentially indeterminate in its meaning. Yet *what* that connection is, is determined by the speaker himself: it is manifest in his speaking in earnest, in jest, in irony, in despair, and so forth. *That* a speaker is essential in the determination of *what* is said is necessary; *what* that relationship is, is radically contingent. Mastered irony reminds us of this radical contingency, of our radical freedom.

Without mastered irony, and the transcendence it affords, the task of actualizing actuality becomes a monumental task, indeed an impossible one; without mastered irony, the task of actualizing actuality is an enslaving burden. Mastered irony lifts us out of an absolute relation to the relative, rescues us from the snares of relativity, and keeps our worldly bonds from disintegrating into our bondage. Mastered irony reminds us of our transcendence, our freedom, and ultimately of the fact that the world and our existence in it are the free gifts of God's grace. In so doing, it rescues us from an ethical arrogance destined to be humiliated; it denounces the ethical goal of willing to be a self by disciplining our lives in steadfast resolve to conform perfectly to the universal demands of the moral law. Mastered irony tempers our ethical task of actualizing actuality for it whispers into our ear the secret that actuality is a gift from the hand of the Eternal, a gift we are invited to receive and to take up as our own.

It is possible to make sense of *owning and owning up to* our words in faithful speech if and only if we recognize our ability to withhold our commitment from them. Mastered irony reminds us of the radical relation of transcendence and freedom that we bear to our words. But mastered irony goes beyond this. It is a healthy, albeit a negative, determination of subjectivity, for after it reminds us of our transcendence and freedom, it points to a renewed commitment to our *positive* and immanent place in the world, and to our positive call to actualize actuality. Irony is unhealthy when it is the instrument of sustained aesthetic detachment, when it is appropriated to avoid indefinitely the bonds to the world and to others entailed by faithful speech; it is healthy when it is appropriated as the instrument which allows us to rest from the demands of such bonding. Mastered irony allows this rest for it recognizes that only the Absolute demands our absolute commitment. As such, mastered irony, as Kierkegaard says, "is extremely important in enabling personal life to gain health and truth" (CI,328).

NOTES

Prologue: Kierkegaard's Critique of the Modern Age

1. I will be using the term 'modern age' in this work to refer not only to that historical period of western culture that extends from the present back some three hundred years (back, that is, from the time of René Descartes [1596–1650]), but also to the eras immediately preceding the seventeenth century—the Renaissance and the Reformation.

2. *Either/Or* (Volumes I & II), edited and translated by Howard V. Hong and Edna H. Hong, with Introduction and Notes (Princeton, N.J.: Princeton University Press, 1987), p. 65. [Hereinafter parenthetically cited as E/O I or E/O II.] I will not follow the Hong and Hong translation, however, on one matter: when referring to the legendary character, Hong and Hong use the term 'Don Juan'; when referring to the operatic character, they use the term 'Don Giovanni'; because my focus is on the musical, I will use the operatic name 'Don Giovanni' for both Mozart's operatic character and for the legendary character of 'Don Juan.' And of course I will use the term *Don Giovanni* for the opera itself.

3. *The Sickness unto Death: A Christian Psychological Exposition for Upbuilding and Awakening*, edited and translated by Howard V. Hong and Edna H. Hong, with Introduction and Notes (Princeton, N.J.: Princeton University Press, 1983), p. 13. [Hereinafter parenthetically cited as SUD.]

4 The idea of the hermeneutical circle is primarily associated with Martin Heidegger, *Being and Time*, translated by John Macquarrie and Edward Robinson (New York: Harper & Row, 1962), pp. 7f., 152f., 314f., 432n.

5. Kierkegaard remarks: "The self is composed of infinitude and finitude. However, this synthesis is a relation and a relation that, even though it is derived, relates itself to itself, which is freedom. The self is freedom" (SUD,29).

6. Even though, for Kierkegaard, the self can, and most often does, become alienated from itself, it cannot be completely so. See SUD,21.

7. Kierkegaard's famous definition of faith—in which the self, in relating itself to itself, is grounded transparently in the power that established it—implies such a covenantal bonding (SUD,13–14).

8. Blaise Pascal, *Pensées*, with an introduction by T. S. Eliot (New York: Dutton, 1958), par. 427. [Hereinafter parenthetically cited as PP.]

9. Ludwig Wittgenstein, *On Certainty*, edited by G. E. M. Anscombe and G. H. Von Wright and translated by Denis Paul and G. E. M. Anscombe (Oxford: Basil Blackwell, 1969), par. 162. [Hereinafter parenthetically cited as OC.] My use of the term 'picture' is similar to the use William H. Poteat makes of it in his *Polanyian Meditations: In Search of a Post-Critical Logic* (Durham, N. C.: Duke University Press, 1985), see especially note 2, p. 293. [Hereinafter parenthetically cited as PM.]

10. This distinction is clearly drawn by Stephen Crites in his essay "Pseudonymous Authorship as Art and as Act," *Kierkegaard: A Collection of Critical Essays*, edited by Josiah Thompson (Garden City, N.Y.: Anchor Books, 1972), p. 210. [Hereinafter parenthetically cited as AA.]

11. J. L. Austin, *How to Do Things with Words*, edited by J. O. Urmson (New York: Oxford University Press, 1965). [Hereinafter parenthetically cited as JLA.]

12. Kierkegaard asserts: "Generally speaking, consciousness—that is, self-con-sciousness—is decisive with regard to the self. The more consciousness, the more self" (SUD,29).

13. See the essay, "The Tragic in Ancient Drama" (E/O I,137–164).

1. Sensuality and Spirit

1. Mircea Eliade, *Cosmos and History: The Myth of the Eternal Return* (New York: Harper Torchbooks, 1959), p. 35. [Hereinafter parenthetically cited as CH.]

2. Thorlief Boman, *Hebrew Thought Compared to Greek* (London: SCM Press, 1960), p. 69 (Boman is quoting this passage from Kleinknecht). [Hereinafter parenthetically cited as HG.]

3. Plato, *Cratylus*, 385b.

4. Don Ihde, *Listening and Voice: A Phenomenology of Sound* (Athens: Ohio University Press, 1976), p. 7. [Hereinafter parenthetically cited as LV.]

5. In all fairness to Professor Poteat's *Polanyian Meditations*, I must note that he uses examples of visual perception other than the obviously static case of seeing the painting from his desk chair. Indeed, the example he begins with is his daily jog through the countryside (PM,53ff.).

6. This contrast between the visual and the auditory—a contrast which is central to this book—has been made by a number of authors. I have already mentioned two works that figure centrally for me, namely, *Polanyian Meditations* and *Listening and Voice*. For two other examples, see Hans Jonas, *The Phenomenon of Life* (New York: Dell, 1966), and Walter Ong, *The Presence of the Word: Some Prolegomena for Cultural and Religious History* (New York: Simon & Schuster, Clarion Books, 1970). [Hereinafter parenthetically cited as PW.] Jonas' commentary on Heidegger in regard to this contrast is especially interesting (pp. 235ff.). I must caution, with regard to Ong's book, that it fails adequately to distinguish the sounds of words from the sounds of music. Poteat takes him to task for this (PM,251ff.).

7. Ihde draws some interesting etymological parallels between listening and obedience (LV,81).

8. Oswald Spengler, *The Decline of the West*, abridged edition by Helmut Werner, English abridged edition by Arthur Helps, translation by Charles Francis Atkinson (New York: Modern Library, 1932), p. 62. [Hereinafter cited parenthetically as DW.]

9. Marjorie Grene, *A Portrait of Aristotle* (Chicago: University of Chicago Press, Phoenix Books, 1963), p. 39. [Hereinafter parenthetically cited as PA.]

10. Professor Grene notes that for both Aristotle and Plato, "it is forms that the knowing mind properly and rightly knows" (PA,65).

11. Plato, *The Republic*, edited by Francis Cornford (London: Oxford University Press, 1945), p. 219.

12. The root sense of theory is intimately connected to seeing, as Eric Partridge has noted in his *Origins: A Short Etymological Dictionary of Modern English*, 4th edition (New York, 1977), pp. 710–711. 'Theory' is here related to 'theatric,' from which we get the English 'theater,' and is in turn related to 'thea,' meaning "a sight," and to 'theasthai,' meaning "to view," which is related to 'thauma,' meaning "a thing compelling the gaze," which is related to 'theorein,' meaning "to look at," which forms the antecedent of the Latin 'theoria,' from which we get the English 'theory.'

13. This way of speaking is reminiscent of Husserl (LV,88).

14. Ong says: "[Speech] leaves no discernible direct effect in space, where the letters of the alphabet have their existence. Words come into being through time and exist only so long as they are going out of existence" (PW,40). Ong's confusion

between the sounds of speech and the sounds of music is evident since what he says of speech has the effect of making it indistinguishable from music.

15. *Word Origins,* p. 278.

16. Hannah Arendt, *The Human Condition* (Chicago: University of Chicago Press, 1958), p. 178. [Hereinafter parenthetically cited as HC.]

17. W. H. Auden, "Dichtung und Wahrheit," *Homage to Clio* (New York: Random House, 1955), p. 36. [Hereinafter parenthetically cited as DUW.]

18. The idea of "owning and owning up to our words" I owe to William H. Poteat in *Polanyian Meditations* (PM,95).

2. *Dabhar* and Existential Immediacy

1. Søren Kierkegaard, *The Concept of Irony: With Continual Reference to Socrates,* edited and translated with Introduction and Notes by Howard V. Hong and Edna H. Hong (Princeton, N.J.: Princeton University Press, 1989), p. 276. [Hereinafter parenthetically cited as CI.] I will diverge (for moral and aesthetic reasons) from the Hong and Hong translation of CI at only one point: I will refer to the "mastered moment" of irony found in Lee M. Capel's translation, rather than to the flat Hong translation of irony as a "controlled element." See *The Concept of Irony: With Constant Reference to Socrates,* translated with an introduction and notes by Lee M. Capel (Bloomington: Indiana University Press, 1965), pp. 324ff.

2. Ludwig Wittgenstein, *Philosophical Investigations,* translated by G. E. M. Anscombe (New York: Macmillan, 1968), pars. 65 and 67. [Hereinafter parenthetically cited as PI.]

3. For an excellent summary of the current philosophical discussions on the theory of action see Hannah Pitkin's *Wittgenstein and Justice: On the Significance of Ludwig Wittgenstein for Social and Political Thought* (Berkeley: University of California Press, 1972), pp. 157–168. [Hereinafter parenthetically cited as WJ.]

4. Even Descartes, whose aim it was to doubt everything that was dubitable, never once called into question the meaning of the words that he relied on to formulate his doubts, his dream hypothesis, and so forth. Perhaps Descartes should have realized that the indubitable starting point for any philosophical inquiry is not doubt but speech; perhaps he should have said, "I speak, therefore I am."

5. Quoted in Stanley Cavell's *The Claim of Reason: Wittgenstein, Skepticism, Morality, and Tragedy* (New York: Oxford University Press, 1979), p. 112. [Hereinafter parenthetically cited as CR.]

6. "The Delta Factor," reprinted in a collection of Percy's essays entitled *The Message in the Bottle* (New York: Farrar, Straus & Giroux, 1981), p. 35.

7. I borrow these characterizations from *Polanyian Meditations,* pp. 17–18.

8. See Virgil Aldridge, "Art and the Human Form," *Journal of Aesthetics and Art Criticism* 29, 3 (Spring 1971), pp. 296–297.

9. "The name [performative] . . . indicates that the using of the utterance is the performing of an action" (JLA,6).

10. I have in mind here the distinction that Wittgenstein makes between depth grammar and surface grammar (PI,par.664).

11. I have put 'extra-linguistic' in scare quotes simply to point out that strictly speaking these elements of the speech-act are not *extra*-linguistic, if that means that they lie outside of the speech-act; indeed, as I understand it, these elements are not only not outside the speech-act, they are integral to it, essentially a part of the whole.

12. Again, I have borrowed the expression "owning one's words before some other" from W. H. Poteat's *Polanyian Meditations.*

13. It is a commonplace to note that for Aristotle actuality precedes potentiality.

See Marjorie Grene, *The Knower and the Known* (London: Faber & Faber, 1966), p. 51. [Hereinafter parenthetically cited as KK.] Also, on the issue of the psychically determined nature of this Aristotelian position, see John Herman Randall's *Aristotle* (New York: Columbia University Press, 1960).

14. On this difference between Aristotle and modern day evolutionary theory, see Grene's *The Knower and the Known*, p. 226.

15. Kierkegaard implies, I believe, that there is a distinction between two senses of givenness. On the one hand, there is the sense of the immediate givenness wherein we find ourselves already in the world at a particular time and in a particular place prior to our forming and appropriating a self-conscious world-picture of the given. This immediate sense of the givenness of ourselves within a world, however, is incomplete and requires, for the full realization of the true nature of that givenness, a self-conscious appropriation of it as *gift*. This appropriation of our immediate givenness as gift grounds our and the world's givenness in a subjective source, a Giver, and orients us toward this source in a posture of gratitude, for without this Giver, there would be nothing.

16. We transcend our words perforce, since we could never say anything, that is, mean what we say and say what we mean, and be responsible for what we mean, and so forth, if we were not always more than what we say.

17. I am thinking here of Logical Positivism. This position takes factual statements alone to be meaningful, that is, to have an ontological efficacy. Other vast segments of our language, for example, value judgments, theological and metaphysical speculations, and aesthetics, are reduced, according to Positivism, to emotive expressions without ontological efficacy.

18. The recent movement called deconstructionism or post-modernism seems to want to go all the way in claiming that no segment of language has ontological efficacy. I will have much more to say about this matter in chapter 5. Here I will discuss some of the works of Jacques Derrida and one recent book on the deconstructionist project, namely, *Radical Hermeneutics: Repetition, Deconstruction, and the Hermeneutic Project*, by John D. Caputo (Bloomington: Indiana University Press, 1987). [Hereinafter parenthetically cited as RH.]

19. For Austin, a constative is a true or false statement of fact or an accurate or inaccurate description of or report on a state of affairs (JLA,3).

20. "Words," in *Collected Shorter Poems* (New York: Random House, 1966), p. 320.

21. By the term 'linguistic determinism,' I mean simply the view that cultures and, as some would have it, even individuals use words to construct their world in whatever way they choose, and so wholly determine with language what is real. I could just as easily have used other synonymous terms, to wit, 'linguistic idealism' or 'linguistic relativism.' See Pitkin's discussion of this issue (WJ,102ff.).

22. Søren Kierkegaard, *Philosophical Fragments* (Princeton, N.J.: Princeton University Press, 1962), p. 93. [Hereinafter parenthetically cited as PF.]

23. By 'modern day nominalism,' I mean the view that names comprise a convenient set of symbols used to designate certain classes of objects. For the modern nominalist names have no ontological significance.

3. Don Giovanni, Music, and the Demonic Immediacy of Sensuality

1. This distinction is developed in Polanyi's Terry Lectures published as *The Tacit Dimension* (Garden City, N.Y.: Anchor Books, 1966). [Hereinafter parenthetically cited as TD.]

2. Michael Polanyi, "Sense-Giving and Sense-Reading (1967) in *Knowing and*

Being: Essays by Michael Polanyi, edited by Marjorie Grene (Chicago: University of Chicago Press, 1969), pp. 181–182. [Hereinafter parenthetically cited as KB.]

3. Michael Polanyi, *The Study of Man* (Chicago: University of Chicago Press, 1958), p. 30.

4. Mark C. Taylor, *Kierkegaard's Pseudonymous Authorship: A Study of Time and the Self* (Princeton, N.J.: Princeton University Press, 1975). [Hereinafter parenthetically cited as KPA]; and *Journeys to Selfhood: Hegel and Kierkegaard* (Berkeley: University of California Press, 1980). [Hereinafter parenthetically cited as JS.]

5. Søren Kierkegaard, *The Concept of Anxiety*, translated by Reidar Thomte and Albert B. Anderson (Princeton, N.J.: Princeton University Press, 1980), pp. 118–154. [Hereafter cited parenthetically as CA.]

6. Søren Kierkegaard, *The Concept of Dread*, translated with an Introduction and Notes by Walter Lowrie (Princeton, N.J.: Princeton University Press, 1957).

7. Louis Mackey, *Kierkegaard: A Kind of Poet* (Philadelphia: University of Pennsylvania Press, 1971), p. 24. [Hereinafter parenthetically cited as KP.]

4. Faust, Romantic Irony, and the Demonic Immediacy of Spirituality

1. *Goethe's Faust*, translated with an introduction by Walter Kaufmann (New York: Doubleday Anchor, 1963). [Hereinafter parenthetically cited by line number.]

2. Thomas Mann, *Doctor Faustus* (New York: Alfred A. Knopf, 1947). See also the excellent commentary on Mann's novel *Faust as Musician: A Study of Thomas Mann's Novel Doctor Faustus* by Patrick Carnegy (New York: New Directions, 1973).

3. Marshall Berman, *All That Is Solid Melts into Air: The Experience of Modernity* (New York: Penguin, 1988). [Hereinafter parenthetically cited as MB.]

4. Harry Redner, *In the Beginning Was the Deed: Reflections on the Passage of Faust* (Berkeley. University of California Press, 1982). [Hereinafter parenthetically cited as BD.]

5. Jean-Paul Sartre, *Being and Nothingness: A Phenomenological Essay on Ontology*, translated by Hazel E. Barnes (New York: Washington Square Press, 1966), p. 557. [Hereinafter parenthetically cited as BN.]

6. William H. Poteat, "Courage, Anxiety and Truth," *Duke Divinity School Review* 31, no. 3 (Autumn 1966), p. 205.

7. In Goethe's version of the story, both Faust and Margaret are finally saved, finally taken up into heaven. I can only speculate that this reflects Goethe's own praise of both Margaret's infatuation with the spirit of infinite negation and Faust's "embodiment" of it. In the final analysis, the play, at least from Goethe's perspective, is no tragedy. From the Kierkegaardian perspective, it is the celebration of the triumph of the demonic.

8. Recently I was on a road trip in the midwest. On an interstate highway I noticed a sign that read: "*Undeveloped* Rest Area Ahead." Further down the same highway I came across another sign that read: "*Modern* Rest Area Ahead." The obvious implication here is that the words 'developed' and 'modern' are virtually synonymous in the modern popular imagination.

9. As Berman notes, Goethe borrows the names of Philemon and Baucis from Ovid's *Metamorphoses* (MB,67).

10. Descartes's project of establishing certainty was prompted by his realization that all of his former opinions, under the pressure of doubt, had dissolved into air. See "Meditations," *The Philosophical Works of Descartes*, translated by Elizabeth S. Haldane and G. R. T. Ross, vol. I (London: Cambridge University Press, 1968), *Mediation I*. [Hereinafter parenthetically cited as MED.]

11. René Descartes, *A Discourse on Method*, translated by Francis Cornford (London: Oxford University Press, 1945), p. 212 [italics added.]

12. Galileo Galilei, "The Assayer," *The Philosophy of the 16th and 17th Centuries*, edited by Richard H. Popkin (New York: Free Press, 1966), pp. 64–68.

13. Floyd Maston, *The Broken Image: Man, Science and Society* (Garden City, N.Y.: Anchor Books, 1966). [Hereinafter parenthetically cited as BI.]

14. E. A. Burtt, *The Metaphysical Foundations of Modern Science* (Garden City, N.Y.: Anchor Books, 1954).

15. Karl Popper, *The Logic of Scientific Discovery* (New York: 1959), p. 279.

16. Alasdair MacIntyre, *After Virtue: A Study in Moral Theory*, 2d ed. (Notre Dame, Ind.: University of Notre Dame Press, 1984), p. 37. MacIntyre's diagnosis of morality within the modern age is correct and incisive: modern subjectivistic assumptions have virtually destroyed the moral fabric of our culture. This subjectivism I have called our demonic worldlessness. When it comes to his prescription to remedy the modern breakdown of morality, MacIntyre betrays his allegiance to the subjectivistic assumptions that he rightly sees as its cause. That this is so becomes obvious in MacIntyre's subsequent book *Whose Justice? Which Rationality* (Notre Dame, Ind.: University of Notre Dame Press, 1989). See Martha Nussbaum's review of this book in *New York Review of Books* (December 7, 1989), p. 41.

17. George Steiner, *Language and Silence: Essays on Language, Literature and the Inhuman* (New York: Atheneum Press, 1958), p. 104. [Hereinafter parenthetically cited as LS.]

18. Joseph Prabhu, "Blessing the Bathwater," *Journal of the American Academy of Religion* 54, no. 3 (Fall 1986), p. 543.

5. Post-Modernism and the Triumph of the Demonic

1. *Personal Knowledge: Towards a Post-Critical Philosophy* (New York: Harper Torchbooks, 1964), p. 142. [Hereinafter parenthetically cited as PK.]

2. See especially the essay "The Retreat from the Word," where Steiner focuses on the impact of mathematics on verbal language (LS,12–35).

3. See John R. Searle, "Reiterating the Differences: A Reply to Derrida." This reply immediately follows Derrida's article "Signature Event Context," in which Derrida is highly critical of J. L. Austin's speech-act theory. Both of these were published in *Glyph: Johns Hopkins Textual Studies* (Baltimore, Md.: Johns Hopkins University Press, 1977), pp. 198–208 and 172–197 respectively. Searle's reply to Derrida provoked (*sic*) Derrida to write his own reply to Searle. Although couched in the mask of Dionysian laughter, the attack is as bitter and as deadly serious a product of *resentiment* as one can imagine. Derrida's reply is entitled *Limited Inc* (Evanston, Ill.: Northwestern University Press, 1988). [Hereinafter parenthetically cited as LI.] Needless to say, my sympathies for the most part lie with Searle. In a later development, Searle takes more swings at Derrida in his review of Jonathan Culler's book *On Deconstruction: Theory and Criticism after Structuralism*. Searle's review of this Derridean book is an occasion for furthering his attack on Derrida's position. See "The Word Turned Upside Down," *New York Review of Books* (October 27, 1983), pp. 74–79. [Hereinafter cited parenthetically as JRS.]

4. Jacques Derrida, *Of Grammatology*, translated by Gayatri Chakravorty Spivak (Baltimore, Md.: Johns Hopkins University Press, 1976), p. 7. [Hereinafter parenthetically cited as OG.]

5. Derrida tries to make good on the claim that the features that are supposed to distinguish writing from speaking apply equally to speaking (LI,9–10). My argument here is that this attempt fails.

6. Searle points out that the deconstructionist's attempt to undermine the so-

called logocentric oppositions, e.g., speaking/writing, male/female, begins by reversing the opposition and ends in subsuming both terms of the oppositions under a "new" concept, e.g., "archi-writing" or "archi-woman" (JRS,74).

7. As Searle points out, the deconstructionist is guilty of making his point by defining terms as he pleases (JRS,76–77).

8. Walter Ong, "*Maranantha*: Death and Life in the Text of the Book," *Journal of the American Academy of Religion* 14, no. 4 (1977), p. 425. Also see my "Scripture: An Auditory Interpretation," *Listening: A Journal of Religion and Culture*, 21, no. 1 (Winter 1986), pp. 25–42.

9. Derrida recognizes that we cannot get completely away from intentionality in our analysis of the meaningfulness of a sentence. But he also claims that "there cannot be a 'sentence' that is fully and actually meaning*ful* and hence (or because) there can be no 'corresponding' (intentional) speech-act that would be fulfilled, fully present, *active* and *actual*" (LI,58).

10. "[A] written sign carries with it a force that breaks with its context, that is, with the collectivity of presences organizing the moment of its inscription. This breaking force is not an accidental predicate but the very structure of the written text" (LI,9).

11. Arendt distinguishes within the *vita activa*, three distinct activities, labor, work, and action (HC,7,177).

12. Michael Polanyi and Harry Prosch, *Meaning* (Chicago: University of Chicago Press, 1975), p. 85. [Hereinafter parenthetically cited as MP.]

13. I refer to the series Kierkegaard and Post-Modernism, Mark C. Taylor, general editor (Tallahassee: Florida State University Press).

14. If my interpretation is correct, Aristotle does not properly posit movement, at least historical movement, for again in Aristotle's philosophy actuality precedes potentiality (possibility); see PF,92.

15. Mackey's characterizations of the differences between the aesthete and the ethical man are to the point (KP,56).

16. Again, Mackey's characterizations of the differences between the aesthete and the ethical man (in particular Judge Wilhelm) are worth noting (KP,67–69).

17. "To invoke a grace from on high is just one more familiar way of bailing out on the flux" (RH,281).

INDEX

Abraham (patriarch), 29, 92, 138
abstract: the structure of sight as, 22, 24; ideas and media as, 38–41; the self as, 101; music as, 112; speech as, 129; the visualism of modern thought as, 145–147; modern mathematics as, 153–154, 165–166; art as, 179–180
abyss, the: Don Giovanni dancing over, 96; of despair, 119; of modern life, 141; hovering above, 191, 198; and the post-modernist ethics of dissemination (Caputo), 195–196
Adam (biblical story of creation), 94, 138; and Eve, 133
aesthetic, the: Kierkegaard's pseudonymous voice not the voice of, 5; sensuous and reflective immediacy, psychical and pneumatic immediacy as species of, 7; and the modern self-understanding, 8; and the plastic arts, 8; the world-picture of, vs. the world-picture of the existential, 9; the immediacy of Faust and Don Giovanni as representative of, 13; as essentially informed by the visual, 26; as natural, organic, 26–27; Plato's forms as within, 29; in music, 37; sculpture and architecture as psychical expressions of, 37ff; music as a pneumatic expression of, 41ff; as a mode of saying, 113–117; flight from the world, 116; and despair, 149; reduction of speech to music, 160; post-modernism as a form of, 178; as distinguished from the existential, 179ff; Derrida on writing and, 182; vs. the ethical, 191; paradigms (Kuhn) as a reflective form of in modern science, 193; the post-modernist collapse of ethics into, 197; et passim
anxiety: about the normative requirements for being human, 62; about conversation, 79; of worldlessness, 94; of Don Giovanni, 97; as the permanent companion of spirit, 99; about unfreedom and freedom, 102–105; about continuity, 108; about the good, 114; in Derrida, 183; and the flux of temporality, 185; faith and, 191; Cartesian vs. human, 195; about stilling the flux of time, 197
Aldridge, Virgil, 209
architecture (and sculpture): contrasted with speech and music as media, 7; as psychical/aesthetic media, expressing the psyche/sensuous relation 8, 26, 37–42, 187; as visual/spatial media, 25–26; as compared to

nature, 26ff; as expressing static, atemporal presence, 51, 182; the passive spectation of, 174
Arendt, Hannah (*The Human Condition*), 47–48, 68–69, 73–75, 84, 130, 135, 141, 149, 152–154, 179, 181, 198, 209, 213
Aristotle, 28, 73, 77, 186, 208–210, 213
art: the idea and medium of, 38; the openness/closedness of, 47; the expressive power of, 50–51; the words of Christ not a work of, 76; of the stage actor, 109; of seduction, 116; and life, 165; and the artist, 178–181;
Auden, W. H. ("Dichtung und Wahrheit"), 32, 50–52, 84, 209
Augustine, of Hippo, 83
Austin, J. L., 10, 47–48, 68–69, 83–84, 87, 176, 201, 207, 210, 212; *How to Do Things with Words*, 207, 209–210

Bacon, Francis, 157
Berman, Marshall (*All That Is Solid Melts into Air*), 130, 133–134, 136, 139–140, 142–143, 211
Bible, 2, 33, 185
Boman, Thorlief (*Hebrew Thought Compared to Greek*), 21, 32–33, 208
break, the: as the key element of the structure of iterability in writing (Derrida), 177–178; of artists/authors from the works they produce in art and writing, 181–182
breath: as psyche (soul) and as pneuma (spirit), 15; of speech, 30; of God, 32
Burtt, E. A. (*The Metaphysical Foundations of Modern Science*), 150, 212

Caputo, John D. (*Radical Hermeneutics*), 175, 183–186, 192–197, 210
Cavell, Stanley (*The Claim of Reason*), 84–85, 209
choice: as an indispensable element, for Kierkegaard, in the actualization of actuality, 1–4; as necessary for relating oneself to oneself, 11; as an element of Greek life at odds with its world-picture, 11; as that which transposes possibilities into actualities, 31; as a manifestation of the transcendent within the immanent, 34; the, of speaking as oneself, 62; as related to temporality, 77; as an essential element of science, 193
concrete: existence as given, but never as

RONALD L. HALL is Professor of Philosophy and Religious Studies at Francis Marion University. His articles have appeared in *Zygon: Journal of Religion and Science, Soundings,* and *The International Journal for the Philosophy of Religion.*